I0820428

LA MESA MEXICANA

ROSA CIENFUEGOS

Photography by Alicia Taylor

Smith Street Books

EL NOROESTE
P. 14→
NORTH PACIFIC OCEAN
EL OESTE
P. 142→
MEXICO

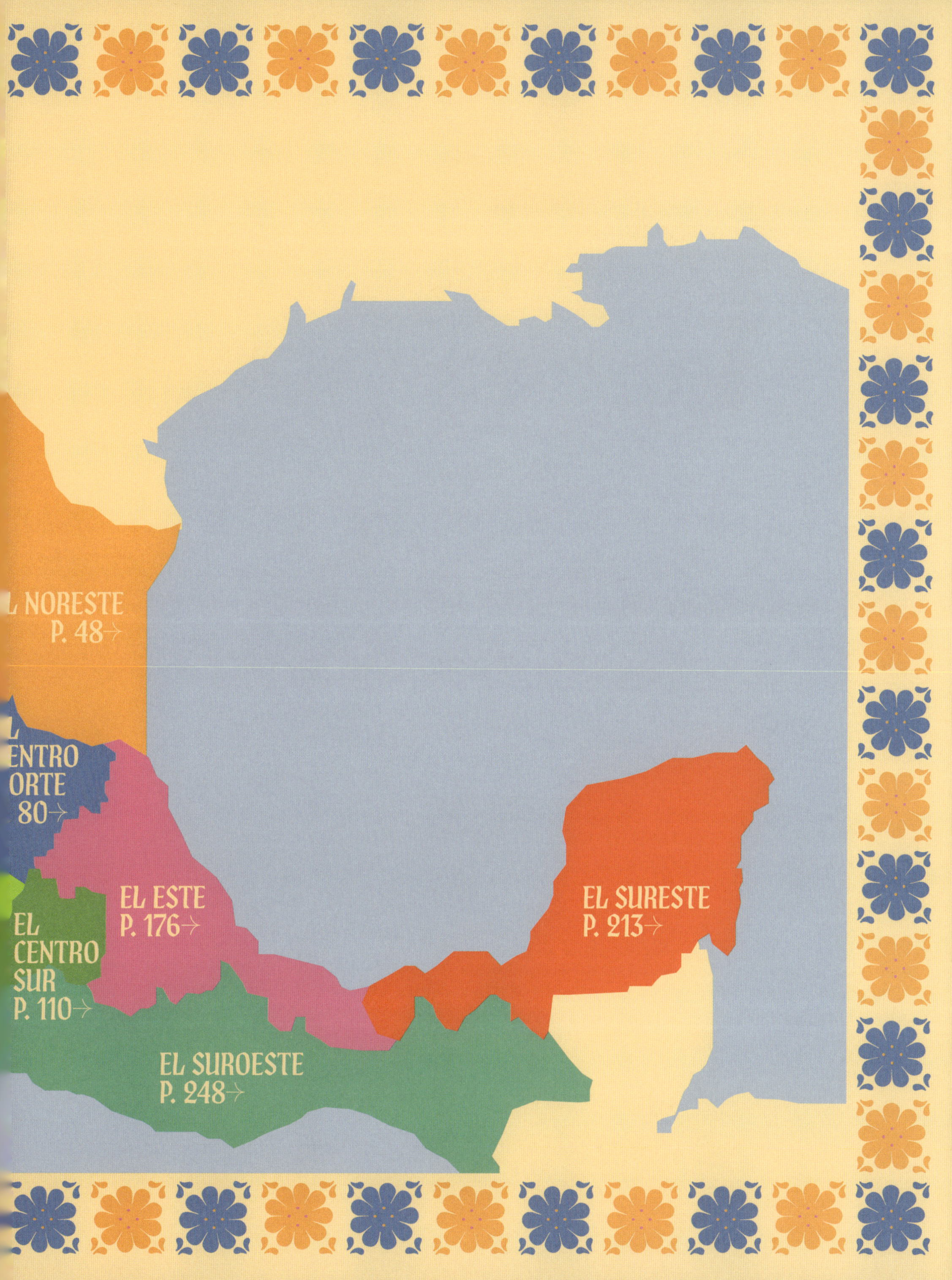

L NORESTE
P. 48→
L
ENTRO
ORTE
80→
EL ESTE
P. 176→
EL SURESTE
P. 213→
EL
CENTRO
SUR
P. 110→
EL SUROESTE
P. 248→

THE MEXICAN TABLE

Mexico isn't just a country: it's a universe of colours, flavours and traditions that has the power to transform everyone who sets foot on its lands.

Here, life has a rhythm of its own. I remember my childhood and young adult life in chaotic, beautiful Mexico City – laughter at the family table, sounds of neighbours singing and calling out, delicious smells from kitchens all around, the vibrant energy of the mercado, kids playing around the food stalls, eating fruit with chilli that left their cheeks stained with chamoy and tajin.

When you're born in Mexico, you inherit roots that make you a storyteller, a guardian of flavours and a keeper of joy. We're not just from Mexico, we are Mexico. Every time we share a recipe, teach someone to dance banda, or explain why a taco is never 'just a taco', we share a piece of who we are.

Mexicans carry a unique pride, one that's rooted in resilience and creativity. Ours is a culture that honours the past while embracing the future, a place where indigenous traditions have blended successfully with modern innovation and multiculturalism. You will see this in the embroidery of the Otomi huipil, the taste of freshly made corn tortillas, and the fireworks that light up the night during the fiestas and ferias (fairs) that are celebrated every week.

So, yes, Mexico is magic. The kind of magic that stays with you – and in you – no matter where you go. It's in the way we celebrate life, even in its simplest moments. As Mexicans, we carry that magic within us, proudly sharing it with the world – one song, one dish, one story at a time.

Mexico is already part of you, and it will make you feel like family. So here we go with another beautiful cookbook to bring love and Mexican flavours to your table, no matter where you are.

My country is large, and for this book I've divided it into eight areas. Mexico from north to south, west to east and everything in between ... Each region has its own ancient landscape, indigenous peoples, history, unique food culture and personality. This mix of cultures makes Mexico a strong, living being and its traditions are treasures that have survived millennia.

The streets of Mexico are alive with laughter – and food. Always food! Street vendors will call out their offerings and follow you, trying to convince you to buy. The tantalising smells are everywhere – and the food is the best you'll ever try ... Tacos, tamales, pozoles and those famous moles. Every meal carries the wisdom of centuries.

Over its vast lands Mexico has everything to offer and every corner of the country tells a story, from turquoise coastlines with warm waters and delicious seafood, to dark forests of ancient trees, snowy mountains and deep valleys, harsh deserts, mysterious pyramids and some of the world's busiest and most vibrant cities. Not to forget the 177 Pueblos Mágicos – the intriguing, beautiful, culturally rich 'magical towns' the government has featured as a special tourism initiative.

Colour and sound is everywhere: hanging pinatas and market stalls topped with fruits and vegetables; the calls of shamans offering candles and magic potions; and small kitchens selling simple home-cooked meals with music playing – maybe a small family band or some norteño music with an accordion and bajo sexto thrumming through a nearby speaker.

Every visit, every city, every Pueblo Mágico, every conversation, every meal – even if it's from a taco stall by the side of the highway in the middle of nowhere – feels like discovering a new piece of Mexico's soul. So, let's take a journey from north to south.

In the northwest you'll find the states of Baja California (divided into North and South), Sonora, Sinaloa, Durango and the country's largest state, Chihuahua. This area is known for its wines, as well as for some of Mexico's most famous and popular exports: fish tacos, Caesar salad and margaritas!

There's a strong ranching tradition across the north – cattle were introduced by the Spanish after conquistador Hernán Cortés arrived in 1519, bringing down the Aztec Empire. Beef is king here, and the famous cheeses of the 'dairy basin' also come from that cattle industry. The climate and landscape are perfect for wheat farming, meaning flour tortillas are – unusually – more popular than corn in this part of the country.

The northeast (Coahuila, Nuevo León and Tamaulipas) is famed for its roasted meats. Carne asada and cabrito are much more than just a meal here – they're a way of life. A perfect weekend for many Monterrey families will usually involve carne asada roasting on the grill, kids running around, music playing ... the vibe is relaxed, communal and always a little smoky!

Let's leave the woodsmoke and head down to the central north – the states of Zacatecas, San Luis Potosi, Aguascalientes, Guanajuato and Querétaro – where the weather and nature start to slowly change. The Huicholes are the indigenous peoples of this area – you can visit a Huichol temple and witness the traditional dances and learn about peyote ceremonies. I was excited to try the traditional food of the area and, of course, enchiladas potosinas were on the table. They were delicious and crispy, with toppings so fluffy that it seemed I would never get full!

The urban hub of Mexico City lies in the Centro Sur (central south region). It's a melting pot of migration from all the other regions, as well as many foreign countries, and its food reflects that. This is where I grew up and, along with the home-cooked pozoles and tamales from our own kitchen, we would always enjoy plenty of street foods such as tacos and tortas. Many modern restaurants in CDMX now focus on traditional pre-Hispanic dishes – you might even find grasshoppers as the main protein in your dinner!

Just north of the city, San Juan Teotihuacán is known as the 'place where Gods are born'. Here are the magnificent Pyramids of the Sun and Moon – they will leave you speechless, and climbing them took my breath away. There is much to explore in this sacred area, with incomparable Aztec figures and engravings. I remember my primary school teacher being excited to talk about them; but at the time I was too young to understand the magnitude of our historical heritage.

As a good chilanga, I have made countless visits to the pyramids with my siblings and, of course, taken my own son, Julio. I have watched the spring equinox over the Sun Pyramid and feel truly lucky to have climbed both, as it's not allowed any more – we realise we have to take care of such a special place. Inside the archaeological zone you won't find seats or any other niceties – it'll be just you, Mexican history and the sun heating your head! Then you must also take time to sit in the town, eat chorizo verde tacos with guacamole and fat, hand-made tlacoyos filled up with beans and topped with nopal (prickly pear cactus), so fresh it seems to have been cut from the restaurant's backyard.

Head west and you will come across one of Mexico's most memorable Pueblos Mágicos – Tequila in the state of Jalisco. Obviously, this town is one of the proudest producers of tequila, Mexico's most famous drink. I went there not long ago with my dad and my best friend, Juan Manuel. Taking a tour to the tequila distilleries in a chilli-shaped truck was fun, up the rocky highways through the blue agave plantations. We hoped to see tejones or armadillos; we didn't have any luck, but maybe we just didn't pay enough attention – it is difficult to concentrate on the wildlife during a tequila tour!

Los Cantaritos el Güero lies halfway between Tequila and Jalisco's state capital, Guadalajara. The food here is magical: perfect aguachile (fresh chilli prawns in salsa negra – the region's special rich, dark sauce), tangy ceviches and, of course, pozole rojo (red pork and hominy stew) were just what we needed to keep us going through the day. On one memorable night, we danced to musica banda until we couldn't stand any more, hugging each other like it was our last day on earth.

The eastern states of Hidalgo, Tlaxcala, Puebla and Veracruz make up Mexico's Gulf Coast. My aunt and cousins live in Hidalgo, so I love this area! The restaurants are filled with smoke from the comales, and you can enjoy delights like slow-cooked barbacoa in the morning with a cold, spicy michelada. The Otomi have lived in this place for thousands of years and their beautiful, colourful and mystical tenangos (embroideries) represent the land, flowers, wild animals and humans. There is always balance and connection between us, it's part of the Otomi vision of the cosmos and the inspiration for their embroidered art that can take months to complete.

Indigenous, Spanish and Afro-Caribbean ingredients are melded in the cooking pots of this region. The Europeans introduced herbs, along with rice, citrus fruits and pineapple, olives, capers and olive oil. Seafood is also high on the menu, so be sure to try the seafood rice dish arroz a la tumbada – along with the complex moles flavoured with spices and chocolate.

The Yucatán Peninsula separates the Caribbean from the Gulf of Mexico, and the food of the southeast states – Tabasco, Campeche, Yucatán and Quintana Roo – has a strong Mayan tradition, such as traditional Yucatán barbecued pork conchinita pibil and citrus-marinated poc chuc. Achiote is the signature spice here, and it gives many of the foods a distinctive reddish tinge. Habaneros are on every table and tropical fruits such as tamarind, plums, mamey, avocados and bitter oranges are common.

Last, but never least, we arrive in the southwest and discover the mountains and deep valleys of the states of Guerrero, Oaxaca and Chiapas. Oaxaca's food was less influenced by the Spanish compared to other parts of the country, so it still has strong ties to the indigenous Mixtec and Zapotec people. Corn tortillas are eaten at every meal, and black beans and chocolate are very popular. We visited the Mercado 20 de Noviembre, and this is when I wished I had two tummies to try everything on offer ... Rows of street stalls selling drinks, fruits and insects – lots of insects! I felt almost dizzy with excitement. I wanted to eat all of the food on offer: queso Oaxaca, sweet breads and more. Of course, we started with tamales. But tamales are not just big here: they are huge!

Too full? There is always enough room left for an earthy mezcal shot, flavoured or straight. It's actually necessary to prepare you for the next food round which was, of course, the 'seven moles' of Oaxaca! Negro, colorado, rojo, verde, amarillo, chichilo and the 'tablecloth staining' manchamantel! They are all different and it's hard to pick your favourite. Dare to try them all: you won't regret it!

Now we've criss-crossed the country, shall we get into the recipes? You might fall in love with them to the point that you realise you just want to be in Mexico or, as we call it, for many reasons: *Mexico lindo y querido!* My lovely, beloved Mexico!

THE MEXICAN PANTRY

Most of the following ingredients are proudly 100 per cent Mexican, and can be purchased from Latin American supermarkets or online.

Achiote

Made from annatto seeds and sold in small blocks, this paste is used to add a radiant colour and sour flavour to food. It is one of the signature ingredients of Yucatán cuisine.

Amaranth

A 'pseudo-cereal' native to North and Central America, amaranth is one of the oldest cultivated crops in the world. In Mexico, the tiny edible seeds are popularly used to make alegrias, a pressed candy bar made with agave syrup, nuts and dried fruit that's commonly eaten as a snack.

Avocados

The avocado was first discovered around 500 BCE by the Aztecs, who named it 'ahuacatl', meaning 'testicle', due to the way the fruit hangs on trees. Today, the humble avocado, of which Mexico is still the world's biggest producer, is found on every table in every Mexican home. It's added to everything from tacos to tortas, dips to salsas, or eaten just on its own, scooped with a spoon. Even if your meal doesn't call for avocado, we still often serve a cheeky avocado taco at the start or end of the main meal.

Beans

These dried legumes are a staple in every Mexican household. Generally speaking, pinto beans are more commonly found in Mexico's north, while black beans are used in central and southern Mexican cooking. Beans are used to make Frijoles refritos (see page 322), which is used as a spread or filling for tacos and tortas.

Cacao

Is there anyone who doesn't like chocolate? Perhaps Mexico's most famous export, cacao was worshipped, used as currency and consumed as a bitter drink before the arrival of the Spanish in the 16th century. They took the cocoa bean to Europe, where sugar was added to make the much-loved treat we all know today (although some Mexicans will argue that Mexican chocolate is still the best). We eat cacao to treat depression, sadness, colds and flu, and use it to make moles or any number of sweet treats.

Cajeta

A thickened syrup made with burned goat's milk, cajeta is considered a type of dulce de leche. Eaten as a snack with warm bolillos (Mexican bread rolls), it can also be used to make jellies and cakes, or to top ice cream and pancakes.

Chamoy

This versatile condiment, made with fresh or dried apricots, chillies and powdered lime, adds a delightful tang to dishes and drinks. It is most commonly served with fruit, fries and chicharrones, and even in cocktails. To make your own chamoy, try the recipe on page 295.

Cheese

One of Mexico's most popular cheeses, Oaxaca (also known as quesillo) is a white semi-hard cheese from – you guessed it – Oaxaca. It is used in any dish that requires melted cheese.

Queso fresco (fresh cheese) is commonly used to top garnachas, soups, enchiladas and tostadas. A mild feta is a good alternative.

Asadero cheese is a semi-hard cheese similar to haloumi that's popular in the north of Mexico.

Requesón is a soft, sour cheese that's also used to top garnachas or tacos. Ricotta is a good substitute.

Chillies

In Mexico, there are more than 150 varieties of chilli – along with countless ways to prepare them. Some of the most popular chillies include serrano, jalapeno, chipotle, guajillo, pasilla, ancho and arbol, and you will find these in many of the recipes in this book, in both their fresh and dried forms. Dried chillies are easy to buy in bulk online.

Clamato

A tomato-based drink mixed with clam broth and spices, Clamato is commonly used as a base for cocktails such as Micheladas (see page 76) and bloody marys. It's also commonly enjoyed on its own with ice, a squeeze of lime and a celery stick. This is a Canadian product but its easily found at Latin American grocers, cocktail supply stores and online. In Australia, V8 vegetable juice is a good substitute.

Corn

The foundation of Mexican cuisine, corn is Mexico's most common grain, with 59 indigenous varieties to choose from. It forms the basis of tamales, tacos, quesadillas, gorditas, tostadas and many desserts and drinks. It is estimated that corn is the main ingredient in more than half of all Mexican dishes, and tortillas are nearly always served with the main meal. In Mexico, white, yellow and blue corn is most commonly ground into flour for tortillas.

Huitlacoche (corn smut) – a corn fungus that grows on some corn – is considered to be a truffle-like delicacy.

Crema

In Mexico, crema has the taste of sour cream, but the consistency of thickened cream, and is a must-have ingredient for topping garnachas, enchiladas and chilaquiles, and for making desserts. Mexican crema can be hard to find, so I like to use a mix of half sour cream and half thickened cream – an Australian ingredient that is slightly dense compared to pure cream. However, you can simply add a bit of milk to sour cream to reach the right drizzling consistency.

Epazote

This aromatic herb, native to Central and South America as well as some parts of Mexico, is often added to beans, quesadillas, soups and teas. It has a strong, almost medicinal flavour, that adds depth to dishes, but it can be an acquired taste to anyone eating it for the first time. Epazote can aid digestion and reduce bloating, although consuming too much can lead to an upset stomach. Fresh epazote is hard to find outside Mexico, but you can buy dried epazote online and from Latin American grocers.

Jicama

Also known as the Mexican yam bean, this tuberous root vegetable is added to salads or eaten as a street snack with various toppings.

Limes

Although not indigenous to Mexico, it's impossible to imagine a Mexican meal without the addition of this ubiquitous citrus. Limes are served with tacos, garnachas, seafood, desserts and in cocktails, where they add a sour tang that helps to cut through rich flavours.

Maggi seasoning

Whether sprinkled over snacks or stirred into Micheladas (see page 76), this sauce adds a salty, umami taste to dishes.

Masa

Masa flour, or masa harina, is made from finely ground corn that has been nixtamalised (soaked in an alkaline solution to break down the outer husk and improve its nutrient availability). Masa is used to make tortillas, quesadillas, gorditas, sopes, huaraches and more. Do not confuse masa flour with regular cornmeal or cornflour (corn starch) when buying flour to make your doughs.

Confusingly, however, masa flour can also be labelled as maize flour, masa lista, maseca and minsa. Just remember that masa flour can be made from white, yellow or blue corn and has a coarse texture. Yellow or blue masa flours are quite distinctive. White masa has a creamy colour, and is easily distinguished from cornflour, which has a very fine, soft consistency.

Nopales

Sold fresh and tinned throughout Mexico, nopales are the edible pads of the nopal cactus (also known as the prickly pear cactus). They have a mild and slightly sour flavour, and are slightly sticky. Sliced and cooked nopales are often added to tacos or served in salads. In Mexico, nopales and the fruit from the cactus are added to juices and smoothies. Outside of Mexico, the tinned variety is readily available.

Onions

As in many cuisines, onions feature heavily in Mexican cooking. White onions, which are sweeter and less astringent than brown onions, are nearly always used. They are often added raw to salsas and salads or used as a garnish.

Oregano

Mexican oregano is used throughout the recipes in this book. It has a stronger flavour and aroma than Mediterranean oregano, with earthy notes that combine perfectly with chillies and Mexican spices. You'll find it in spice shops, Latin American grocers and online.

Piloncillo

Piloncillo is a raw, dark unrefined sugar made from boiled sugar cane juice. It has a long history dating back to pre-Hispanic times, when the Aztecs used sugar cane juice for sweetening. Piloncillo is still produced traditionally and is widely used in Mexican cuisine, especially in drinks and desserts. It is sold in densely packed and distinctively shaped solid cones. Soft brown sugar can be used instead.

Pork lard

Pork lard is used extensively in Mexican cooking, even for pastries and sweet breads. It enhances the flavour of dishes and adds a soft or fluffy texture to the end result. You will find it in most supermarkets or your local butcher might sell it. Substitute vegetable shortening for a vegan or vegetarian alternative.

Tajin seasoning

A chilli, lime and salt mix with a sour taste that's often sprinkled on fruit, vegetables, soups, beer, popcorn and even lollies. It goes with everything!

Tama-Roca sticks

Mexican candy sticks made with tamarind, chilli, lime and salt. They are often added to slurpees or Micheladas (see page 76), but can also be enjoyed on their own.

Tomatillos

Also known as the Mexican husk tomato, tomatillos are not related to tomatoes, despite their name. The fruit has a tangy, sour taste and can be eaten cooked or raw.

Tomatoes

A global ingredient now synonymous with Mediterranean cuisine, it's hard to believe that Europe has only grown this fruit for 500 years. Archaeological evidence suggests the Aztecs were cultivating and cooking tomatoes as early as 500 BCE. By the 16th century, Cortés and his fellow invaders spread this versatile fruit around the world … and the rest, as they say, is history.

Valentina sauce

This famous Mexican condiment is a staple in kitchens throughout Mexico. It combines cayenne chillies, vinegar and salt to produce a hot sauce that's drizzled on nearly everything. Valentina sauce comes in two varieties – hot and extra hot. You can replace it with Buffalo, Tapatio or Botanera hot sauces, but Valentina sauce is the most traditional.

Vanilla

Another indigenous ingredient, vanilla comes from the orchid family and grows in tropical areas. Pollination is required to produce the vanilla 'fruit' with its dark, shiny skin and strong perfume. Vanilla seeds are added to many Mexican desserts.

Baja California ❋ Baja California Sur ❋

ROESTE
ora Sinaloa Chihuahua Durango

EL NOROESTE

I'm trying hard not to be biased, but I can't imagine another part of the world that has more than northwest Mexico ... more geography, more history, more intriguing food traditions. This area – made up of the states of Baja California, Baja California Sur, Sonora, Sinaloa, Chihuahua and Durango – truly has it all.

It's a thrilling blend of ancient and modern, blessed with wildly different landscapes from the arid deserts of Chihuahua and Sonora to the lush coastline of Baja California. The region's food reflects that, too. From the ancient tradition of barbecuing in a pit in the ground, to the Caesar salad that was quickly thrown together in a Tijuana hotel kitchen, to the rise of fish tacos on the world stage in the 1970s, northwest Mexico is always proudly creating and reinventing.

For centuries, if not millennia, the indigenous peoples of this region fed themselves well from the ingredients of the desert, mountains and coastline. The desert communities thrived on drought-resistant crops and foraged foods – maize, beans and squash as staples, flavoured with chillies, herbs and wild plants. Coastal groups like the Seri feasted on seafood, while the inlanders cooked hardy grains, such as amaranth, and foraged juicy nopales (cactus pads) and agave.

Throughout the region, people used different parts of the agave plant for food, drinks or to feed their animals. The quiote (flower stalk) was cooked for its sweet, fibrous texture. The piña (core) was roasted in underground pits to release its natural sugars; it was sometimes eaten as a sweet treat or used to ferment beverages. The pencas (leaves) were occasionally cooked or softened to feed animals during droughts. Some agave species were used to make mezcal, while others provided fibres for household items such as ropes, brooms and even roofs.

When the Spanish arrived in the 1500s, they brought with them livestock, wheat and spices, which gradually merged with local ingredients. The climate in Mexico's northwest is drier than in the south, making it better suited to growing wheat – and so flour tortillas, rather than the traditional corn tortillas, became a staple, particularly in Sonora and Chihuahua. The drier climate and grassy plains were also perfect for Spanish ranch culture and the northwest became famed for its beef and dairy, especially cheeses, and is today known as the 'dairy basin' of Mexico.

The ancient barbacoa method of slowly cooking meat to juicy perfection in a pit in the ground, covered with agave leaves, is thought to be the origin of the English term 'barbecue' – and fall-apart slow-cooked 'pulled' meats are now a hallmark of northwestern cooking. Foods in this region were often preserved by smoking and drying, which also enhanced their flavour. Machaca (see page 22) was originally made with deer meat dried under the desert sun, then seasoned and shredded using a metate (a flat stone mortar and pestle). With the arrival of Spanish cattle, beef took over as the main ingredient in machaca and other meat dishes.

Chilorio – preserved meat from the Sinaloa region – was made in pre-Hispanic times by cooking deer and wild boar with chillies. The Spanish introduced pork, which is now the favourite ingredient – a wonderful flavour-packed example of the blending of Spanish and local cultures.

The Mennonites arrived in Chihuahua, Mexico's largest state, in the early 20th century, bringing their cheese-making skills. It's incredible that a community once thought of as isolated could have such a lasting impact. The local cheese they produced is known today as 'Mennonite cheese' or 'Chihuahua cheese'. Mild yet rich, it melts perfectly, making it ideal for dishes like Chile con queso (see page 18), another of Chihuahua's iconic dishes that's now a staple in every Mexican restaurant. Another key ingredient of the region is the native long, green chilaca chilli. When dried it's called a pasilla chilli; when used fresh, it adds a distinct flavour and just the right amount of non-spicy heat to balance the creamy cheese.

South of Chihuahua, in the 'dairy basin' of the Comarca Lagunera (Region of Lagoons, which spans the states of Durango and neighbouring Coahuila), farm workers created their own unique dish by cooking pieces of meat communally on an old plough disc to make a shared lunchtime feast, which became known as Discada (see page 36), after the disc on which it was cooked. Now every restaurant and every family in the region has their own version of this recipe.

By contrast, Baja California, in the very northwest of Mexico bordering California, is famed for its seafood, with fish tacos being one of its most famous modern exports. They were originally a humble snack cooked up by exhausted fishermen on the beach at the end of the day, and packed into a corn tortilla with cabbage and pico de gallo. Since the 1970s they've hitched a lift on every trendy food truck and travelled across the world, proudly showcasing their home region.

Tamales barbones (see page 31), made with fresh prawns (shrimp) whose barbas (whiskers) stick out cheekily through the tops of the corn husks, are a culinary tradition from the small town of Escuinapa de Hidalgo in south Sinaloa. At the other end of the food scale is the showy Torre de Mariscos (see page 28). Nothing humble here. It's an extraordinary tower of fresh seafood invented to showcase the fabulous range and quality of local Sinaloan seafood.

Mexico's northwest is a vibrant, living example of how food reflects culture, geography and history. Local cooking methods and recipes many thousands of years old remain intact, but globalisation has brought new twists, and local chefs are cleverly working indigenous ingredients into modern dishes. Watch this space: this is a kitchen story that continues to evolve, one plate at a time.

Chile con Queso

Spicy cheese

Serves 4

This dish holds a special place in my heart because my father spent a lot of time working in Chihuahua, where this dish originated, and he often makes it for us now that we live in Sydney. His chile con queso fills our home with the warmth of his memories and the richness of its flavours, and to me the combination of melted Chihuahua cheese and roasted chilaca chillies is pure comfort. It's a dish that reminds me not only of my family roots, but how food connects us across continents, from the Mennonite farmers in the Chihuahuan desert, to our kitchen in Australia. When my father cooks chile con queso, it's as if we're back in Mexico, if only for a moment. It's amazing how a simple dish can carry so much history and personal meaning.

Ingredients

- 4 fresh poblano or banana chillies
- 1 tablespoon vegetable oil
- 1 white onion, finely sliced
- 1 teaspoon crushed garlic
- 1 teaspoon table salt
- 250 g (9 oz) mild cheddar, grated (or Chihuahua cheese if you can get it)
- 100 g (3½ oz) mozzarella, grated
- 1 tablespoon sour cream
- Totopos, to serve Page 318 →

Method

Preheat a barbecue grill or use a stovetop gas flame to char the chillies, turning occasionally, until the skins are blackened and blistered. Using tongs, immediately transfer the chillies to a large zip-lock bag and let them sweat for 5–10 minutes – this will make peeling them much easier. Once the chillies are cool enough to handle, cut off the stems, peel away the skins and carefully remove and discard the seeds. Slice the chillies into thin strips.

Heat the oil in a saucepan over medium heat and saute the onion and garlic for 2–3 minutes, until translucent and fragrant. Add the chilli strips and saute for another 2–3 minutes.

Sprinkle with the salt and stir well. Reduce the heat to low, add the cheese and mozzarella and let them melt for 3 minutes, or until fully combined. Add the sour cream and stir until you have a creamy mixture.

The chile con queso is best served straightaway, for the cheese to have the perfect consistency.

Serve as a dip with totopos or corn chips, or use to stuff tacos, quesadillas or burritos.

Ensalada Cesar

Caesar salad

Serves 4

The Caesar salad was invented in 1924 at Caesar Cardini's restaurant in Tijuana. It was a dish created out of necessity. Cardini, an Italian restaurateur from a family of immigrants, had to use what was on hand when his kitchen was short on ingredients after being overwhelmed by diners' orders, leading to the delicious – and now classic – mix of cos lettuce, croutons, parmesan and an iconic creamy dressing.

In Mexico, Caesar salad is often topped with grilled meats and enjoyed as a main ... and the recipe has of course evolved with many local twists, with restaurants adding avocado, spicy chillies and different cheeses – but in Tijuana you will find the original. Chefs prepare the salad tableside, showcasing the fresh ingredients and making the beautiful fusion of Italian and Mexican flavours a full dining experience. The dressing is the star of the show.

Ingredients

- 3 baby or 1 large cos (romaine) lettuce, about 300 g (10½ oz), large leaves torn
- 50 g (1¾ oz) parmesan

Croutons

- 100 ml (3½ fl oz) olive oil
- pinch of garlic powder
- pinch of freshly ground black pepper
- 1 teaspoon table salt
- 250 g (9 oz) bread, cut into 2 cm (¾ in) cubes

Dressing

- 2 egg yolks
- 1 teaspoon crushed garlic
- 4 anchovy fillets, finely chopped
- juice of 1 lemon
- 1 teaspoon dijon mustard
- 50 ml (1¾ fl oz) olive oil

Method

Preheat the oven to 160°C (320°F) fan-forced and line a baking tray with baking paper.

To make the croutons, pour the olive oil into a large bowl, add the garlic powder, pepper and salt and stir together. Add the bread cubes and toss to coat, then arrange in a single layer on the baking tray, transfer to the oven and bake for 10–15 minutes, until lightly golden and crisp.

Now for the dressing – which is traditionally mixed in a large wooden bowl with a wooden spoon! Whisk together the egg yolks, garlic, anchovy fillets (don't skip these: they're the secret ingredient), lemon juice, mustard and olive oil. Keep whisking the dressing until it's creamy and smooth, with a mayonnaise-like consistency. Season with salt and pepper.

To assemble, add the lettuce to the bowl of dressing and toss well, making sure every leaf gets coated. Add the croutons and shave the parmesan over the top and serve immediately.

If you're feeling fancy you could add some grilled chicken, but remember that the original recipe is just as delicious without any other ingredients.

Burrito Machaca

Beef jerky burrito

Makes 10

Machaca is beloved in northern Mexico, especially in Chihuahua. It was originally made with deer meat that had been dried under the searing hot sun, then seasoned with salt and garlic and pounded and shredded using a metate (a flat stone mortar and pestle). It was the perfect way to preserve meat in arid desert areas.

Today, beef is more commonly used, and it is dried in an oven, then cooked in a sauce of tomatoes and chilli. Machaca is often made in large portions, so it's ready whenever the craving hits, perhaps for a cazuela (stew), or served with eggs in a burrito, or in a Torta de la barda (see page 70). I make this in Sydney for my friends from Chihuahua – and even if I'm not using the traditional method, it's always packed with flavour and brings a taste of home to those who are missing it.

The machaca can be prepared well ahead. It will keep in an airtight container in the fridge for up to 2 months.

Ingredients

- 2 kg (4 lb 6 oz) minute steaks
- 30 g (1 oz) table salt
- 2 tablespoons minced garlic

Machaca sauce

- 2 tablespoons vegetable oil
- 1 white onion, finely diced
- 1 teaspoon crushed garlic
- 2 fresh jalapeno chillies, finely diced
- 2 roma (plum) tomatoes, finely diced
- 8 eggs, whisked together

To serve

- 10 large Tortillas de harina, about 30 cm (12 in) in size — page 316 →
- 1 × quantity Frijoles negros refritos — page 322 →
- 400 g (14 oz) mozzarella, shredded or sliced
- Salsa de Cacahuate y Chile de Arbol — page 304 →

Method

Preheat the oven to 130°C (270°F) fan-forced.

Spread the steaks on a wire rack over a large deep baking tray. Sprinkle generously with the salt and garlic on both sides. Transfer to the oven and bake for 1 hour, or until the meat is slightly dry.

Increase the oven temperature to 180°C (350°F) fan-forced and bake for another 45 minutes. The meat should be dry on the outside, but still soft inside. Allow to cool.

Pulse the meat briefly in a food processor to shred it. The meat will reduce down and become a sort of fine 'powder' (similar to Asian pork floss).

To make the machaca sauce, heat the oil in a large saucepan over medium heat and saute the onion and garlic for 2–3 minutes, until softened. Add the chilli and the shredded meat and cook for 8 minutes, or until the machaca looks golden and slightly fried. Stir in the tomato and cook for 5 minutes. Finally, add the egg to the pan and stir regularly for about 3 minutes, until cooked through.

Working in batches, spread each tortilla with a generous portion of refried beans and 40 g (1½ oz) mozzarella. Add some machaca sauce to each burrito, wrap it up and toast in a comal or heavy-based frying pan for about 2 minutes on each side, until the cheese has melted.

Serve with the salsa.

Quesabirrias

Spiced beef quesadillas

Makes 12

Birria is a traditional goat soup from Guadalajara, while quesabirrias (cheese birrias) have become an incredibly popular social media phenomenon in recent years, particularly in the United States. Regardless of if you eat them in Tijuana or San Diego, quesabirrias have a definite northern Mexican heritage, whether made with beef, lamb or the traditional goat. I couldn't stop myself mixing it up a bit though, adding more chillies for a beautiful rich colour.

Method

To make the marinade, place the chillies in a saucepan and cover with 1 litre (4 cups) water. Bring to the boil, then reduce the heat and simmer for 5 minutes, or until the chillies are soft. Pour the chillies and their cooking water into a blender and add the salt. Blend until smooth.

Heat the oil in a saucepan over medium heat, add the chilli mixture and cook for 7–10 minutes, until it darkens slightly. Remove from the heat. Place the remaining marinade ingredients in the blender and blitz until smooth, then transfer to a large bowl, stir in your chilli sauce and season. Add the beef to the marinade and toss to coat. Cover and marinate in the fridge overnight, turning the beef occasionally.

The next day, pour 2.5 cm (1 in) water into a saucepan, add the bay leaves, peppercorns and cloves and bring to a simmer. Place the marinated meat in a steamer basket, put the lid on, then set the steamer over the pan. Steam over low heat for 8 hours, or until the meat is completely tender – check regularly and top up the water in the pan as needed. Allow the meat to cool slightly, then shred.

Using a slotted spoon, remove the bay leaves, peppercorns and cloves from the birria broth, then add about 1 litre (4 cups) water and gently heat. Taste, and add a little more water if the flavour is still very strong.

Heat ¼ teaspoon of lard in a chargrill pan over medium heat. Take a tortilla and dip it in the birria broth. Add the tortilla to the hot pan and let it warm up for a minute. Sprinkle a handful of shredded cheese on one half of the tortilla, top with a generous helping of shredded beef, then fold the tortilla in half and give it a gentle press with a spatula so it sticks together. Cook on both sides until the tortilla is golden and crispy. Transfer to a plate and keep warm while you cook the rest.

Serve with the coriander, onion and lime wedges, and some broth for each person to dip their quesabirrias into.

Ingredients

- 1 kg (2 lb 3 oz) boneless beef, cut into 5 cm (2 in) chunks
- 3 bay leaves
- 5 whole black peppercorns
- 2 whole cloves
- 1 tablespoon pork lard
- 12 Tortillas de maiz page 314 →
- 300 g (2 cups) shredded Oaxaca or mozzarella cheese

Marinade

- 2 dried guajillo chillies, stems removed
- 2 dried pasilla chillies, stems removed
- 2 dried cascabel chillies, stems removed
- 4 dried ancho chillies, stems removed
- 1 teaspoon table salt
- 1 tablespoon vegetable oil
- 2 tomatoes, roughly chopped
- 1 white onion, roughly chopped
- 1 teaspoon ancho chilli powder
- 1 teaspoon dried Mexican oregano
- 1 teaspoon finely grated fresh ginger
- 1 garlic clove, peeled
- 1 teaspoon ground cumin
- 330 ml (11 fl oz) bottle of Mexican lager
- 2 tablespoons white vinegar

To serve

- 1 bunch of coriander (cilantro), chopped
- 1 white onion, finely chopped
- 3 limes, cut into wedges

QUESO CHIHUAHUA

When we were living in Mexico City, Dad would bring home delicious wedges of buttery, crumbly Chihuahua cheese from his work trips to the north, and Mum would make sticky cheese quesadillas or chayotes (chokos) stuffed with cheese – my favourite! Dad always asked for Mum's choriqueso, a dip made with melted Chihuahua cheese and crispy chunks of Mexican chorizo, perfect for tacos made with flour tortillas, just the way he enjoyed them in Chihuahua.

In northern Mexico, Chihuahua cheese is a staple in so many dishes. Its meltability makes it ideal for anything that needs oozy, melty, gooey cheese: quesadillas, tacos, burritos and stuffed chillies, and the local creamy Chile con queso (see page 18). It's also sometimes called 'queso asadero' because it's great for grilling, topping grilled meats and for making baked cheese.

You'll find this famous cheese in almost every home and restaurant in this part of the world, a symbol of the region's dairy heritage. Its origins are closely tied to the Mennonite migrations of the 16th century. The Mennonites fled Germany and the Netherlands to escape religious persecution, settling initially in rural Poland, then Canada. Centuries later, in 1922, about 3000 Mennonites from the Canadian province of Manitoba reached an agreement with the Mexican President, Álvaro Obregón, to settle in Chihuahua, where they bought large areas of land and were allowed to keep their language, traditions and beliefs. By 1927 their numbers had grown to 10,000 and they were established in the states of Chihuahua, Durango and Guanajuato.

Similar to the Amish communities of Pennsylvania, the Mennonites are committed to following a simple way of life. Even today they use almost no electricity or internet, and shun cars for personal use. The community supports itself through centuries-old farming traditions, growing corn, chillies, cotton and onions – and, of course, making their famous dairy products. A few Mennonites married Chihuahuenses or other Mexicans, but they often kept within their own communities. It's still easy to recognise them in the towns – almost every pale-skinned person in the state is a 'Menonita'!

Almost as soon as they'd settled in Chihuahua, the Menonitas put their dairy skills to good use and started mass-producing their favourite products, including their cheese, adapting their methods to local conditions. Similar to pale cheddar or America's Monterey Jack, in Chihuahua this cheese is called 'queso menonita'. Everywhere else in Mexico it's known as 'queso Chihuahua'. Within the Mennonite communities it's called 'cheddar' or 'chester' cheese.

Queso Chihuahua today holds a crucial role in the state's agricultural and economic activities. It's produced in such large quantities that whole families rely on cheese-making for their household income. You can even buy it cut and packaged in the shape of the state of Chihuahua! My friends in Sydney who come from Chihuahua tell me it's the cheese they miss more than anything.

If you're lucky enough to travel through Chihuahua, be sure to sit down and enjoy a local chile con queso with totopos while you're there.

Torre de Mariscos

Seafood tower

Serves 4

The original fabulously flamboyant seafood tower, created about a decade ago by restaurateur Paul Peñuelas to showcase the abundance and freshness of local seafood off the coast of Sinaloa, is a mix of prawns, octopus, fish and scallops. Marinated in a zesty sauce of lime juice, tomatoes and coriander, it's often served with totopos or tostadas to add a contrasting crunch.

This recipe is dedicated to my friend Fabián, who introduced me to the local seafood in Sydney. We collaborated to create a version that closely resembles the original, using ingredients easily found in supermarkets. We told stories while we cooked and enjoyed the process of creating something special to share with friends and family, making memories along the way.

Preparing this amazing dish is an adventure. If you're cooking the octopus yourself, it's best to do so a day in advance. I layer my seafood towers in a plastic cylinder (from a milk or orange juice bottle), about 15 cm (6 in) high, with the top and bottom cut off. Easy!

Ingredients

- 1 red onion, very finely sliced
- 10 dried piquin chillies, crushed into flakes
- 600 ml (20½ fl oz) fresh lime juice (or enough to cure all the seafood separately)
- 300 g (10½ oz) firm white fish fillet, such as barramundi, cut into 2 cm (¾ in) chunks
- 2 roma (plum) tomatoes, seeds removed, finely diced
- 2 fresh jalapeno chillies, finely diced
- 2 tablespoons finely chopped coriander (cilantro), plus extra to serve
- table salt
- 300 g (10½ oz) raw prawns (shrimp), peeled, deveined and cut into 2 cm (¾ in) chunks
- 300 g (10½ oz) scallops, cut into quarters, roe removed
- 300 g (10½ oz) cooked octopus, cut into 1 cm (½ in) chunks (see Note overleaf)
- 2 avocados
- 1 cucumber, halved, seeds removed, then cut into 5 mm (¼ in) chunks
- 1 × quantity Salsa negra page 298 →
- Tostadas or Totopos, to serve page 318 →

Method

Combine the onion and chilli flakes in a non-metallic bowl, add 1 tablespoon of the lime juice and set aside to lightly pickle while preparing all the seafood.

Place the fish in a non-metallic bowl and add enough lime juice to cover. Leave to marinate for 20 minutes. Add the tomato, jalapeno chilli and coriander, stir together gently and add a pinch of salt to make a light ceviche.

Meanwhile, place the prawns, scallops and octopus in separate non-metallic bowls. Add enough lime juice to each bowl to cover all the seafood, then leave to marinate for 15 minutes.

Dice one of the avocados and slice the other avocado.

Once all the seafood is ready to go, use a tall plastic cylinder, about 10 cm (4 in) in diameter, to create an individual seafood tower on each person's plate, following the instructions overleaf.

Recipe continues →

Start by layering one-eighth of the cucumber inside the cylinder, then one-eighth of the fish ceviche, pressing down firmly with your hand to pack it well and create distinct layers. Next, add a layer of scallops, then some of the diced avocado. Add a layer of octopus, a little of the red onion mixture, and then prawns. Repeat in the same order to create a second round of layers, and finish by decorating the top with the sliced avocado and extra chopped coriander. Once the tower is tightly packed, pour a quarter of the salsa negra over the top. Carefully lift the plastic container upwards, ensuring the tower holds its shape and sits beautifully on the plate.

Repeat to make another three seafood towers. Serve immediately, with tostadas or totopos.

Note

If cooking your own octopus, buy a medium-sized one and start by cleaning it if this hasn't been done for you. Remove the beak, eyes and any leftover insides. Rinse under cold water to get rid of any grit or slime.

To tenderise the octopus, freeze it overnight and then thaw before cooking – this breaks down the meat fibres naturally.

To cook, in a deep stockpot, bring 2 litres (2 qts) water and 2 bay leaves to the boil over medium–high heat. Using tongs, grab the octopus by the head and dip the tentacles in and out of the boiling water three times. This makes them curl up nicely and helps keep the texture tender. Now lower the whole octopus into the boiling water, reduce the heat and simmer gently for 40 minutes or until a knife slides easily into the thickest part of the tentacles. (The cooking time will depend upon the size of your octopus.)

Tamales Barbones

Bearded prawn tamales

Makes 10

Let's talk tamales! They're my star dish in my tamaleria in Sydney, so in this cookbook you'll find lots of different tamal recipes from all across Mexico. From the city of Escuinapa de Hidalgo, in the south of Sinaloa bordering the state of Nayarit, comes the rare, unique and utterly delicious tamales barbones, which takes its amusing name from the way these richly flavoured tamales are prepared and presented. Traditionally, they are made with large fresh prawns, whose barbas (whiskers) show through the top of the corn husks in which they are wrapped – the street vendors in Escuinapa skilfully handle these tamales by their barbas.

Eating prawns has never been this much fun. Prepare to get your hands messy!

Ingredients

- 20 dried sweetcorn husks (see Notes overleaf)
- 3 dried guajillo chillies, stems removed
- 1 roma (plum) tomato
- ¼ white onion
- 100 g (3½ oz) pork lard
- 1 teaspoon baking powder
- 1 teaspoon prawn (shrimp) powder (see Notes overleaf)
- table salt
- 500 g (1 lb 2 oz) white or yellow masa flour
- 3 dried arbol chillies, stems removed
- 10 large raw prawns (shrimp), kept whole

Method

Soften the sweetcorn husks in a large bowl of warm water for about 5 minutes, then drain to remove any excess water.

Meanwhile, put the guajillo chillies in a saucepan with 1 litre (4 cups) water and bring to the boil. Leave to boil for 10 minutes, then remove from the heat and scoop out the chillies. Strain the cooking water, reserving both the water and the contents of the strainer. Set aside.

Toast the tomato and onion in a hot comal or heavy-based frying pan, turning often, for 5–7 minutes, until charred and well roasted. Set aside.

Place the lard and baking powder in a bowl and whip the mixture as fast as possible using a wooden spoon – the lard needs to soften and look spongy. Don't stress if this takes a long time; it can take up to 15 minutes to achieve the right consistency.

Pour 650 ml (22 fl oz) of the reserved chilli water into a blender. Add the rehydrated guajillo chillies, prawn powder and 1 teaspoon salt and blend until smooth. Pour the blended chilli mixture over the whipped lard, then add the masa flour and 1 tablespoon salt and mix well until completely combined. (Depending on the brand of masa flour you've used, you may need to add a little more water to achieve the right consistency.) To test if the dough is ready, drop a small ball of dough into a cup of cold water; if it floats to the top you're good to go! (If the dough doesn't float, mix the dough a little longer until it does float.)

Recipe continues →

Put the roasted tomato and onion in a blender. Add another 150 ml (5 fl oz) of the reserved chilli water and the leftover guajillo chilli seeds from your strainer. Add another 1 teaspoon salt and the arbol chillies. Blitz into a dense and chunky sauce.

To assemble the tamales, spread 100 g (3½ oz) of the dough over each corn husk, starting from the narrow end (the tip) and spreading it up to the middle, leaving a 4 cm (1½ in) border around the edge. Place a prawn lengthways on each corn husk, over the dough, ensuring its whiskers stick out from the tip of the husk. Drizzle about 2 tablespoons of the chunky sauce over each prawn, then spread another 40 g (1½ oz) of dough over each to seal the filling.

Place another sweetcorn husk over the filling, then wrap up the tamale by overlapping the sides and folding over the bottom edge towards the top to enclose the filling, but leaving the prawn whiskers sticking out the top. Secure with kitchen string and set aside. Repeat with the remaining husks and ingredients to make 10 tamales.

Stand the tamales upright in a large steamer. Fit as many tamales as you can into the steamer, but be careful not to pack them in too tightly or they may burst, leaving you with empty tamales. Place the steamer over a saucepan of simmering water and steam for 45 minutes.

The best way to check your tamales are cooked is to remove one from the steamer, let it cool for 5 minutes, and then unwrap the husk. If the dough doesn't stick to the husk and looks shiny and fluffy, then your tamales are ready.

Let the tamales cool for 15–20 minutes inside the steamer before serving.

The tamales will keep in an airtight container in the fridge for up to 2 days.

Notes

You can buy dried sweetcorn husks from Latin American supermarkets or online. It's better to buy more than you need, as they are unpredictable and can sometimes be small or break. They can be frozen, or kept in an airtight container in the pantry.

You'll find prawn powder in Asian grocery stores.

Tacos de Pescado

Fish tacos

Makes 16

After a long day at sea, the fishermen of Baja California would grill or fry their catch on the beach, then wrap it in corn tortillas and add whatever toppings they had to hand – shredded cabbage, pico de gallo, a drizzle of creamy chipotle sauce, or maybe just a squeeze of lime.

By the 1970s, with the rise of seafood restaurants and food trucks, fish tacos were no longer a local secret, and their popularity surged in the United States, especially California. Today, this fisherman's dinner is found at street stalls, and in pubs, fish and chip shops and even upmarket dining establishments around the world.

The combination of fresh fish with the textures and flavours of the condiments is essential – so never hesitate to add all the toppings.

Ingredients

600 g (1 lb 5 oz) skinless firm white fish fillets, such as barramundi, cut into strips about 8 cm (3¼ in) long and 3 cm (1¼ in) thick

vegetable oil, for deep-frying

Batter

250 g (9 oz) plain (all-purpose) flour

1 teaspoon baking powder

1 teaspoon table salt

1 teaspoon freshly ground black pepper

1 egg

250 ml (1 cup) Corona lager

To serve

16 Tortillas de maiz page 314 →

¼ cabbage (green or purple), shredded

Pico de gallo page 290 →

Mayonesa de chipotle page 288 →

Method

Place all the batter ingredients in a blender and mix until combined, thick and smooth. Transfer to a shallow bowl, add the fish and turn to coat.

Heat the oil in a deep-fryer or large heavy-based saucepan over medium–high heat to 190°C (375°F) on a kitchen thermometer. To check it's hot enough, drop a small amount of the batter into the oil – if it floats to the surface and starts bubbling, you're good to go!

Working in batches, lift the fish from the batter and gently lower it into the hot oil. Slowly fry for about 4 minutes, until lightly golden. Remove and drain briefly on paper towel.

Serve immediately, piling the fried fish into the tortillas with the cabbage, pico de gallo and chipotle mayo.

Discada

Durango-style asado

Serves 4

Legend has it that this dish originated with the workers of the 'dairy basin' in the Comarca Lagunera region as a communal lunchtime meal. A shared lunchbreak and limited utensils prevented everyone from cooking separately at the same time, so they would all bring whatever meat they happened to have at home, and toss it onto an old, worn-out, heated plough disc to cook together as a shared meal – and discada was created.

Nowadays, there are official discada 'recipes', and every family has its own particular take on it. Some throw in prawns (shrimp) or beer to give it a unique twist. Each version tells a story of family creativity – my advice is to use all the leftovers in your fridge and create your own family's tradition! This is also a wonderfully fun, festive dish for big reunions or informal gatherings.

Method

You'll need to use a cooking pot large enough to fit all the ingredients comfortably. Heat the lard in the pot over medium heat until it begins to melt. Add the chicken and cook, turning occasionally, for about 5 minutes, until lightly browned.

Add the pork and let it start releasing its fat, then add the beef and bacon. Stirring constantly, so all the meat cooks evenly and doesn't stick to the base of the pan, cook for about 10 minutes, until the meat is starting to brown and crisp up. Season with the salt and black pepper.

Once the meats are fully seared, add the lager to the pot, followed by the potato, onion, bell pepper, tomato and passata. Stir well, then continue to cook, stirring occasionally, for 15 minutes or until the potato is tender, the vegetables have softened and the lager has reduced slightly. The consistency should be juicy but not watery, with everything fully cooked and coated in the flavoursome sauce.

Serve immediately with tortillas and guacamole falso for a bit of kick.

Ingredients

- 100 g (3½ oz) pork lard
- 4 chicken drumsticks
- 250 g (9 oz) boneless pork, cut into 4 cm (1½ in) chunks
- 250 g (9 oz) boneless beef, cut into 4 cm (1½ in) chunks
- 150 g (5½ oz) bacon, diced
- 1 teaspoon table salt
- 1 teaspoon freshly ground black pepper
- 330 ml (11 fl oz) Corona lager
- 100 g (3½ oz) potato, cut into 2 cm (¾ in) dice
- 1 white onion, very finely sliced
- 2 green bell peppers (capsicums), cut into 2 cm (¾ in) dice
- 2 roma (plum) tomatoes, cut into 2 cm (¾ in) dice
- 100 ml (3½ fl oz) tomato passata (pureed tomatoes)

To serve

Tortillas de maiz page 314 →
Guacamole falso page 299 →

Chilorio

Sinaloan-style spicy pork

Serves 4

Today, you can buy chilorio in cans all across Mexico, but nothing compares to making it fresh at home, following the traditional methods used for generations. This rich, robust dish dates to pre-Hispanic times, when indigenous groups in the Sinaloa region made it with deer or wild boar, as well as salt and chillies to help preserve the meat. The arrival of the Spanish in the 1500s introduced pork to the local diet, which eventually became the main ingredient of this dish. Chilorio not only tells a story of indigenous techniques but also of the blending of Spanish and local cultures, giving us the rich flavours we enjoy today.

Method

Put the pork shoulder, bay leaves and salt in a large saucepan with 400 ml (14 fl oz) water. Cook at a gentle boil over medium heat for 20 minutes, until the water has almost evaporated and the meat is soft, dry and fall-apart tender. Discard the bay leaves.

Leaving the pork shoulder in the pan, shred the meat using two forks. Add the lard and fry the pulled pork meat over medium heat for 5–8 minutes, until lightly golden.

Meanwhile, to make the sauce, put the chillies in a small saucepan with 500 ml (2 cups) water and boil for 10 minutes, or until they are soft. Put the chillies in a blender with 100 ml (3½ fl oz) of their cooking water. Add the remaining sauce ingredients and blend to a smooth consistency.

Strain the sauce over the pulled pork and stir over low heat for 3–5 minutes, until warmed through.

Serve the chilorio with Mexican rice and refried beans – or with Salsa borracha if using it to fill a taco or burrito.

The chilorio will keep in an airtight container in the fridge for up to 3 days.

Ingredients

- 1 kg (2 lb 3 oz) boneless pork shoulder, diced
- 4 bay leaves
- 2 teaspoons table salt
- 60 g (2 oz) pork lard

Chilorio sauce

- 3 dried guajillo chillies
- ½ dried pasilla chilli
- 1½ teaspoons ground cinnamon
- 1½ teaspoons ground cloves
- 1 bay leaf
- 1½ teaspoons dried oregano
- 1 garlic clove, crushed
- pinch of ground cumin
- 2 teaspoons white vinegar

To serve

Arroz Mexicano	page 327 →
Frijoles negros refritos	page 322 →
Salsa borracha (optional)	page 290 →

Wakabaki

Sonora-style beef stew

Serves 4

For the Yaqui people of Sonora, this hearty beef stew, brimming with vegetables and chickpeas, is steeped in spiritual significance and is a vibrant celebration of culture. According to legend, their ancestors would make wakabaki after sacrificing a deer in tribute to their gods. Unlike other beef stews, which typically feature simple seasonings and focus on the flavour of the meat, wakabaki features a unique and rich blend of spices and local ingredients to create a complete meal that warms the soul.

Ingredients

- 500 g (1 lb 2 oz) beef ribs, separated
- 500 g (1 lb 2 oz) skirt steak, cut into 3 cm (1¼ in) chunks
- 4 bay leaves
- 1 teaspoon table salt
- 400 g (14 oz) tinned chickpeas (garbanzo beans), drained and rinsed
- 2 fresh poblano or banana chillies
- 2 roma (plum) tomatoes, each cut into 6 chunks
- 300 g (10½ oz) pumpkin (winter squash), cut into 3 cm (1¼ in) chunks
- 2 carrots, cut into 3 cm (1¼ in) chunks
- 200 g (7 oz) green beans, trimmed and halved
- 2 sweetcorn cobs, cut into 5 cm (2 in) chunks
- ½ green cabbage, roughly chopped
- 1 small bunch of coriander (cilantro), roughly chopped
- Tortillas de maiz, to serve page 314 →

Method

Pour 4 litres (4 qts) water into a large stockpot and place over medium heat. Add the beef ribs and skirt steak, bay leaves, salt and chickpeas. Bring to a gentle boil, then cook over medium heat for 1 hour, allowing the flavours to develop and the meat to become tender. Discard the bay leaves.

Meanwhile, preheat a barbecue grill or use a stovetop gas flame to char the chillies, turning occasionally, until the skins are blackened and blistered. Using tongs, immediately transfer the chillies to a large zip-lock bag and let them sweat for 5–10 minutes – this will make peeling them much easier. Once the chillies are cool enough to handle, cut off the stems. Peel away the skins and carefully remove and discard the seeds. Slice the chillies into strips.

Add the chilli strips to the pot, along with the tomato chunks, and simmer for 20 minutes. You should have a smooth, slightly chunky broth as the tomato breaks down.

Stir in the pumpkin, carrot, green beans and sweetcorn and simmer for another 20 minutes, until the vegetables start to become tender. Add the cabbage and coriander and simmer for another 10 minutes. Taste the broth – it should be rich and flavoursome – and adjust the seasoning if needed.

Serve the wakabaki with warm tortillas. Any leftovers will keep in an airtight container in the fridge for up to 3 days.

Colache

Zucchini and corn casserole

Serves 4

Mexican food is not just about meats and chillies. Colache, a traditional vegetarian dish celebrated for its vibrant colours and inviting aroma, is particularly popular in Sonora and Sinaloa. It's made with calabacita, a type of squash, mixed with fresh vegetables such as corn, tomatoes and onions, and served as a side dish or a main with rice and corn tortillas.

The western state of Michoacán has a very similar version of colache, which also features sauteed zucchini. I've included this variation on my menu at La Casa Latina in Sydney.

Ingredients

- 1 tablespoon vegetable oil
- 1 white onion, finely diced
- 1 teaspoon crushed garlic
- 3 zucchini (courgettes), cut into 1 cm (½ in) dice
- 2 fresh jalapeno chillies, seeds removed and finely chopped
- 1 tomato, finely diced
- 125 g (4½ oz) fresh or tinned sweetcorn kernels
- 1 teaspoon table salt
- 200 g (7 oz) firm ricotta or queso fresco, crumbled

Method

Heat the oil in a saucepan over medium heat. Add the onion, garlic, zucchini and chilli and saute for 5–7 minutes, until softened. Add the tomato and sweetcorn and cook, stirring occasionally, for 10 minutes, until just softened and combined.

Remove from the heat and stir in the salt and cheese. Serve with Mexican rice and warm tortillas.

The colache will keep in an airtight container in the fridge for up to 3 days, and can also be enjoyed cold or at room temperature.

To serve

Arroz Mexicano page 327 →
Tortillas de maiz page 314 →

Maizduros

Corn cookies

Makes about 20

These traditional baked biscuits from Durango are known for their crunch and slightly sweet corn flavour. The name combines 'maiz' (corn) and 'duros' (hard), describing their characteristic crispness.

Maizduros are part of the special Easter feast in Durango, but are also enjoyed with coffee, milk or traditional Mexican hot chocolate all year round. They have a unique smoky aroma from the wood-fired ovens they're traditionally cooked in and remind me of the delicious bakeries you can find in Pueblos Mágicos all over Mexico.

The sweet smell of cinnamon and piloncillo while these cookies are baking fills me with happiness and excitement, nostalgia and memories.

Ingredients

- 300 g (10½ oz) yellow maize flour
- 300 g (2 cups) plain (all-purpose) flour
- 50 g (1¾ oz) ground cinnamon
- pinch of table salt
- 1 tablespoon baking powder
- 150 g (5½ oz) piloncillo or brown sugar
- 100 g (3½ oz) pork lard or vegetable shortening
- 2 tablespoons natural vanilla extract
- 4 large eggs
- 370 ml (12½ fl oz) evaporated milk

Method

Preheat the oven to 160°C (320°F) fan-forced and line two baking trays with baking paper.

In a large mixing bowl, combine the flours, cinnamon, salt, baking powder and sugar. Add the lard and begin kneading. Gradually incorporate the vanilla, eggs and evaporated milk, kneading until you have a consistent dough that doesn't stick to your hands.

On a clean work surface, roll out the dough to about 1 cm (½ in) thick. Cut out shapes using a cookie cutter of your choice and arrange on the baking trays, leaving about 5 mm (¼ in) space between them.

Bake for 10 minutes, then turn all the cookies over and bake for another 5 minutes. Remove from the oven and leave to cool completely on a wire rack before serving.

The cookies will keep in an airtight container at room temperature for up to 2 weeks.

Tepache

Serves 6

Tepache is a traditional Mexican drink that originated with the fermentation of corn. However, when the Spanish arrived and introduced fruits, it began to be made with pineapple. Seeing freshly brewed tepache on offer at your favourite spot is a sure sign of instant refreshment.

The transformation from pineapple peel and spices to this fizzy, golden brew is like magic in a jar. The beauty of tepache is that no two batches are ever identical. Each one has its quirks, like a little fermented fingerprint – that's the charm of working with something alive. Even better, it's a brilliant way to use up pineapple skins that otherwise get discarded.

If you're after a boozy vibe, you can leave your tepache to ferment an extra day or two. Just don't get carried away – over-fermenting can make it a bit too tangy for most palates.

Feeling adventurous? Some people mix in a splash of beer for added fizz and a malty kick, while others spice things up with star anise or allspice to create their own signature twist.

Ingredients

- 1 large ripe organic pineapple
- 200 g (7 oz) piloncillo or soft brown sugar
- 1 cinnamon stick
- 2 cloves

Method

Prepare your pineapple by peeling the fruit and keeping the skin and core – they're the stars of the show here. Use the fruit to make dishes such as Tacos al pastor (see page 122), or just eat it with a sprinkling of Tajin seasoning and Chamoy sauce (see page 295).

Chop the pineapple skin and core into 10 cm (4 in) chunks and place in a large container or pitcher. Pour in 2 litres (2 qts) water, then stir in the sugar, cinnamon stick and cloves until the sugar dissolves. Cover the container with plastic wrap and secure with elastic bands to keep out insects.

Leave the tepache to sit at room temperature for 2–3 days, stirring occasionally. You'll notice it starting to bubble as it ferments – that's when you know the magic is happening! (How long it takes depends on the weather; fermentation happens more quickly when it's hot.) Once your tepache is tangy and just sweet enough, strain out the solids, chill the liquid, and serve over ice.

If you want a little fizz, let it ferment for an extra day, but be careful – it can get too strong if left too long! Dilute with cold water to create the perfect sip. I like it strong but not sweet, while some people prefer it sweeter ... your choice!

Once fermented, the tepache will keep in an airtight container in the fridge for up to 3 days.

EL
Coahuila
Nu

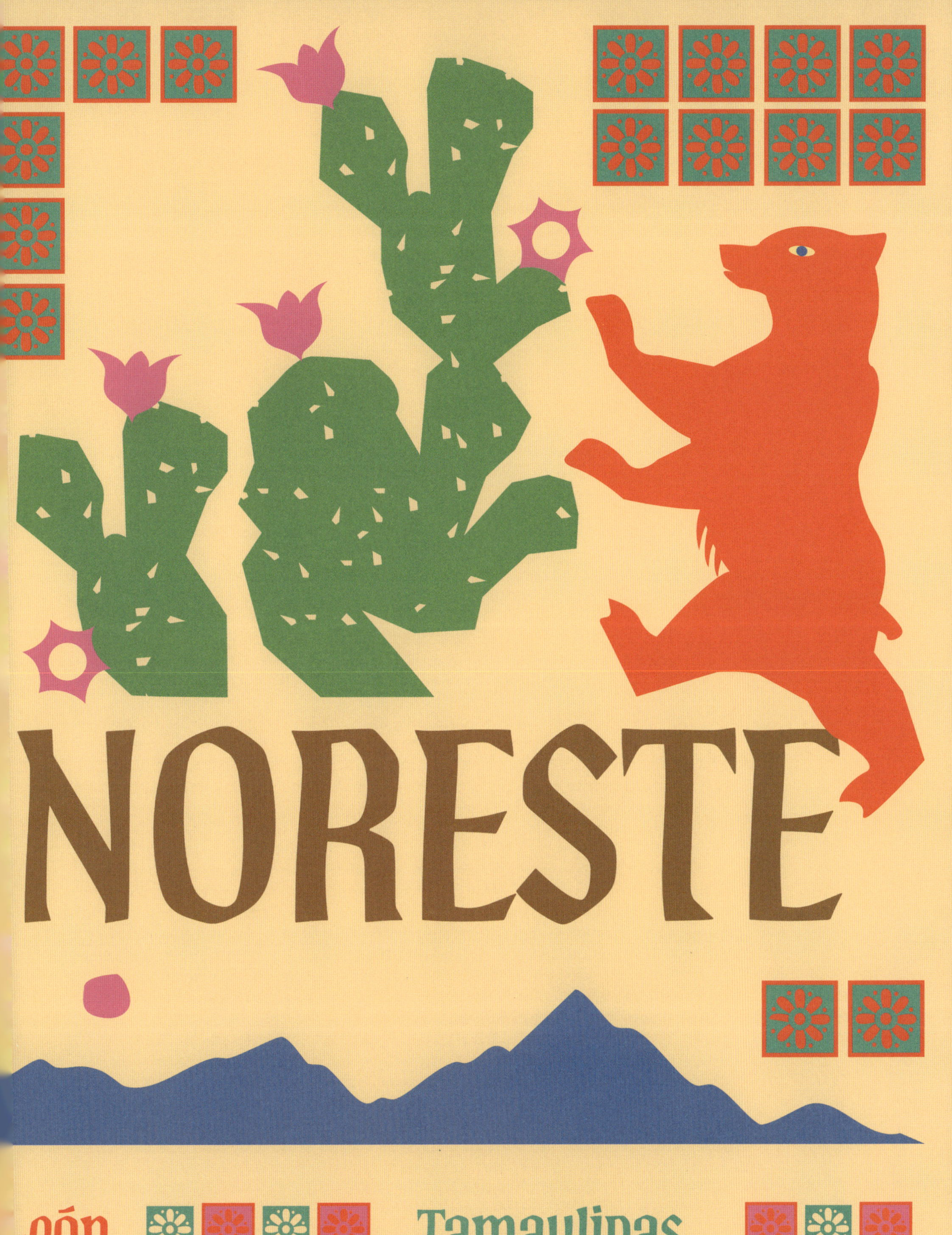
NORESTE
León
Tamaulipas

EL NORESTE

Mesquite, prickly pear and sotol: that's quite a diet! The indigenous peoples of this region – the Coahuiltecans, Chichimecas and Janambres – were experts at surviving in the tough, semi-arid environment of northeast Mexico. For 2000 years they relied on a variety of native plants, which they would eat and make drinks from.

Mesquite is a shrub or small tree commonly found in Mexico's arid and semi-arid regions. Its fruit contains edible seeds, which can be ground into a sweet, highly nutritious flour that is rich in fibre, protein and minerals. Mesquite honey is another gift from this tree, as well as a kind of jelly-like gum known as chucata, which has long been used to heal wounds and to ease digestive and inflammatory problems. The tree's dense and durable wood is highly valued for making furniture and tools, and is heavily used in carpentry. Its also prized for making charcoal, adding a smoky flavour to any asado. With so many uses, it's perhaps not surprising that mesquite's popularity has led to overharvesting in some areas, so steps must be taken to preserve this important resource.

The sotol plant grows in the deserts of Mexico, resembling a small palm tree with long, spiky leaves. The plant has been used for multiple purposes, including making baskets, mats, petates (woven bedrolls), bags, decorations and various other crafts. Its bulbs were also consumed by the indigenous peoples of the area – but the most popular use of sotol today is the famous alcoholic spirit of the same name that is produced from it. Sotol has a strong, earthy, smoky taste, and many compare its flavour to that of tequila or mezcal, although these are made from agave, a completely different plant.

In the pre-Hispanic period, indigenous peoples of this region would also occasionally feast on wild game, hunted using techniques honed over centuries. The area's harsh climate led to the creation of techniques such as pit-roasting and sun-drying to preserve meat for long periods. As in the northwest, new ingredients and cooking methods arrived with the Spanish in the 16th century. Livestock, such as cattle, goats and sheep, altered the look of the grassy plains, and the food landscape too. Wheat growing became the norm, and flour tortillas gained popularity. Gorditas from the north of Mexico are often thicker and made with wheat flour, unlike their corn-based southern counterparts.

This area is now famed for its great meats, especially the states of Coahuila and Nuevo León, where they typically grill over charcoal. Grilling over mesquite wood is still a hallmark of the region, imparting that strong smoky flavour.

The Monterrey tradition of cabrito asado (roasting a whole baby goat over an open flame) is closely connected to the arrival of the Spanish over 400 years ago – their goats skipped off the boats and thrived on the land. Cabrito asado (see page 56) isn't just a dish in Monterrey: it's a weekend tradition that has become almost a sacred ritual! The process of preparation is slow and meticulous, requiring both patience and plenty of beer! It's all about taking the time to let the meat roast to perfection, and is as much about sharing the moment with family and friends as it is about the culinary results. The preparation becomes a central part of any weekend gathering.

Fried pork chicharron (see page 54) has likewise been perfected in Monterrey, at La Ramos, a butchery that closely guards its cooking technique and seasoning secrets. I know they make theirs with pork belly or cheeks, instead of the skin that's generally used. It tastes meatier and more substantial than the chicharron made in the rest of the country.

It's difficult to overstate the importance of agriculture in the northeast. As well as beef and goats, the Spanish brought irrigation that watered the fertile river valleys of Tamaulipas. Suddenly beans, maize, squash and other crops were growing everywhere – and today, the vineyards in Coahuila also produce some of Mexico's finest wines.

As in so much of Mexico, the food of this region is ever evolving and the food-makers are ever creative. The famous 'sandwich at the wall' Torta de la barda (see page 70) – originally filled with beans, sardines and pico de gallo, although sardines are now less common – was invented at a lunch stand in the Tampico railway yard back in 1928.

Nachos, on the other hand, were invented as an improvised supper for a group of hungry American late-comers at a Coahuila hotel in 1943. While the dish has evolved into a globally popular pub dinner that now includes meats, beans and guacamole, you'll find traditional nachos in almost every cinema in Mexico, topped with nothing more than melted cheese, jalapeno chillies and perhaps a salsa. Just the way they were first made.

There is a strong sense of community in this inhospitable region, and food plays an essential role in this. Traditional feasts are often centred around shared meals, where old recipes are prepared using techniques that are over a thousand years old. Preparation is a communal activity, with people coming together to celebrate the harvest, religious holidays, or even the changing seasons. Not a single ingredient goes to waste. For weddings, the juices from the traditional pork stew, Asado de bodas (see page 102), are used to cook Nuevo León's traditional Frijoles con veneno (beans with poison, see page 58) to serve alongside the feast. The juices from the pork stew add depth and richness to the beans, but also reflect the resourcefulness of the home cooks of northeast Mexico in wringing out every last bit of flavour from every dish.

Nachos

Mexican-style corn chips

Serves 8–10

Legend has it that in 1943, Ignacio Anaya was working in the kitchen of a hotel in Piedras Negras, Coahuila, when a group of hungry Americans came into the restaurant at closing time. With nothing to serve them, Ignacio had to improvise. He took some corn tortillas, cut them into triangles, and fried them until crisp. Then he added melted cheese and a few chopped jalapeno chillies, and created a simple dish his customers loved! When asked its name, Ignacio thought he was asked, 'What's your name?' – and so he replied 'Nacho', the Spanish diminutive of Ignacio. So, nachos were born, a celebration of delicious resourcefulness and linguistic misunderstanding.

Ingredients

- 10 g (⅓ oz) butter
- 1½ teaspoons cornflour (corn starch)
- 100 ml (3½ fl oz) milk
- 250 g (9 oz) cheddar, grated (or Chihuahua cheese if you can get it)
- 90 g (3 oz) cream cheese
- 1 teaspoon sweet paprika

To serve

- 2 × quantities Totopos page 318 →
- Chiles en vinagre page 330 →

Method

Melt the butter in a pan over medium–low heat. Stir in the cornflour and cook, stirring, for 1–2 minutes until thickened. Add the milk slowly, stirring continuously until the sauce has thickened.

Stir in the cheddar, cream cheese and paprika. Simmer, stirring frequently, for about 5 minutes, until you have a thick cheesy sauce.

To serve, divide the totopos among plates or wide shallow bowls. Pour the cheesy sauce over the totopos and serve immediately, with sliced pickled chillies scattered over the top and more on the side.

Chicharron de la Ramos

Monterrey-style pork crackling

Serves 4

La Ramos, the Monterrey establishment that made this rich and succulent chicharron popular, keeps its cooking technique and seasonings well guarded. Instead of the pork skin typically used in other regions, they use pork belly or cheeks, imparting a unique character to their chicharron. The pork is marinated in a blend of spices, then fried to the perfect balance of juicy tenderness and crunch – setting it apart from the lighter, airier chicharron I've eaten as a snack in Mexico City.

Method

Preheat the oven to 100°C (210°F) fan-forced, or as low as your oven will go.

Score the skin of the pork belly at 2 cm (¾ in) intervals, so you can slice it more easily after cooking. Then turn it over and make several incisions on the underside, to allow the seasoning to penetrate the meat.

Mix together the garlic and salt and rub thoroughly all over the pork belly, ensuring the seasoning gets into the cuts on both sides.

Put the pork belly, skin side up, on a wire rack over a roasting tin and bake for 1 hour. The skin should be as dry as possible and have turned a translucent, pinkish colour. This step is crucial for a perfect crispy texture.

Remove the pork belly from the oven and allow it to rest for about 10 minutes. Using a sharp knife, slice the pork into strips, cutting along your earlier incisions.

Heat the lard in a large frying pan over medium–low heat. When hot, carefully add the pork belly strips, skin side down. Fry for about 8 minutes, or until the skin starts to bubble and has a crunchy, crackling texture. Remove from the pan and drain on paper towels to remove the excess fat.

Serve the crackling with guacamole and pico de gallo.

The crackling will keep in an airtight container in the fridge for up to 4 days.

Ingredients

- 1 kg (2 lb 3 oz) piece of boneless pork belly
- 1 teaspoon crushed garlic
- 1 tablespoon table salt
- 100 g (3½ oz) pork lard

To serve

Guacamole page 299 →
Pico de gallo page 290 →

Cabrito Asado

Slow-roasted goat

Serves 6

My dad would make this celebrated Monterrey dish for our Tuesday Mexican specials at his Sydney restaurant, El Cuervo Cantina. The aroma of slow-roasting goat would fill the air, drawing in customers. My friend Paco was a regular, calling in to satisfy his cravings for authentic Mexican food. He would wait eagerly at the bar, chatting with me while Dad prepared the cabrito to perfection. The dish was always a highlight for what Dad called our 'regiomontanos customers' ('regiomontanos' being a nickname for people from Nuevo León's capital, Monterrey), as it showcased the rich culinary traditions of their culture. Those evenings were filled with laughter, good food and the warmth of community and special memories.

Ingredients

- 100 g (3½ oz) salt
- 1.5 kg (3 lb 5 oz), goat leg, bone in
- 4 rosemary sprigs

To serve

Frijoles charros page 323 →

Tortillas de harina page 316 →

Salsa taquera page 294 →

Method

Dissolve the salt in 500 ml (2 cups) hot water and place in a large shallow ceramic dish. Add the goat leg and rosemary and set it aside to soak in the brine for at least 30 minutes.

Preheat the oven to 180°C (350°F) fan-forced.

Cover the dish with a layer of baking paper followed by a layer of foil, then transfer to the oven and roast for 3 hours. Increase the oven temperature to 220°C (430°F).

Remove the foil and baking paper and drain off all but 60 ml (¼ cup) of the liquid in the base of the dish. Return the goat leg to the oven and roast, uncovered, for a further 35–40 minutes, until golden and crisp.

Let the goat leg rest for 20 minutes before carving. Serve with the beans, tortillas and salsa.

Any leftovers will keep in an airtight container in the fridge for up to 3 days.

Frijoles con Veneno

Poison beans

Serves 4

Don't let the literal translation of this recipe name scare you. The term 'veneno' actually refers to the specific type of seasoning in this unique dish that is popular across Nuevo León.

Originally, the 'veneno' came from the broth left over from a traditional pork wedding stew, asado de bodas, that was used to cook the beans, adding depth and richness to the dish. In Zacatecas, 'poison beans' and the pork wedding stew are often served together.

My friend Claudia Garcia, who is originally from Monterrey, often makes these poison beans and asado de bodas at her gatherings in Melbourne, so I've been lucky enough to try the real deal made with an authentic Monterrey touch.

Ingredients

- 2 teaspoons pork lard (or use the skimmed fat from the Asado de bodas) page 102 →
- 1 × quantity Frijoles negros, made with dried pinto beans instead of black beans page 322 →
- 150 ml (5 fl oz) broth from Asado de bodas page 102 →

Method

Heat the lard in a frying pan over medium heat. Add the beans and the broth. Stir together for about 7 minutes, until the beans have reached a creamy consistency. Using a potato masher, crush the beans until they are half mashed, adding a little extra water if the mixture is very thick.

Serve as a side for dishes such as Asado de bodas, Carne asada (see page 62), Cabrito asado (see page 56), or any dish with rice.

The beans will keep in an airtight container in the fridge for 4 days.

CERRO DE LA SILLA

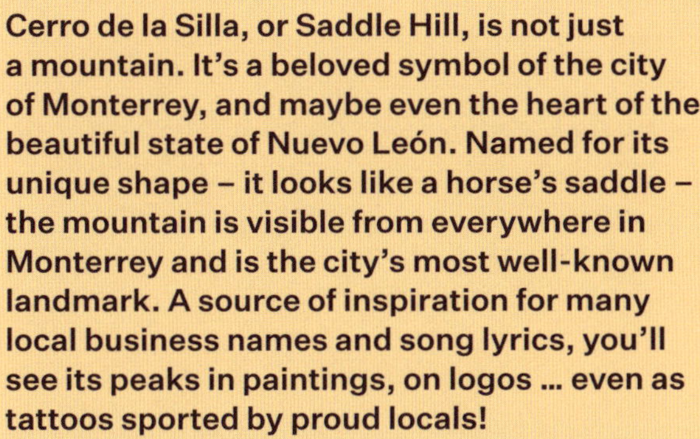

Cerro de la Silla, or Saddle Hill, is not just a mountain. It's a beloved symbol of the city of Monterrey, and maybe even the heart of the beautiful state of Nuevo León. Named for its unique shape – it looks like a horse's saddle – the mountain is visible from everywhere in Monterrey and is the city's most well-known landmark. A source of inspiration for many local business names and song lyrics, you'll see its peaks in paintings, on logos ... even as tattoos sported by proud locals!

The Cerro de la Silla has four main peaks, each with its own distinct features. The 'Norte' peak is the mountain's most iconic part. The second peak, the 'Sur', is the most dangerous and challenging to climb, due to the rocky formations around it. The third is the 'Antena', the most visited of the mountain's peaks, with plenty of tourist-friendly access points and the state's television antenna. The fourth and lowest is the 'Virgen', from which you can enjoy stunning views of the mountain.

Hiking the Cerro de la Silla is a rite of passage. The trails are steep and rocky, but the views make it all worth it. Starting early is key, not just to avoid the heat, but to catch a magical sunrise and watch the first morning rays hit Monterrey.

Near the base of the mountain is a waterfall, the Cascada de Guadalupe. The path leading there is slippery, so tread carefully, but don't be surprised if you stumble across a Zumba class or workout group when you reach it! Everyone in Monterrey keeps an eye on the Cascada, as there are years when the waterfall runs dry. When it flows well in a hot summer, the entire city rushes there to have a dip and cool off, in a long-running local tradition.

One of the best things about Cerro de la Silla is the wildlife. Armadillos casually cross the trails, while eagles fly above. If you're lucky, you might spot a white-tailed deer.

At the base of the mountain you'll find families picnicking in shaded areas, carne asada cooking on portable grills, kids running around ... It's a perfect weekend for any Mexican family, with a classic Monterrey vibe – relaxed, communal and always a little smoky!

The local communities say the mountain holds a spirit, and on Cerro de la Silla it certainly feels as if you're part of something bigger and that nature is looking after you.

Carne Asada

Grilled beef

Serves 10

The north of Mexico is famed for its great meats, especially Coahuila, Sonora, Chihuahua and Nuevo León. While all these states have their own, often very similar, methods of grilling over charcoal, Monterrey-style carne asada is not just a dish, but a sacred ritual.

Typically made from high-quality cuts such as flank, skirt steak or scotch fillet, carne asada is brilliant in its simplicity. The meat is often marinated with nothing more than salt – a minimalist approach that allows the natural flavours to shine.

Authentic carne asada must always be cooked over charcoal. As the meat grills over an open flame, it develops that characteristic smoky char. Just add some norteño music, a couple of cold beers and a few different side dishes for a true north Mexican vibe.

Ingredients

- 4 potatoes, unpeeled, cut into 4 cm (1½ in) chunks
- table salt
- olive oil
- 300 g (10½ oz) asadero cheese or haloumi, cut into 1 cm (½ in) thick slices
- 10 spring onions (scallions)
- 1 kg (2 lb 3 oz) beef short ribs
- 2 kg (4 lb 6 oz) skirt steak

To serve

- Salsa de Habanero con mango page 310 →
- Guacamole page 299 →
- Tortillas de maiz page 314 →
- lime wedges

Method

For a true Monterrey-style carne asada, you need to use a charcoal grill – the smoky flavour from the coals is essential. Start by lighting charcoal and letting it burn until the flames die down and you have glowing coals.

Toss the potato with a little salt and olive oil and wrap in foil. Cook on the grill for about 30 minutes, until the potato is tender. Meanwhile, wrap the cheese slices up in one foil packet and leave on the grill for about 10 minutes, just to warm through and pick up a smoky aroma. The spring onions can go straight on the grill to soften and char slightly.

Season all the meat on both sides with salt and grill to your liking. For rare, cook for about 4 minutes per side. For medium, cook for about 6 minutes per side. For well done, cook for about 8 minutes per side.

When everything is cooked, serve the meat, potato, cheese and spring onions on individual plates. Serve with the salsa, guacamole, tortillas and lime wedges for everyone to make their own individual feast.

Any leftover meat will keep in an airtight container in the fridge for 4 days. Use for Discada (see page 36), or serve with Arroz Mexicano (see page 327) and Frijoles con veneno (see page 58).

Tamales Nortenos

Northern-style tamales

Makes 20

It's always a challenge to make food for friends who are craving the dishes they loved in their childhood. While some considered my tamales small in comparison to the ones they grew up with in Mexico City, I would get comments from my norteño (northern Mexican) friends about my tamales being 'very big'. When I heard about tamales de dedo (finger tamales), it all made sense. These are common in the north of the country and are small and cute.

I'd like to thank Miriam Cuellar and Paco Sandoval for sharing their tamale memories and stories with me over the years.

Ingredients

- 40 dried sweetcorn husks (see Note overleaf)
- 800 g (1 lb 12 oz) boneless pork shoulder or leg, skin on, cut into 5 cm (2 in) chunks
- 2 bay leaves
- 1 onion, halved
- 4 teaspoons table salt
- 1 dried pasilla chilli
- 1 dried ancho chilli
- 2 dried guajillo chillies
- 2 garlic cloves, peeled
- pinch of ground cumin
- 200 g (7 oz) pork lard
- 1 teaspoon baking powder
- 500 g (1 lb 2 oz) masa flour, sifted

Method

Soften the corn husks in a large bowl of warm water for about 5 minutes, then drain to remove any excess water.

Put the pork in a large saucepan and pour in 2 litres (2 qts) water. Add the bay leaves, half an onion and 1 teaspoon of the salt. Bring to the boil, then reduce the heat and simmer gently for 1 hour, or until the pork is fully cooked. Transfer the pork to a large bowl, reserving the stock, and shred with two forks.

Add all the chillies to the pan of pork stock and boil for 10 minutes, or until soft. Scoop out the chillies, discard the stems and seeds, then place in a food processor with the garlic, cumin, remaining onion half, and another 1 teaspoon salt. Blend to a smooth salsa, then strain out any small bits of chilli.

Place the lard and baking powder in a large bowl and whip the mixture as fast as possible using a wooden spoon – the lard needs to soften and look spongy. Don't stress if this takes a long time; it can take up to 15 minutes to achieve the right consistency.

Heat 1 teaspoon of the beaten lard in a saucepan over medium heat, add the chilli salsa and stir until it changes colour. Set aside.

To the bowl of beaten lard, add the masa flour and remaining 2 teaspoons salt. Pour in 650 ml (22 fl oz) of the warm pork stock and mix well until completely combined. (Depending on the brand of masa flour you've used, you may need to add a little more water to achieve the right consistency.) To test if the dough is ready, drop a small ball of dough into a cup of cold water; if it floats to the top you're good to go! (If the dough doesn't float, mix the dough a little longer until it does float.)

Recipe continues →

Spread 40 g (1½ oz) of the dough in the middle of a damp sweetcorn husk, leaving a 4 cm (1½ in) border around the edge. Add 50 g (1¾ oz) of the shredded pork, 50 ml (1¾ fl oz) of the chilli salsa, then cover with another 20 g (¾ oz) of dough. Place another sweetcorn husk over the filling, then wrap up the tamal by overlapping the sides and folding over the top and bottom edges towards the centre to enclose the filling. Secure with kitchen string and set aside. Repeat with the remaining husks and ingredients to make 20 tamales.

Stand the tamales upright in a large steamer. Fit as many tamales as you can into the steamer, but be careful not to pack them in too tightly or they may burst, leaving you with empty tamales. Place the steamer over a saucepan of simmering water and steam for 45 minutes.

The best way to check if your tamales are cooked is to remove one from the steamer, let it cool for 5 minutes, and then unwrap the husk. If the dough doesn't stick to the husk and looks shiny and fluffy, then your tamales are ready.

Let the tamales cool for 15–20 minutes inside the steamer before serving.

The tamales will keep in an airtight container in the fridge for 3 days.

Note

You can buy dried sweetcorn husks from Latin American supermarkets or online. It's better to buy more than you need, as they are unpredictable and can sometimes be small or break. They can be frozen, or kept in an airtight container in the pantry.

Tampiquena

Tampico-style steak

Serves 4

My dad used to serve this at his restaurant in Sydney and it was always the most popular dish. I wonder if our guests understood its cultural importance? Every part of this recipe represents an element of the northern port city of Tampico. The beans symbolise the fertility of the land; enchiladas verdes the lush green fields; cheese the purity of its people; guacamole the fruits of the region; and strips of steak the Pánuco River. (Tampico, it is claimed, produces the best meat in the country.) Even the oval platter the dish is traditionally served on is said to represent the shape of La Huasteca region.

A feast of a meal, this dish really is Tampico on a plate.

Ingredients

- 1 × quantity Frijoles negros refritos page 322 →
- 1 × quantity Guacamole page 299 →
- 4 × 250 g (9 oz) beef rump steaks, fat trimmed
- table salt and freshly ground black pepper
- vegetable oil, for drizzling

Enchiladas verdes

- 500 g (1 lb 2 oz) boneless, skinless chicken breasts
- 2 bay leaves
- 1 tablespoon table salt
- 500 g (1 lb 2 oz) fresh or tinned tomatillos
- 1 white onion
- 1 small garlic clove, peeled
- 2 fresh green jalapeno or serrano chillies, stems removed
- 250 ml (1 cup) chicken stock
- 80 ml (⅓ cup) vegetable oil
- 12 Tortillas de maiz page 314 →
- 200 ml (7 fl oz) crema
- 200 g (7 oz) queso fresco, Cotija or feta, crumbled

To serve

- Arroz Mexicano page 327 →
- lime wedges

Method

To make the enchiladas verdes, place the chicken in a saucepan and cover with cold water. Add the bay leaves and 1½ teaspoons of the salt. Bring to the boil, then reduce the heat and simmer for 20 minutes, or until the chicken is just cooked through. Drain the chicken and set aside until cool enough to handle, then shred with two forks.

Place the tomatillos in a food processor. (If you are lucky enough to find fresh tomatillos, first remove the husks and thoroughly wash the fruit.) Roughly chop half the onion and add to the processor with the garlic, chillies, chicken stock and the remaining 1½ teaspoons salt. Blitz until smooth.

Finely slice the other onion half and set aside.

Heat 2 tablespoons of the oil in a saucepan over medium heat, then add the tomatillo sauce. Simmer for 10 minutes, or until the sauce darkens in colour, adding a little water if necessary – the sauce needs to be runny.

Heat the remaining oil in a frying pan over medium heat. Working in batches, cook the tortillas for 15–20 seconds on each side, until pliable and just starting to become crisp. Using tongs, dip the tortillas in the tomatillo sauce until completely coated, then place three tortillas, folded in half, on each serving plate. Spoon the remaining tomatillo sauce over the enchiladas and top with the crema, cheese, shredded chicken and finely sliced onion.

Recipe continues →

Make sure you have all the components ready to go before you start cooking the steaks. Arrange the refried beans and guacamole on each serving plate alongside the enchiladas, ensuring you leave enough space for the steaks.

Heat a chargrill pan over high heat. Season the steaks with salt and pepper and drizzle with oil. For rare, cook the steaks for about 4 minutes each side. For medium, cook for about 6 minutes each side and for well done, cook for about 8 minutes each side.

Transfer the steaks to each diner's plate and serve with the rice and lime wedges on the side.

Torta de la Barda

Sandwich from the wall

Makes 1

The famous 'sandwich from the wall' was invented in Tamaulipas in 1928 by José María Bracamontes, who started serving tortas filled with sardines, beans and pico de gallo. His stand was strategically located at the wall that separates the bustling centre of the city of Tampico from the customs area near the railway yard. The tortas quickly proved a hearty meal for tired and hungry dockworkers, and the unique location of the sandwich stand gave the dish its name.

Today, the torta's fame has spread far beyond northeast Mexico, although the sardines have fallen out of fashion and been replaced by various meats, cheeses and vegetables. If you can get presswurst (queso de puerco) at your local deli, this is the time to use it!

Ingredients

- 1 teaspoon vegetable oil
- 50 g (1¾ oz) Mexican-style fresh chorizo, skin removed and crumbled
- 1 French bread roll
- 60 g (2 oz) Frijoles negros refritos page 322 →
- 2 slices ham
- 2 slices American-style cheese
- 50 g (1¾ oz) shredded Machaca page 22 →
- 1 avocado, sliced
- ½ tomato, sliced
- ½ white onion, sliced into rounds
- 1 slice presswurst (optional)
- 2 tablespoons crumbled queso fresco, Cotija or feta
- 15 g (½ oz) pork crackling (see Note)

To serve

- Salsa verde page 286 →
- Chiles en vinagre page 330 →

Method

Heat the vegetable oil in a small frying pan over medium heat, add the chorizo and cook for 1–2 minutes, until lightly browned and cooked through. Remove from the pan and set aside.

Slice the bread roll in half lengthways, without cutting all the way through.

Once you have all the other ingredients ready, lightly toast the bread roll over low heat in the frying pan you cooked the chorizo in.

Open the roll out and smear the beans inside the roll. Add a slice of ham and American cheese, then the machaca, avocado, chorizo, tomato, onion and presswurst, if using. Finish with the queso fresco and remaining ham and cheese slices.

Top with the pork crackling, slather on some salsa verde, and serve with pickled chillies on the side.

Note

Pork crackling is often stocked in supermarkets in the chips (crisps) aisle.

Gorditas de Trigo

Wheat pockets

Makes 6

Gorditas from the north of Mexico are often made with wheat flour, distinguishing them from their corn-based counterparts in the south. These thick tortillas are versatile and can be enjoyed sweet or savoury, meaty or vegetarian. Go crazy with your fillings!

I tried these for the first time at my friend Paco's house in Melbourne, which is where I met Claudia – an amazing cook who is proud of her northern Mexican heritage. She was patiently making gorditas, one by one, filling them with pork asado. We've been good friends ever since, sharing recipes, stories and memories. Gracias, Claudia.

The recipe below makes snack-sized gorditas, but some stalls in Mexico City serve ones weighing up to 200 g (7 oz), so just make them to the size you prefer. Enjoy!

Ingredients

- 250 g (1⅔ cups) plain (all-purpose) flour
- 1 tablespoon baking powder
- 1½ teaspoons table salt
- 150 ml (5 fl oz) milk, at room temperature
- 50 g (1¾ oz) pork lard
- 100 g (3½ oz) Frijoles con veneno, warmed page 58 →
- Salsa verde de chile asado, to serve page 298 →

Method

In a bowl, mix together the flour, baking powder and salt. Gradually add the milk and mix to combine. Add the lard and begin kneading the mixture into a dough. Knead for 8 minutes, or until you have a smooth dough that doesn't stick to your hands. It's important to knead the dough well to achieve the right texture.

Divide the dough into six equal portions, about 80 g (2¾ oz) each. Roll each portion into a small ball, then use a rolling pin to flatten each ball into a thick round about 1 cm (½ in) thick.

Heat a comal or large heavy-based frying pan over medium heat. Once hot, and working in batches, cook the gorditas for 1–2 minutes per side, flipping them frequently to avoid burning. Make sure the heat isn't too high, so they cook evenly.

Transfer the gorditas to a chopping board and leave to cool for a couple of minutes. Use a sharp knife to carefully open them along one side, making a pocket – they'll still be hot!

Spoon about 1 tablespoon of warm veneno beans into each gordita and serve with the salsa.

The gorditas will keep in an airtight container in the fridge for 5 days.

Jaibas Rellenas

Stuffed crabs

Serves 2

I have fond memories of my friend Coral. She was studying in Sydney when the pandemic started. She couldn't leave the country and she didn't have anywhere to live, so I opened my house to her and we became very good friends. She was always talking about jaibas rellenas – stuffed crabs – from her home town in Tamaulipas and how delicious they were. We made them once together and I fell in love with them. The crab meat is delicious, and the idea of crumbing and frying it in the shells is inspired. Coral was right!

Method

If using fresh crabs, place them in a large saucepan of boiling water and boil for 15 minutes. Drain and let cool.

Carefully clean out the crab meat, keeping the shells for filling. This takes a lot of time, so be patient – you will love the result! Using a small knife, crack off the legs and claws, being careful to avoid damaging the top shells, as we are going to use these. Gently lift the top part of the shell from the body – don't apply too much pressure, as we don't want the shell to crack. Once the top is removed, use your fingers to carefully take out all the meat, as well as the inner organs, and reserve these for the filling. Break the legs and claws and extract the meat from these as well. Rinse the shells with cold water.

Melt the butter in a saucepan, then saute the garlic and onion for 2–3 minutes, until softened. Add the tomato, parsley, salt, pepper and all the crab meat. Cook gently for about 8 minutes, then allow to cool a little.

Tip the breadcrumbs and flour into two separate shallow bowls. Beat the eggs in a third bowl. Fill the crab shells with the crab mixture, pressing it in firmly. Dip the filling into the flour, then the beaten egg, then coat in the breadcrumbs.

Heat the oil in a deep heavy-based frying pan over medium–high heat to 180°C (350°F) on a kitchen thermometer. Add the stuffed crab shells, filling side down, and fry for 2 minutes, until crispy and light golden. Drain on paper towel and serve with the rice and salsa.

Note

Some crabs don't have enough meat for this dish, so this recipe includes some extra crabmeat, which you can buy from good fishmongers. Buy cooked dressed crabs if you're not confident with pulling out the meat.

Ingredients

- 4 large blue swimmer crabs, or 4 cooked dressed crabs, plus 200 g (7 oz) crabmeat (see Note)
- 100 g (3½ oz) unsalted butter
- 1 tablespoon crushed garlic
- 1 white onion, finely diced
- 1 roma (plum) tomato, finely diced
- 1 small bunch of parsley, finely chopped
- 1 teaspoon table salt
- pinch of freshly ground black pepper
- 150 g (5½ oz) dried fine breadcrumbs
- 100 g (⅔ cup) plain (all-purpose) flour
- 2 eggs
- 200 ml (7 fl oz) vegetable oil

To serve

Arroz Mexicano page 327 →
Salsa de chipotle page 288 →

Michelada

Mexican chilli beer

Makes 1

In Monterrey, a michelada is the go-to drink for any occasion, whether that's simply cooling off in the heat, or kicking back with family and friends during a Carne asada (see page 62) cook-fest. It's all about bold flavours and being brave enough to make your michelada your own! Locals mix light beer with lashings of lime juice, spice and seasonings – and always plenty of ice. Rim the glass with Tajin powder for extra kick and pure Mexican vibes.

Method

Combine the chamoy, Tajin seasoning and a pinch of salt in a small bowl. Dip the rim of a tall chilled beer glass into the mixture, then sprinkle the rim of the glass with more Tajin.

Pour the lime juice, Clamato, Tabasco, Maggi seasoning and worcestershire sauce into the glass. Add the remaining pinch of salt and stir until fully dissolved.

Pour in the beer, decorate with Skwinkles or Salsagheti, if you like, and enjoy!

Ingredients

- 2 tablespoons Salsa chamoy (store-bought or homemade) page 295 →
- 3 shakes of Tajin seasoning, plus extra for sprinkling
- 2 pinches of table salt
- juice of 2 limes
- 80 ml (⅓ cup) Clamato
- 1 teaspoon Tabasco sauce
- 1 teaspoon Maggi seasoning
- 1 teaspoon worcestershire sauce
- 355 ml (12 fl oz) bottle of Mexican lager
- Skwinkles or Salsagheti, to serve (optional)

Glorias

Glory bites

Makes 15

Made from a rich, creamy blend of goat's milk and sugar, and with some crunch from pecans or almonds, these traditional Mexican sweets are officially known as Glorias de Linares – named for their birthplace, the small city of Linares in Nuevo León, where the woman who first crafted them reputedly claimed that they tasted like 'glory'.

Over the years, glorias have spread across the country, easily recognisable by their vibrant red cellophane wrappers. They're often given as sweet tokens of love at celebrations such as baptisms, first communions and family or friend reunions, and they evoke great nostalgia for many older Mexicans.

You will need about 15 pieces of red cellophane, cut into 12 cm (4¾ in) squares, for wrapping these wonderful sweets.

Ingredients

- 250 ml (1 cup) milk
- 250 ml (1 cup) goat's milk
- 350 g (12½ oz) soft brown sugar
- 1 teaspoon natural vanilla extract
- pinch of baking soda
- 250 g (9 oz) pecans or almonds, chopped

Method

In a large saucepan, warm the milk and goat's milk over medium heat, stirring occasionally until the mixture comes to a gentle boil.

Stir in the sugar, vanilla and baking soda. Cook over low heat, stirring often, for about 1 hour, or until the mixture thickens to a caramel-like consistency (similar to dulce de leche). It's important to keep the heat low to prevent the caramel splattering and burning.

Remove from the heat and leave to cool for about 15 minutes. When the caramel is warm but not hot, stir the pecans or almonds through.

Have at least 15 squares of red cellophane ready before starting the next step.

When the caramel mixture is cool enough to handle, using a spoon, take 2 tablespoons of the mixture and roll it into a cylinder, about 4 cm (1½ in) long. Place the caramel cylinder on a piece of cellophane and wrap it tightly, twisting the ends to seal. Repeat with the remaining caramel mixture.

Let the glorias set at room temperature for a few hours, so the caramel firms up and the sweets can be easily removed from the cellophane wrappers.

Glorias will keep in an airtight container in the fridge for 1 month.

EL
CENTR
Zacatecas
San Luis Potosí
Agu

NORTE
lientes Guanajuato Querétaro

EL CENTRO NORTE

The central north region of Mexico, which includes the states of Zacatecas, San Luis Potosi, Aguascalientes, Guanajuato and Querétaro, can sometimes be overshadowed by the more well-known and (as the north might say) more showy food regions of Mexico. But this area has its own quiet culinary identity that is as rich as its history.

In fact, the indigenous peoples of this region – the Huichol, Otomi, Chichimeca and the Pame – have contributed greatly to the Mexican food culture that is loved around the world today. The Chichimecas, known for their survivalist ways, were adept at using the land's natural resources. They relied heavily on corn, beans and squash – the rather grandly named 'Mesoamerican triad' – as the backbone of their diet.

The area's dry climate was good for growing chillies and herbs such as epazote. These, along with wild plants like agave and prickly pear, were key ingredients in ancient meals. San Luis Potosi even has a traditional indigenous dessert made with tunas, the fruit of the prickly pear cactus. I've decided not to include 'queso de tuna' in this book, as this fruit is very difficult to find outside Mexico, but please look it up if you're interested.

In Querétaro, nestled between the Sierra Gorda mountains and the Bajío plains, the highland climate could grow crops such as chillies, beans and corn – which the Otomi people used in an exciting variety of ways, including grinding corn to make masa flour for their tortillas and tamales, a practice that continues to this day. In other parts of Querétaro, the soil is ideal for growing one of Mexico's most famous crops, the pitaya (dragon fruit), with its beautiful pink skin and refreshing flavour.

Guayaba, or guava, holds a prominent place in the country's culinary and medicinal traditions. Known for its sweet, tangy flavour and high nutritional value, it's a staple ingredient in desserts, drinks and sauces. In the state of Aguascalientes, where guava orchards flourish, the fruit's abundance has inspired cooks to experiment over the years, adding a local signature to traditional dishes and using up surplus fruit. Not surprisingly, Aguascalientes has developed a huge variety of sweet and savoury guava recipes for jams, salsas, jellies and drinks … and even mole!

When you're travelling through the central north region of Mexico, you must stop off to snack on 'poisoned tacos' (see page 84), preferably in their home town of Zacatecas, in the state of the same name, where they were invented in the 1940s. You'll only find them here, usually sold as a snack or late-night treat in the region's vibrant street markets. Don't be frightened by the name: it was simply a cunning 1940s sales ploy!

In Mexico's central north, no wedding is complete without Asado de bodas (see page 102), a celebratory pork wedding stew. Almost the entire northern region of Mexico claims to have given rise to this delicious stew, but Zacatecas is popularly viewed as its birthplace. Traditionally, it's served with 'poison beans' from neighbouring Nuevo León (see page 58), showing how food travels across regional borders – especially for a wedding – with the beans being cooked in the broth from the pork stew. Once again, don't be put off by its 'poisonous' name – we Mexicans have a sense of humour!

While you're passing through the Guanajuato countryside, you must stop at the stands selling Peanut tamales (see page 97). These are something out of the ordinary and hard to find in other regions. The esquites (corn in a cup, see page 86) from the small village of Bernal in the state of Querétaro are also a treat not to be missed.

In the Bajío plains that stretch across parts of Aguascalientes, San Luis Potosi, Querétaro, Zacatecas, Guanajuato and the neighbouring state of Jalisco, a common cooking characteristic is the use of traditional metates (a flat stone mortar and pestles) for grinding spices and flattening meat to make simple but delicious spiced meat patties known as Pacholas (see page 88).

When the Spanish arrived in this region in the 16th century, they brought with them a whole array of new ingredients, such as rice, broad (fava) beans, almonds and cloves, leading to dishes such as Pollo almendrado (see page 100). This meal hold special resonance for me. My grandmother, Tete, would make pollo almendrado for special occasions in her home. Some of my happiest memories are of times in her kitchen, nibbling on a warm tortilla while she added the finishing touches to the almond sauce that represented an unbelievably delicious fusion of our country's different cultures.

Tacos Envenenados

Poisoned tacos

Makes 20

The story goes that these tacos were invented by Don Lauro, who began selling them in a store near the railway station in Zacatecas in the 1940s. He would never reveal the secret of the filling, simply saying it was made of 'veneno' (poison)! This claim proved cleverly intriguing and only added to their allure.

These tacos are usually sold as a snack or late-night treat in the region's vibrant street markets. Each vendor has their own unique recipe, adding to the excitement and novelty.

I like to serve these tacos with a roasted green chilli salsa – but feel free to be adventurous.

Ingredients

- 5 potatoes, scrubbed
- 100 g (3½ oz) Mexican-style fresh chorizo, skin removed, crumbled
- 400 g (14 oz) Frijoles con veneno page 58 →
- 20 Tortillas de maiz, warmed page 314 →
- 100 g (3½ oz) pork lard
- 250 g (1 cup) sour cream
- 100 g (3½ oz) queso fresco, Cotija or feta, crumbled
- ½ iceberg lettuce, finely shredded
- Salsa verde de chile asado, to serve page 298 →

Method

Pour 2 litres (2 qts) water into a large saucepan, add the potatoes and bring to the boil. Cook over medium heat for 30 minutes, or until tender. Drain the potatoes, then leave to cool in the fridge for 20 minutes. Peel the potatoes and mash the flesh, leaving some chunky bits.

Combine the chorizo and beans in a saucepan and warm over low heat for 10 minutes, stirring often. Stir in the mashed potato to make a thick filling. Remove from the heat and set aside to cool for 30 minutes.

Spread each warm tortilla with 2 tablespoons filling, then fold in half.

Heat the lard in a frying pan over medium–low heat. Working in batches, fry the tacos for 1–2 minutes on each side, until lightly crisp. Drain on paper towel.

Serve the tacos topped with the sour cream, cheese, lettuce and salsa.

Esquites de Bernal

Bernal corn in a cup

Serves 4

A few years ago, my friend Luis landed a great job in Querétaro. Although it saddened me to know we might not see each other as often, it gave us the chance to long-distance bond over new foods.

Both of us are huge fans of elotes and esquites – elotes being boiled sweetcorn cobs served on a stick and spread with mayo, cheese, chilli and lime juice, and esquites being a cup of cooked corn kernels topped with those same toppings. It's a tradition for us to try different stalls and crown a favourite. And, let me tell you, the esquites from the magical small town of San Sebastian de Bernal in Querétaro take creativity to new heights, with over ten different variations. No wonder Luis always raves about them!

Among the standouts are esquites featuring prawns (shrimp), habanero chilli, jalapeno chilli, green mole, epazote, bone marrow in red chilli – and, of course, the classic original, simply served with epazote, butter and chilli. This makes it almost impossible to visit Bernal just once.

Ingredients

- 4 × 5 cm (2 in) beef marrowbone chunks (ask your butcher to cut them for you)
- 2 dried guajillo chillies, stems removed
- 1 dried ancho chilli, stems removed
- 1 dried arbol chilli, stems removed
- 1 garlic clove, roughly chopped
- ½ white onion, roughly chopped
- 1 teaspoon table salt
- 40 g (1½ oz) unsalted butter
- 2 teaspoons dried epazote (optional)
- 3 white or yellow sweetcorn cobs, husks and silks removed, kernels stripped; you'll need about 450 g (1 lb) corn kernels
- 80 g (2¾ oz) whole-egg mayonnaise
- juice of 4 limes
- 100 g (3½ oz) queso fresco, Cotija or feta, crumbled
- cayenne pepper or Tajin seasoning, for sprinkling

To serve

- Salsa de siete chiles page 306 →
- lime wedges

Method

Pour 2 litres (2 qts) water into a large saucepan. Add the marrowbones, then cover and cook for 1 hour, or until the marrow is popping out of the bones. During this time, stir occasionally to make sure the bones remain completely submerged, adding more water if necessary. Drain, reserving the broth.

Place the dried chillies in a saucepan with 500 ml (2 cups) water and bring to the boil. Cook over high heat for 5 minutes, or until soft.

Transfer the chillies and their cooking water to a food processor, along with the garlic, onion and ½ teaspoon of the salt. Blend until fully combined.

Melt the butter in a large saucepan over medium heat, add the remaining ½ teaspoon of salt and the epazote, if using. Add the blended chilli mixture and the corn kernels and cook, stirring frequently, for 10 minutes, or until lightly golden. Add 1 litre (4 cups) of the reserved marrowbone broth and stir until heated through and well combined.

To serve, spoon half the corn kernels into four cups. Top with half the mayonnaise, half the lime juice and half the cheese, and sprinkle with cayenne pepper or Tajin seasoning. Repeat the layering with the remaining ingredients.

Finish with a good amount of salsa and a marrowbone perched on top, and serve with lime wedges.

Pacholas

Thin beef patties

Makes 12

These simple meat patties are made with basic ingredients that are easy to find in any Mexican kitchen.

Sweet pacholas are popular in Querétaro, where they were traditionally made from corn flavoured with piloncillo and cinnamon, and enjoyed with a Café de olla (see page 138).

This is the meat version in the Guanajuato style and includes ancho chillies for extra punch.

Method

Place the chillies in a saucepan, pour in 500 ml (2 cups) water and bring to the boil. Leave to boil for 5 minutes, then remove from the heat and set aside to cool for 10 minutes.

Pour 100 ml (3½ fl oz) of the chilli cooking water into a blender. Add the rehydrated chillies, onion, garlic and milk and blend to a thick sauce.

Crack the eggs into a large bowl. Add the parsley, pepper and breadcrumbs and mix together. Add the beef, pork and the blended chilli sauce, then knead together in the bowl until you have a meaty paste, like you'd use for a burger patty.

Divide the meat mixture into 12 even portions. Place a plastic food bag over the bottom half of a tortilla press. Place a patty in the middle of the press, cover with another plastic food bag, then close the tortilla press and gently press the patty until evenly flattened. Open the tortilla press, remove the top plastic bag and set the patty aside while you flatten the remaining patties. (If you don't have a tortilla press, you can simply roll out the patties between sheets of baking paper to about 12 cm (4¾ in) in diameter and about 5 mm (¼ in) thick.)

Heat a small amount of oil in a comal or heavy-based frying pan or chargrill pan over medium heat. Cook the pacholas in batches for 30 seconds on each side, or until cooked through.

Serve warm, with the lettuce, tomato and salsa.

The cooked pacholas will keep stored between sheets of baking paper in an airtight container in the fridge for 4 days.

Ingredients

- 2 dried ancho chillies, stems and seeds removed
- ½ white onion, roughly chopped
- 2 garlic cloves, crushed
- 50 ml (1¾ fl oz) milk
- 2 eggs
- 1 small bunch of parsley, finely chopped
- 1 teaspoon ground white pepper
- 70 g (2½ oz) dried breadcrumbs
- 300 g (10½ oz) minced (ground) beef
- 100 g (3½ oz) minced (ground) pork
- vegetable oil
- ½ iceberg lettuce, shredded
- 2 tomatoes, cut into wedges
- Salsa macha verde, to serve page 302 →

Mole de Guayaba

Guava mole

Serves 4

The guava mole, a lesser-known but innovative gem of Mexican cuisine, originated in the state of Aguascalientes, where guava orchards thrive. The town of Calvillo, nestled in a mountain valley, has become known as the 'world capital of guava' – particularly high-quality apple guava – and the town holds an annual guava fair allowing local farmers to showcase their iconic crop.

Over the years, the fruit's abundance in this region has inspired its cooks to experiment, adding a local signature to traditional dishes and using up surplus fruit. Not surprisingly, Aguascalientes has developed a huge variety of sweet and savoury guava recipes – including guava mole!

Ingredients

- 4 chicken marylands, skin on
- ½ white onion
- 4 bay leaves
- 1 tablespoon table salt
- steamed white rice, to serve

Guava mole

- 1 corn tortilla
- 60 ml (2 fl oz) vegetable oil
- ½ white onion, finely chopped
- 5 dried pasilla chillies, stems and seeds removed
- 5 dried guajillo chillies, stems and seeds removed
- 2 dried mulato chillies, stems and seeds removed
- 50 ml (1¾ fl oz) tequila
- 1 teaspoon dried thyme
- 80 g (½ cup) sesame seeds
- 8 ripe guavas, halved
- pinch of ground cumin
- pinch of ground cinnamon

Method

Put the chicken in a large saucepan with the onion, bay leaves, salt and 2 litres (2 qts) water. Bring to the boil, then reduce the heat and simmer for 30 minutes, or until the chicken is cooked through. Lift out the chicken and set aside, reserving the broth.

To make the guava mole, char the tortilla in a large heavy-based frying pan over medium heat for 5 minutes on each side, until the tortilla is hard, dehydrated and slightly black. Remove from the pan and set aside.

Wipe out the pan if needed, then heat 2 tablespoons of the vegetable oil over medium heat. Add the onion and saute for about 5 minutes, until translucent. Add the chillies, reduce the heat to medium–low and cook, stirring frequently, for 5 minutes, until softened.

Add the tequila and the charred corn tortilla to give the mole its characteristic smoky flavour. Cook for 3 minutes, stirring constantly to prevent the chillies burning. Add the thyme, sesame seeds, guava and 2 litres (2 qts) of the reserved chicken broth (add a little water, if needed, to get to this amount). Bring to the boil over medium heat, then remove from the heat and leave to cool a little.

Tip the mixture into a blender and blitz until smooth, then strain the sauce to give it a velvety texture.

In the same frying pan, heat the remaining oil, then pour in the strained sauce, stirring constantly over medium heat – the sauce should be thick yet smooth. Add the cumin and cinnamon and stir until the sauce comes to a gentle boil. Reduce the heat, add the chicken and simmer for 10 minutes to heat through.

Serve hot, on a bed of steamed white rice.

ENCHILADAS

As amazingly varied as they are, enchiladas are simply corn tortillas, filled, rolled or folded and smothered in sauce. They're so beloved in modern Mexican restaurants and pubs that you might think they're a recent invention, but their origins go back hundreds of years, when the Aztecs would fill corn tortillas with beans and roll them up to eat. The modern enchilada developed after the Spanish arrived, bringing their beef and melty cheese which were quickly embraced as fillings. The name 'enchilada' comes from the Spanish 'enchilar', meaning 'to season with chilli' … and also 'to irritate'!

Every corner of Mexico takes pride in its own unique twist on the classic enchilada – especially when it comes to the toppings. Even just in this central north region you'll find so many exciting variations.

Hailing from Guanajuato, enchiladas mineras are corn tortillas that are smothered in a red chilli sauce and fried in pork lard. They're filled with ranchero cheese and chopped onion, then topped with lettuce, more cheese, pickled chilli strips, carrot and boiled potatoes. There's a lot going on, but it's all utterly delicious.

Enchiladas potosinas (see page 94) come from San Luis Potosi, and they're made with masa dough that's been painted with guajillo chilli. They're like fried quesadillas filled with fresh cheese and tomatoes, decorated with chopped onion, sour cream and lettuce – everything that makes a dish pop!

After being dipped in guajillo chilli sauce, enchiladas queretanas are fried and stuffed with a mix of onion, potato and carrot, then topped with lettuce, cream and cheese. Simple yet scrumptious.

Zacatecas enchiladas also have a guajillo chilli sauce base. Filled with onion and cheese, they're finished off with shredded cabbage, sour cream and more cheese – a comforting, classic combination.

Enchiladas suizas are the elegant princesses of the enchilada family. Their fancy twist is that they have melted Chihuahua cheese on top and are baked in the oven. You can make them with either Salsa verde or Salsa roja (see page 286), depending on your mood.

The versatility of enchiladas is boundless. Any tortilla dipped in sauce could become an enchilada. With the huge variety of salsas out there, the possibilities are similarly endless. And all moles can be turned into enmoladas. It's the same concept – mole sauce over a tortilla, filled with whatever you fancy and topped with cream and cheese. Vegetables? Sure! Add them as you like.

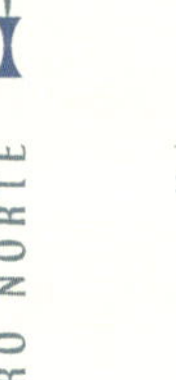

Enchiladas Potosinas

San Luis Potosi-style enchiladas

Serves 4–5

My friend Mon had family in San Luis Potosi and always bragged about the famous enchiladas potosinas there. Her aunt would occasionally come to Mexico City, and one day Mon invited us to her house to try the delicious treats her aunt had brought with her. Enchiladas potosinas are part of the cuisine of the Huasteca Potosina region and a source of pride for people from this area. After tasting them, we understood why – they are delicious!

Ingredients

- 8 dried guajillo chillies, stems and seeds removed
- 500 g (1 lb 2 oz) masa flour
- 1 teaspoon table salt
- 1 teaspoon sweet paprika
- vegetable oil, for shallow-frying

Filling

- 2 roma (plum) tomatoes
- 2 green tinned tomatillos or green bell peppers (capsicums)
- 3 fresh serrano or jalapeno chillies
- 2 garlic cloves, peeled
- pinch of table salt
- 2 tablespoons vegetable oil
- 250 g (9 oz) firm ricotta

To serve

- ½ iceberg lettuce, finely shredded
- ½ white onion, finely diced
- 2 avocados, sliced
- 250 ml (1 cup) crema

Method

Place the dried chillies in a saucepan with 1.5 litres (6 cups) water and bring to the boil. Cook over high heat for 10 minutes, or until they are soft. Remove from the heat and leave the chillies in the water to cool a little.

Pour 500 ml (2 cups) of the chilli cooking water into a food processor, reserving the remaining chilli water. Add the softened chillies to the blender and blitz until fully mixed.

Strain the chilli sauce into a large bowl and add another 350 ml (12 fl oz) of the chilli cooking water. Add the masa flour, salt and paprika and mix until the dough is soft and doesn't stick to your hands. Leave in the bowl, covered with plastic wrap, while you make the filling.

Heat a comal or heavy-based frying pan over medium heat. Once hot, char the tomatoes, tomatillos, chillies and garlic for about 5–7 minutes, until they are slightly charred. Remove from the heat and leave to cool for 15 minutes. Remove the stems from the chillies and the seeds and membranes from the bell peppers, if using. Place the charred ingredients in a food processor with the salt and blend to a smooth salsa.

Heat the oil in a saucepan over medium heat. Add the charred tomato mixture and cook for 5 minutes, until it has darkened slightly. Remove from the heat and leave to cool for 20 minutes. Add the ricotta and stir well until you have a dense filling.

Recipe continues →

To make enchiladas potosinas, you'll follow the same procedure as you would for making any tortilla. Place a plastic food bag over the bottom half of a tortilla press. Roll 50 g (1¾ oz) of the dough into a ball about the size of an apricot and place it in the middle of the press. Cover with another plastic food bag, then close the tortilla press and gently press to flatten the dough to about 15 cm (6 in) in diameter. Open the tortilla press and remove the top plastic bag. Add 20 g (¾ oz) of the filling to one half of the tortilla, then fold the tortilla to seal the edges and make a half-moon shape. (If you don't have a tortilla press, you can roll out the dough between sheets of baking paper using a rolling pin.)

Repeat with the remaining dough and filling; you should end up with about 20 enchiladas.

Heat enough oil in a frying pan over medium heat to come halfway up the sides of the enchiladas. Working in batches, fry the enchiladas for about 2 minutes on each side, until golden and crisp. Drain on paper towel.

Serve hot, with lettuce, onion, avocado and a drizzle of crema on top.

Tamales de Cacahuate

Peanut tamales

Makes 10

Peanut tamales are common at lunch spots or traditional tamale street stands in the state of Guanajuato. My friend Joaquín studied at the university there, and I visited him many times for the Cervantino festival. Amid the guacamayas (bread rolls filled with chicharron, avocado, boiled egg and spicy salsa) and the extra-spicy quesadillas that made me cry, the delicious peanut tamales always stood out.

The traditional method for preparing these tamales involves spreading out all the dough, scattering it with the sauce and peanuts, rolling up the dough into a baguette shape, and then cutting it into pieces. The dough in the version below is the same ... but I prepare the tamales using the same method as for my tamales in Sydney. I think it's more practical and manageable for everyone!

Ingredients

- 20 sweetcorn husks (see Note overleaf)
- 4 dried guajillo chillies, stems and seeds removed
- 150 g (5½ oz) piloncillo or soft brown sugar
- 1 cinnamon stick
- 1 garlic clove, peeled
- 200 g (7 oz) pork lard
- 1 teaspoon baking powder
- 500 g (1 lb 2 oz) masa flour
- pinch of table salt
- 200 g (7 oz) raw skinless peanuts
- 200 g (7 oz) ricotta

Method

Soften the sweetcorn husks in a large bowl of warm water for about 5 minutes, then drain to remove any excess water.

Bring 1 litre (4 cups) water to the boil in a saucepan and add the chillies, sugar and cinnamon stick. Simmer over medium heat for 10 minutes, then leave to cool. Discard the cinnamon stick.

Pour 650 ml (22 fl oz) of the chilli cooking water into a blender. Add the rehydrated chillies and garlic and blend until fully combined.

Place the lard and baking powder in a bowl and whip the mixture as fast as possible using a wooden spoon – the lard needs to soften and look spongy. Don't stress if this takes a long time; it can take up to 15 minutes to achieve the right consistency.

Sift the masa flour into a large bowl with the salt. Using a blender or molcajete, finely grind the peanuts, then mix them through the flour. Add the beaten lard and knead until combined, then add the blended chilli mixture and knead again until you have a soft dough. Finally, add the ricotta and knead until well combined, smooth and soft. (Depending on the brand of masa flour you've used, you may need to add a little more water to achieve the right consistency.)

Recipe continues →

Spread 150 g (5½ oz) of the dough in the middle of a damp sweetcorn husk, leaving a 5 cm (2 in) border around the edge. Place another sweetcorn husk over the filling, then wrap up the tamale by overlapping the sides and folding over the top and bottom edges towards the centre to enclose the filling. Secure the ends with kitchen string and set aside. Repeat with the remaining husks and dough to make 10 tamales.

Stand the tamales upright in a large steamer. Fit as many tamales as you can into the steamer, but be careful not to pack them in too tightly or they may burst, leaving you with empty tamales. Place the steamer over a saucepan of boiling water and steam for 45 minutes.

The best way to check if your tamales are cooked is to remove one from the steamer, let it cool for 5 minutes and then unwrap the husk. If the dough doesn't stick to the husk and it looks shiny and fluffy, your tamales are ready.

Let the tamales cool for 15–20 minutes inside the steamer before serving.

The tamales will keep in an airtight container in the fridge for 4 days.

Note

You can buy dried sweetcorn husks from Latin American supermarkets or online. It's better to buy more than you need, as they are unpredictable and can sometimes be small or break. They can be frozen, or kept in an airtight container in the pantry.

Pollo Almendrado

Almond chicken

Serves 4

Rooted in the state of Querétaro, almond chicken has always been a staple in my home and on the tables of many Mexican families. My grandmother, Tete, would make it for special occasions and serve it with white rice, but I also remember how delicious it was with handmade tortillas, slightly charred from the comal. Thank you, Tete, for all the recipes that will always be in my heart.

Ingredients

- 4 chicken marylands, skin on
- ½ white onion
- 3 bay leaves
- 1 tablespoon table salt
- 2 tablespoons vegetable oil
- 2 garlic cloves, peeled
- 1 teaspoon freshly ground black pepper
- 2 teaspoons dried breadcrumbs

Almond sauce

- ½ white onion, roughly chopped
- 2 garlic cloves, peeled
- 4 roma (plum) tomatoes
- 2 dried ancho chillies, stems and seeds removed
- 2 dried guajillo chillies, stems and seeds removed
- 1 cinnamon stick
- 2 cloves
- 4 whole black peppercorns
- 150 g (5½ oz) whole almonds
- 1 tablespoon table salt
- 2 chipotle chillies in adobo sauce

To serve

- steamed white rice
- Frijoles negros refritos page 322 →
- Tortillas de maiz page 314 →

Method

Put the chicken in a large saucepan with the onion, bay leaves, salt and 2 litres (2 qts) water. Bring to the boil, then reduce the heat and simmer for 30 minutes, or until the chicken is cooked through. Lift out the chicken and set aside, reserving the broth. Discard the onion and bay leaves.

To make the almond sauce, place a large saucepan over high heat and add the onion, garlic cloves and tomatoes. Cook for 5 minutes, stirring and turning constantly, until slightly charred. Add the dried chillies and stir regularly for another 7 minutes, making sure the chillies don't burn. Pour in 500 ml (2 cups) of the reserved chicken stock, then cover and simmer over medium heat for 5 minutes. Set aside to cool.

In a dry saucepan, lightly toast the cinnamon stick, cloves and peppercorns for 3 minutes, being careful not to let them burn. Add the almonds and toast them for about 5 minutes, stirring constantly to prevent burning.

Tip the toasted almonds and spices into a food processor. Add the charred vegetable mixture, along with the salt and chipotle chillies. Pour in 1 litre (4 cups) of the reserved chicken broth and blend until smooth.

Heat the oil in a large saucepan over medium heat, add the garlic and fry on both sides for 1–2 minutes, until golden. Remove the garlic and discard it; we're only using it to infuse the oil. Pour in the blended almond sauce and the remaining chicken broth. Stir in the black pepper and bring to a simmer over medium heat. Stir in the breadcrumbs to thicken the sauce – it should be a thick but smooth consistency. Stir often.

Add the chicken to the sauce and simmer for 10 minutes to heated through. Serve hot with steamed white rice, refried beans and tortillas.

Any leftover almond chicken will keep in an airtight container in the fridge for 4 days.

Asado de Bodas

Pork wedding stew

Serves 4

There is no wedding in Mexico's central north without asado de bodas. Legend has it that this pork wedding stew originated around 1910 during the Mexican Revolution, when Pancho Villa arrived with his troops at an ejido (cooperatively run farm) in Zacatecas, in the state of Morelos, and asked for a victory dinner to be made with pork and chilli. It is now one of the most requested dishes at celebrations.

It is still traditional in some regions for asado de bodas to be offered by the groom's family to the bride's family, in a gesture symbolising riches for the newlyweds.

Method

Melt the lard in a large saucepan over medium–high heat. When the lard is hot, add all the meats, along with the salt, pepper, orange peel, bay leaves and garlic. Cook, stirring often, for about 10 minutes, until the meat is sealed and beginning to brown. Pour in 500 ml (2 cups) water, reduce the heat to low and simmer for another 30 minutes. Remove the bay leaves and orange peel.

Meanwhile, place the dried chillies in a saucepan with 1 litre (4 cups) water and bring to the boil. Cook over medium heat for 5 minutes, or until softened. Remove from the heat and leave the chillies in the water to cool.

Heat a comal or heavy-based frying pan over medium heat. Once hot, cook the tomato and onion for about 5–7 minutes, until slightly charred.

Transfer the tomato and onion to a food processor, along with the softened chillies and 200 ml (7 fl oz) of the chilli cooking water. Add the sugar, cinnamon, oregano, cumin and cloves, season with salt and blend until smooth.

Add the sauce to the pan of meat and leave to simmer together for 30 minutes over low heat, allowing the flavours to meld and the oils from the meat and chillies to rise to the top. Skim off the excess fat with a spoon and reserve it for preparing the Frijoles con veneno.

Serve the stew with rice, freshly made frijoles con veneno and tortillas.

Any leftover stew will keep in an airtight container in the fridge for 4 days.

Note

Reserve the juices from this stew to make the traditional matching wedding dish, Frijoles con Veneno.

Ingredients

- 100 g (3½ oz) pork lard
- 250 g (9 oz) pork ribs
- 250 g (9 oz) boneless pork shoulder
- 250 g (9 oz) pork neck
- 2 teaspoons table salt, plus extra for seasoning
- pinch of freshly ground black pepper
- peel of 1 navel orange
- 4 bay leaves
- 1 tablespoon crushed garlic
- 5 dried guajillo chillies, stems and seeds removed
- 1 dried ancho chilli, stems and seeds removed
- 2 dried arbol chillies, stems and seeds removed
- 1 roma (plum) tomato
- ½ white onion
- pinch of brown sugar
- 1 teaspoon ground cinnamon
- 1 tablespoon dried Mexican oregano
- 1 teaspoon ground cumin
- 1 teaspoon ground cloves

To serve

Arroz Mexicano page 327 →
Frijoles con veneno (see Note) page 58 →
Tortillas de maiz page 314 →

Pollo San Marcos

San Marcos-style chicken

Serves 4

Pollo San Marcos is not just a dish, it's a tradition and a love story that dates back to the early days of the national fair (Feria de San Marcos) in Aguascalientes. Don Florent, a wealthy, successful and charming rancher known for his incredible luck, seemed to have it all, yet his life felt incomplete – until he met Doña Lala at the fair. Their connection was immediate and before the three weeks of the fair ended, they were already married and living in Don Florent's beautiful hacienda surrounded by huge gardens.

But one challenge emerged in their perfect marriage: Don Florent was allergic to red meat. For months, the couple endured repetitive meals of fried and boiled chicken, until Doña Lala decided it was time for a change.

Inspired by the bounty from their gardens, the talented Doña Lala created a new dish with potatoes, chillies, chorizo and aromatic spices. Don Florent was amazed and invited neighbours to come and dine. Doña Lala's chicken became a sensation, and it soon became one of the star dishes traditionally served at the Aguascalientes Feria de San Marcos.

Ingredients

- 4 chicken marylands, skin on
- ½ white onion
- 3 bay leaves
- 1 tablespoon table salt
- 30 g (1 oz) pork lard
- 200 g (7 oz) Mexican-style fresh chorizo, skin removed, crumbled
- 2 potatoes, peeled and finely sliced
- Chiles en vinagre, to serve page 330 →

San Marcos sauce

- 1 teaspoon ground allspice
- 1 teaspoon ground cloves
- 1 teaspoon ground cinnamon
- 1 teaspoon dried Mexican oregano
- 2 teaspoons white vinegar
- 3 roma (plum) tomatoes, roughly chopped
- ½ white onion

Method

Put the chicken in a large saucepan with the onion, bay leaves, salt and 2 litres (2 qts) water. Bring to the boil, then reduce the heat and simmer for 30 minutes, or until the chicken is cooked through. Lift out the chicken and set aside, reserving the broth.

For the San Marcos sauce, place the spices and oregano in a blender with the vinegar, tomato, onion and 150 ml (5 fl oz) of the chicken broth. Blend until the mixture has a thick adobo-like consistency. Transfer to a bowl, add the chicken and leave to marinate for about 10 minutes.

Heat the lard in a large heavy-based frying pan over medium heat. Remove the chicken from the marinade (reserving the marinade) and fry for 2 minutes on each side. Remove the chicken from the pan and set aside.

Add the chorizo to the pan and cook for 5 minutes, stirring frequently. Add the potato and cook, stirring, for another 10 minutes, ensuring everything is well mixed. Pour in the reserved marinade and bring to the boil, then reduce the heat to low, cover and simmer for 10 minutes. Add the chicken, then cover and simmer for another 10 minutes, until the potato is tender and the chicken is thoroughly heated through.

Serve in bowls with the pickled chillies.

Any leftover chicken will keep in an airtight container in the fridge for 4 days.

Agua de Guayaba

Guava water

Serves 4

While it's ridiculously simple to make, there's something almost magical about agua frescas. Fruit, ice, maybe a few seeds, a touch of sugar, and boom – you have yourself a refreshing drink. Here's the kicker: you'd think this concept would be everywhere, but I've never seen another country do it quite like Mexico.

There are classics such as agua de jamaica (hibiscus water) and agua de tamarindo (tamarind water). Some are made with seasonal fruits – mango, guava, orange, mandarin, strawberry, watermelon, lime and chia seeds ... whatever the local market has on offer. If it grows in Mexico, chances are someone's turned it into an agua fresca. You could try a different agua fresca every day of the month and still have more to taste, and it would be a lie to say I have a favourite.

During guava season, this is what they make in Aguascalientes, the 'guava capital of the world'. You'll find massive glass jars filled to the brim with this refreshing, cooling drink in the ice-cream shops and market stalls.

You can use guavas of any colour – but the pink ones are sweetest.

Ingredients

- 5 ripe guavas (see Note)
- 3 tablespoons caster (superfine) sugar
- 1 litre (4 cups) chilled water
- ice cubes

Method

Cut the guavas in half and place in a blender with the sugar and water. Strain into a jug and serve over ice.

The agua de guayaba will keep in an airtight container in the fridge for up to 2 days.

Note

If you don't have guava, you could instead use the flesh of half a rockmelon (cantaloupe), and just 2 teaspoons caster sugar, adding more sugar if needed.

Chancaquillas

Pepita brittle

Makes 12

Chancaquillas, or pepitorias, are a traditional sweet from Rioverde in San Luis Potosi, made with green pepitas or peanuts and piloncillo, and then shaped like a cookie. You can find them pretty much anywhere in Mexico – I remember going to my local mercado where vendors would sell huge baskets of chancaquillas, along with a mix of other sweet delicacies. The combination of indigenous ingredients makes them the perfect traditional sweet treat.

Ingredients

- 300 g (10½ oz) pepitas (pumpkin seeds)
- 2 teaspoons ground cinnamon
- 1 teaspoon pure anise extract
- 500 g (1 lb 2 oz) piloncillo or soft brown sugar

Method

Line a large baking tray with baking paper.

Toast the pepitas in a comal or heavy-based frying pan over medium heat for 5 minutes, stirring constantly and keeping your eye on them so they don't burn. Add the cinnamon and anise extract and toast, stirring constantly, for another 5 minutes. Set aside.

Put the sugar and 100 ml (3½ fl oz) water in a heavy-based saucepan. (If you have a traditional clay pot, use it here – it keeps the temperature stable so the caramel doesn't burn.) Stir constantly over low heat for 15–20 minutes, until the sugar has dissolved and the mixture has transformed into a dense caramel. Take great care not to burn it or you will need to start again. Remove from the heat, add the toasted pepitas and stir constantly – the caramel will look a bit runny and dark in colour.

The next stage has to be done quickly, otherwise the caramel dries and will be hard to handle. It's also sticky and hot, so I pop on a pair of thick cotton gloves with plastic gloves over the top. Working with about 2 tablespoons of the mixture at a time, roll into balls and pat down gently to flatten.

Leave to cool and set at room temperature.

The chancaquillas will keep in an airtight container in the fridge for 2 weeks.

EL
Edo de Mexico

CENTRO
SUR
Morelos

EL CENTRO SUR

As someone from Mexico City, I can tell you this part of the country is a culinary playground, where every corner offers something delicious that's also steeped in history. It's not just about tacos, tamales and quesadillas – although these are, of course, fantastic! From its indigenous roots to today's bustling streets, this region offers an ever-evolving, ever-intriguing story of food, culture and Mexican identity.

The Centro Sur is deeply connected to ancient Mesoamerican civilisations, particularly the Mexica, who lived in the Valley of Mexico and built the great city of Tenochtitlan (founded around 1325, in the heart of what is now Mexico City), long before Spanish colonisation in the 1500s.

The Mexica's deep understanding of food has left a lasting legacy in the valley. This is where pre-Hispanic ingredients, such as maize, beans, chillies, amaranth and squash, laid the foundations for modern Mexican cuisine. For more than 2000 years the indigenous people here were master cultivators. The Mexica had spectacular farming techniques, even creating floating gardens (chinampas) on Lake Texcoco on which to grow their crops.

Dishes such as Pipian verde (see page 128) date back to pre-Hispanic times, when the Aztecs and Mayans relied on native ingredients such as pepitas (pumpkin seeds). The name of the dish comes from the Nahuatl word 'pipitl', meaning 'seed'. Roasted and ground into a paste, these were mixed with local chillies and water to make a thick sauce that was eaten with local turkey, duck or rabbit. Simpler to make than mole – with its often-complex blend of spices and chocolate – this early version of pipian was more accessible and affordable for ordinary Mexicans.

Today, Mexico City is a place where cultures collide, resulting in great food. Tacos al pastor (see page 122) is the result of immigrants arriving from the Middle East in the 1960s, introducing locals to lamb shawarma, gyros and the vertical grill. Once settled, they swapped the lamb for local pork and beef, and incorporated Mexican spices and chillies into their cooking. Pita breads became corn tortillas, and a pineapple was added to the spit so the sweet juice could run down into the meat as it cooked. That's fusion!

Tepoztlán, in the neighbouring state of Morelos to the south of Mexico City, is a place where pre-Hispanic traditions and modern tastes meet. Whether you're exploring the town's mystical energy, wandering its colourful markets, or enjoying the view of the Tepozteco Mountain, Itacates (see page 116) – triangular corn tortilla pockets stuffed with fillings and cooked on a hot griddle – are a must-try experience. They look similar to gorditas, but the pork lard flavour makes all the difference!

The fillings for itacates range from simple and traditional to more elaborate creations. Common ingredients include quelites (edible wild greens), beans, cheese or even meat. In Tepoztlan, it's not unusual to find itacates filled with toasted chapulines (grasshoppers), a source of protein dating back to pre-Hispanic times.

Among the iconic dishes of Morelos, with its warm climate and fertile soil, Cecina (see page 132) probably tops the list. Living in Mexico City, it was common for us to take a weekend trip to Morelos, and return home with a kilo of this irresistible dried salted meat to last us through the week. Walking through the Morelos market stalls, sampling different varieties and finding our favourite was always well worth the trip.

Another place not to miss is Toluca, the capital of Mexico State. Among its many culinary delights, chorizo verde (see page 114) stands out, given its vibrant colour and flavour from the inclusion of ingredients such as spinach, parsley, oregano, chillies and pepitas. For us chilangos (residents of Mexico City), it was traditional to return from a Toluca weekend with a generous portion of this iconic sausage!

Having been born in Mexico City, the food there will always hold a special place in my heart. When growing up, I spent countless hours exploring markets and local eateries with my family. Some of my fondest memories include making tamales and salsas with my aunt and grandma, the whole house filling with the enticing smells of chicken broth, chillies, luscious pork lard and the unique scent of corn husks as we all gathered together in the kitchen and took turns mixing and steaming masa dough around flavoursome fillings. Sweet pink tamales were always on the menu with a delicious café de olla (see page 138), and there was always a sense of joy and community that came with the food.

In recent years, the rise of fine dining in Mexico City has led to a renewed interest in indigenous ingredients and ancient cooking techniques. Chefs are looking to the past for inspiration, creating unique dishes that pay homage to Mexico's rich food history.

Tacos de Chorizo Verde

Green chorizo tacos

Serves 6

For us chilangos – residents of Mexico City – it's customary to return from a trip to the nearby city of Toluca with a parcel of its famous green chorizo sausage, freshly made and bursting with authentic flavour. Being an artisanal product, there are many versions of this herbaceous and slightly spicy sausage, which is a must-try whenever you find yourself in Toluca.

When we arrived in Australia, my dad decided to make his own version. With a touch of curiosity and a lot of determination, he dusted off a small sausage-stuffing machine and recreated this Toluca classic from scratch. Though we rarely use the machine now, it's a treasured keepsake, a symbol of his love for food and a connection to our culinary roots.

Here's a great way to bring a small piece of Toluca to your table. Besides being delicious in these tacos, you can serve the chorizo mixture with scrambled eggs, or in Discada (see page 36), quesadillas and burritos.

Method

Toast the pepitas in a comal or heavy-based frying pan over medium heat for 5 minutes, stirring constantly and keeping your eye on them so they don't burn. Remove the pepitas from the pan.

Add the parsley and spinach to the pan and cook, stirring often, for 2 minutes.

Tip the parsley and spinach into a food processor, along with the pepitas. Add the tomatillos, chillies, bay leaves, spices and vinegar. Blend until finely chopped.

Transfer the mixture to a large bowl, then mix the pork through. Cover and leave in the fridge overnight for the flavours to meld.

When ready to cook, heat the oil in a comal or large heavy-based frying pan over medium heat. Add the pork and fry for about 10 minutes, stirring occasionally, until browned and cooked through.

Serve in warm tortillas, topped with guacamole.

The cooked chorizo mixture will keep in an airtight container in the fridge for 4 days.

Ingredients

- 100 g (3½ oz) pepitas (pumpkin seeds)
- 1 small bunch of parsley, roughly chopped
- 300 g (10½ oz) baby spinach leaves
- 10 tinned tomatillos
- 4 fresh jalapeno chillies, stems removed
- 1 fresh poblano chilli, stem removed
- 10 bay leaves
- 10 allspice berries
- 1 teaspoon coriander seeds
- 100 ml (3½ fl oz) white vinegar
- 1 kg (2 lb 3 oz) minced (ground) pork
- 1 tablespoon vegetable oil

To serve

Tortillas de maiz page 314 →
Guacamole page 299 →

Itacates de Tepoztlan

Tepoztlan-style triangular corn pockets

Makes 8

In the indigenous traditions of the Nahua people, corn has always been at the heart of every meal. The Nahuatl word 'itacatl' means a 'bundle' or 'package of food', often carried by travellers or workers – and today, itacates are triangular pockets made from masa flour, stuffed with fillings and cooked on a hot chargrill. They might look a bit similar to gorditas, but the strong lard flavour makes all the difference! Itacates can be made from yellow, white or blue corn – each bring a unique flavour and texture.

The itacates below are filled with tinga de pollo, one of the top sellers at my deli. A flavourful and versatile Mexican dish, it consists of shredded chicken cooked with onions in a smoky, slightly spicy tomato-based salsa. Chipotle is definitely my favourite chilli flavour in a chicken tinga – I just love the way it adds a warm and comforting taste.

For filling the itacates, this chicken tinga recipe is on the drier side, but you can easily cook it with extra salsa if you'd like it a bit saucier for other dishes.

Ingredients

¾ × quantity Tortilla de maiz dough page 314 →

250 ml (1 cup) crema

250 g (9 oz) queso fresco, Cotija or feta, crumbled

Mayonesa de chipotle , to serve page 288 →

Tinga de pollo

80 ml (⅓ cup) vegetable oil

1½ white onions, finely sliced

600 ml (20½ fl oz) Salsa de chipotle page 288 →

500 g (1 lb 2 oz) cooked shredded chicken breast

2 teaspoons table salt

Method

To make the tinga de pollo, heat the oil in a large saucepan over medium–high heat and saute the onion for 5 minutes. Add the salsa and stir for 3 minutes, or until the salsa turns dark orange. Add the shredded chicken and salt and cook for 5 minutes, or until heated through. Transfer the mixture to a bowl, then cover and set aside in the fridge to cool.

Take 100 g (3½ oz) of the tortilla dough and roll into a ball, then gently flatten the ball into a thick tortilla no bigger than the size of your hand. Place 50 g (1¾ oz) of the tinga filling in the centre, then fold the tortilla over to enclose the filling, and form it into a triangle. Flatten the triangle slightly with your hands until it is about 12 cm (4¾ in) long. Repeat with the remaining dough and filling to make eight itacates.

Heat a comal or heavy-based frying pan over medium heat. Working in batches, fry the itacates on one side for 3 minutes, then flip and cook for another 5 minutes, until lightly golden.

Serve warm, topped with the crema and cheese, and with chipotle mayo on the side.

Tlacoyos

Thick oval tortillas

Makes 6

Tlacoyos are a favourite dish at my tamaleria. Made with blue corn masa flour and filled with refried beans, they have the perfect texture – crisp on the outside and soft inside. Many customers love them so much they ask for the recipe. I send them off happy with all the ingredients they need and a few of my personal tips.

Ingredients

- ¾ × quantity Tortilla de maiz dough, made with blue masa flour page 314 →
- 300 g (10½ oz) Frijoles negros refritos page 322 →

Topping

- 500 g (1 lb 2 oz) tinned nopales (prickly pear pads), cut into 3 cm × 1 cm (1¼ in × ½ in) strips
- 2 tomatoes, diced
- 1 small white onion, diced
- 2 tablespoons chopped coriander (cilantro) leaves
- 100 g (3½ oz) queso fresco, Cotija or feta, crumbled

To serve

- crema, for drizzling
- Salsa taquera page 294 →

Method

Take 100 g (3½ oz) of the tortilla dough and roll it into a ball. Using your hands, gently flatten the ball into a thick tortilla no bigger than the size of your hand. Place 50 g (1¾ oz) of the refried beans in the centre of the tortilla, then fold the tortilla over to enclose the filling and roll into a large ball. Repeat with the remaining dough and refried beans to make six balls.

Heat a comal or heavy-based frying pan over medium heat. Place a tortilla ball in the pan and use a spatula to flatten it into an 18 cm (7 in) oval with pointed ends. Cook the tlacoyo, flipping frequently, for 3 minutes, until lightly brown in spots. Remove from the pan and repeat with the remaining tortilla balls.

Meanwhile, combine all the topping ingredients in a bowl. Spoon the topping onto the warm tlacoyos and finish with a drizzle of crema and a little salsa.

Pozole Blanco

White hominy soup

Serves 4

Although it originated in the southern Mexican state of Guerrero, pozole blanco has managed to break through regional boundaries and become a staple across the country, especially in Mexico City.

This dish is special for me because it connects me to my family's history. My paternal grandfather, Tomás, was born and raised in the town of Tixtla in Guerrero, a place known for its authentic pozole blanco. Growing up in Mexico City, I enjoyed the capital's version of the dish, which incorporates some subtle local adaptations, being lighter and less greasy and served with lots of avocado, tostadas, sour cream and salsa verde, rather than trotters and chiles capones (pickled chillies).

I've also been fortunate to savour the original and I love them both.

Ingredients

- 800 g (1 lb 12 oz) tinned hominy, drained
- 400 g (14 oz) boneless pork shoulder, cut into 5 cm (2 in) chunks
- 4 bay leaves
- ½ white onion
- 2 teaspoons table salt
- 400 g (14 oz) chicken breasts, skin off

Toppings (choose your favourites)

- 4 sardine fillets in oil
- 1 avocado, chopped
- ½ white onion, finely chopped
- dried Mexican oregano
- chilli powder

To serve

- 8–12 Tostadas page 318 →
- 200 g (7 oz) sour cream
- 200 g (7 oz) queso fresco, Cotija or feta, crumbled
- Salsa verde page 286 →
- Chiles capones page 260 →
- lime wedges
- pork crackling (see Note)

Method

Pour 3 litres (3 qts) water into a large saucepan and add the hominy, pork shoulder, bay leaves, onion and salt. Bring to the boil, then reduce the heat and simmer gently for 45 minutes. Add the chicken and cook for another 30 minutes, or until the hominy has burst and all the meat is fully cooked. Remove and discard the onion and bay leaves. Lift out the pork and chicken, shred the meat with two forks, then return it all to the soup.

When ready to serve, set up the table with all the toppings laid out. Prepare the tostadas by spreading them with sour cream, crumbled cheese and salsa verde. Ladle the soup into bowls for guests to add all their favourite toppings to. Serve the chiles capones, lime wedges and pork crackling on the side.

The pozole blanco will keep in an airtight container in the fridge for up to 4 days.

Note

You can use the Chicharron de La Ramos pork crackling from page 54, or buy ready-made pork crackling from the chips (crisps) aisle in supermarkets.

Tacos al Pastor

Shepherd-style tacos

Serves 4–5

These are some of my best-selling tacos at my Sydney shop, and one of my personal favourites.

A wonderful culinary fusion, this dish is a perfect example of how simple ingredients and a bit of ingenuity can come together to create something really amazing. When Middle Eastern immigrants arrived in Mexico in the 1960s, they brought with them lamb shawarma and gyros, which quickly took on a more 'Mexican' flavour when made with local ingredients – the finishing touch being the brilliant addition of a pineapple to the roasting spit so the sweet juice could run over the grilling meat!

Little wonder it is becoming more common to see tacos al pastor in Mexican restaurants around the world. Meanwhile, my friend Alan has been practising how to torch the al pastor meat from my deli to get that extra crispy, smoky flavour, replicating the experience of eating it at street stalls in Mexico City.

Strangely, pineapple isn't always served on these tacos these days. I always ask my taquero to add a few slices because, for me, it's the sweet and savoury balance that makes al pastor truly exceptional.

Ingredients

- 1 teaspoon achiote paste
- 3½ tablespoons guajillo chilli powder
- 2 teaspoons table salt
- 50 ml (1¾ fl oz) white vinegar
- 1 kg (2 lb 3 oz) boneless pork leg, sliced 5 mm (¼ in) thick
- 500 g (1 lb 2 oz) beef cheeks, sliced 5 mm (¼ in) thick
- 2 white onions, finely sliced
- ¼ pineapple, peeled, cored and finely sliced
- 40 Tortillas de maiz, about 11 cm (4¼ in) in size page 314 →

To serve

- 1 white onion, diced
- 1 small bunch of coriander (cilantro), leaves chopped
- Salsa taquera page 294 →
- lime wedges

Method

Place the achiote paste in the small bowl of a food processor with the chilli powder, salt and vinegar. Blend to make a thick marinade.

Place the pork and beef in a large non-metallic bowl and rub the achiote marinade into the meat. Cover and set aside in the fridge to marinate for at least 3 hours, but preferably overnight.

Preheat the oven to 180°C (350°F) fan-forced. Arrange the marinated pork and beef in a large roasting tin, overlapping the meat in a single layer and adding the onion in between the slices of meat. Cover the tin with foil, then roast for 1 hour.

Remove the roasting tin from the oven and discard the foil. Place the pineapple slices over the meat. Roast, uncovered, for a further 30 minutes.

Roughly slice the meat again as finely as you can (like shaved kebab meat). Divide the meat among 20 warm double-thickness tortillas (stacking two tortillas slightly offset on top of each other). Top the tacos with the onion, coriander, roasted pineapple and some salsa.

Serve immediately, with lime wedges.

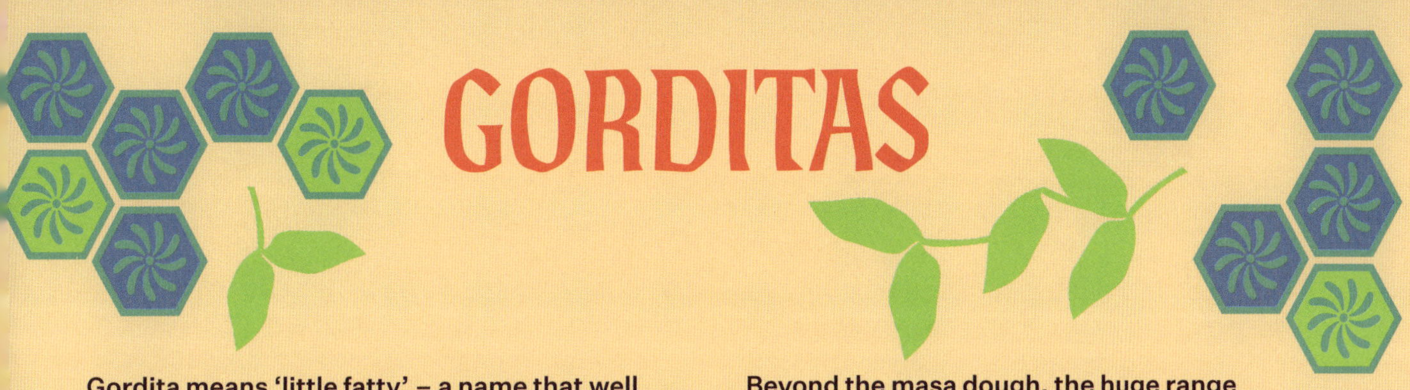

GORDITAS

Gordita means 'little fatty' – a name that well describes these plump, soft mini tortillas that are turned into little pockets and stuffed with any number of fillings. The masa dough is divided into small balls and flattened into thick discs, about the size of a small pancake, cooked in a comal until the crust is golden, and then sliced open to be filled.

Gordita fillings vary widely from region to region and include stews, meats, cheese, beans, potatoes and even chicharron (pork crackling), usually with crema and salsa piled on top. Some gorditas are stuffed before being cooked, while others are filled afterwards.

Few dishes evoke as much nostalgia and joy as the famous gorditas from Doña Tina in the bustling market of Cuernavaca, between Mexico City and Morelos. Since 1968 these mouthwatering creations have been delighting everyone who's lucky enough to try them. Doña Tina's stand has become a landmark for locals and visitors, offering not just food but the taste of tradition.

The secret to Doña Tina's iconic gorditas lies in the masa dough, which is lovingly prepared with lard so it has a richness and depth of flavour that sets it apart. Once shaped, the gorditas are fried to perfection in pork lard, giving them a golden, crispy exterior and a tender, juicy interior that leaves everyone wanting more. Every bite seems to be a perfect balance of texture and taste, testament to the care and expertise that goes into each gordita.

Beyond the masa dough, the huge range of toppings on offer has also made these gorditas famous – including chicken tinga (see page 116), rich umami mushrooms, chicharron (see page 54) and savoury picadillo (see page 126). Every gordita is carefully finished with a generous portion of sour cream, a sprinkle of queso fresco and a drizzle of spicy salsa that adds the perfect kick.

I crave these gorditas and would make a special trip from Mexico City when I lived there. Doña Tina's gorditas are thinner and slightly bigger than those in Mexico City, irresistibly crispy on the outside – and the garnishes are all on top of the gordita instead of inside.

For over five decades Doña Tina's gorditas have been a cornerstone of comfort food in Cuernavaca. As soon as you enter the market, the aroma leads you to the gordita stand. These are a culinary legacy, so, if you're ever passing through Cuernavaca, stop by the market and taste them. It's an experience you won't want to miss.

Gorditas de Picadillo

Minced beef gorditas

Serves 6–8

Filling up a gordita with picadillo is a genius idea! It's like carrying around a delicious minced beef corn pocket that can satisfy any cravings.

Ingredients

1 × quantity Tortilla de maiz dough	page 314 →
250 g (1 cup) sour cream	
250 g (9 oz) queso fresco, Cotija or feta, crumbled	
Chiles en vinagre, to serve	page 330 →

Picadillo

- 5 roma (plum) tomatoes, cut into large chunks
- 2 carrots, cut into 1 cm (½ in) chunks
- 2 potatoes, cut into 1 cm (½ in) chunks
- 2 tablespoons pork lard
- 2 garlic cloves
- 1 white onion, finely diced, plus ½ onion extra, roughly chopped
- 500 g (1 lb 2 oz) minced (ground) beef
- 2 teaspoons table salt
- 1 teaspoon freshly ground black pepper
- 1 sweetcorn cob, husks and silks removed, kernels stripped
- 100 g (3½ oz) green beans, trimmed and sliced
- 2 bay leaves
- vegetable oil, for shallow-frying

Method

Start by making the picadillo. Place the tomato in a saucepan with 500 ml (2 cups) water and bring to the boil over medium heat. Cook for 2 minutes, or until soft, then remove using a slotted spoon and set aside to cool. Add the carrot and potato to the water and cook for 10 minutes, until soft, then strain the liquid, reserving 250 ml (1 cup). Allow the carrot and potato to cool.

Heat the lard in a frying pan over medium heat, add one garlic clove and cook until slightly burnt (this adds a bitter edge to the sauce), then remove and discard. Add the finely diced onion and saute for 5 minutes, or until softened. Add the beef and salt, breaking up the mince with the back of a wooden spoon, then reduce the heat to low and cook for 10 minutes, or until the beef is cooked.

Place the cooked tomato in a food processor with the remaining garlic clove and the extra chopped onion. Add the black pepper and reserved cooking water and blend until smooth. Pour the sauce over the cooked beef and add the corn kernels, green beans, bay leaves and the cooked carrot and potato. Cook, stirring occasionally, for 10 minutes, or until thickened slightly. Remove and discard the bay leaves. Allow to cool slightly.

Take 100 g (3½ oz) of the tortilla dough and roll it into a ball. Gently flatten the ball into a thick tortilla, no bigger than the size of your hand, and place 50 g (1¾ oz) of the picadillo in the centre. Fold the tortilla over to enclose the filling and roll into a large ball. Flatten slightly with your hands until it is about 12 cm (4¾ in) in diameter. Repeat with the remaining dough and picadillo until all the ingredients are used.

Heat enough oil for shallow-frying in a large heavy-based frying pan over medium heat. Working in batches, shallow-fry the gorditas for 3 minutes on one side, then flip and cook the other side for 5 minutes, until lightly golden.

Serve warm, topped with the sour cream and cheese, and with pickled chillies on the side.

The picadillo filling will keep in an airtight container in the fridge for up to 3 days.

Pollo en Pipian Verde

Chicken with pepita verde

Serves 4

This pipian sauce dates back to pre-Hispanic times, when indigenous cultures, including the Aztecs and Mayans, relied on native ingredients such as pepitas. It has a simpler composition than mole, which often includes a complex blend of spices and chocolate. Here, it's the flavour of the sweet, nutty pepitas that takes centre stage.

During Día de los Muertos (Day of the Dead) celebrations, pipian (made with chicken, pork, potatoes or squash) is the main dish prepared for ofrendas (offerings) in this region, symbolising both vibrant nourishment and enduring connection to loved ones who have passed.

Ingredients

- 4 chicken marylands, skin on
- ½ white onion
- 3 bay leaves
- 1 tablespoon table salt

Pipian verde

- 100 g (3½ oz) pepitas (pumpkin seeds)
- 50 g (1¾ oz) unsalted peanuts
- 20 g (¾ oz) sesame seeds
- 800 g (1 lb 12 oz) fresh tomatillos or green bell peppers (capsicums)
- 3 cos (romaine) lettuce leaves
- 1 bunch of coriander (cilantro)
- 1 bunch of radish leaves
- 4 fresh jalapeno chillies, stems removed
- 2 fresh poblano chillies, stems removed
- 1 parsley sprig
- 1 teaspoon dried epazote (or Mexican oregano)
- 3 garlic cloves, peeled
- 3 tablespoons vegetable oil
- ½ white onion, roughly chopped

To serve

- steamed white rice
- Tortillas de maiz page 314 →

Method

Put the chicken in a large saucepan with the onion, bay leaves, salt and 3 litres (3 qts) water. Bring to the boil, then reduce the heat and simmer for 30 minutes, or until the chicken is cooked through. Lift out the chicken and set aside, reserving the broth.

To make the pipian verde, toast the pepitas, peanuts and sesame seeds in a comal or heavy-based frying pan over medium heat for 5 minutes, or until lightly golden, stirring constantly. Tip them all into a blender, blitz into a fine paste and set aside.

Roughly chop the tomatillos, lettuce, coriander, radish leaves and chillies. Place in a food processor with the parsley sprig, epazote and one of the garlic cloves. Blend with enough of the reserved chicken broth to achieve a smooth consistency.

Heat the vegetable oil in a large saucepan over medium heat. Add the onion and remaining two garlic cloves and stir for about 3 minutes, or until golden. Leaving the oil in the pan, transfer the onion and garlic to the processor and blitz again until smooth.

Add the toasted seed paste to the oil in the pan. Stirring constantly, cook over medium heat for about 4 minutes, until starting to crisp. Slowly start adding the blended green sauce to the pan, mixing until fully combined with the seed paste. Season with salt to taste.

Reduce the heat to low, then cover and simmer for 15 minutes, stirring occasionally. Stir in another 500 ml (2 cups) of the reserved chicken broth to loosen the sauce. Return the chicken to the pan, then cover and cook for another 15 minutes, until the chicken is thoroughly heated through.

Serve warm, with steamed white rice and warm tortillas.

Tacos Acorazados

Armoured tacos

Makes 8

The story of these tacos begins with a local train service. At each station along the way from the city of Cuautla, in Morelos, to Ozumba in the State of Mexico, women would sell their produce to the passengers – including these hearty tacos, which legend tells us were created by Señora Felicita, who at the age of 13 began selling them as she travelled to the north and back during the Mexican Revolution. Señora Felicita moved to different parts of the state over the years, and during World War II she established a taco stall in Morelos. The name 'acorazado', meaning 'armoured', was inspired by the strong ships and submarines of the time, and when applied to her tacos, refers to the double layer of thick tortillas used to hold the filling – stuffed with simple yet satisfying ingredients such as boiled eggs, strips of jalapeno and sometimes chicken feet, ideal for feeding hungry workers and travellers.

As their fame grew, tacos acorazados became a staple in Morelos. It is said that Señora Felicita operated the stall until her death in the late 1970s, and her grandchildren now continue the tradition. The base is always a generous serving of red rice with chiles rellenos (stuffed chillies), but now you'll find around 20 different toppings on offer, such as chicharron (pork crackling) in green or red salsa, milanesa (veal schnitzel), pork ribs, boiled eggs, mole, gizzards, moronga (pork blood sausage), pork steak or spicy chorizo.

A good taco acorazado is always completed with a topping of fresh salsa and perhaps a sprig of papalo – a fragrant local herb that enhances its flavour.

Below is the base recipe – take your pick of what to serve on top!

Method

Double stack the tortillas, slightly offset from each other, to create 10 double-thickness tortillas.

Fill each one with 2 tablespoons of rice, one chile relleno and some of the salsa.

Add whatever other toppings you fancy and serve immediately.

Ingredients

16 Tortillas de maiz, warmed	page 314 →
200 g (7 oz) Arroz Mexicano	page 327 →
8 Chiles rellenos, with their Salsa de tomate	page 332 →

Cecina

Salted dried meat

Serves 4

When I was growing up in Mexico City, it was common to take a weekend trip to visit friends in the neighbouring state of Morelos and return home with a big bag of this delicacy to keep us going through the week. The preparation of this iconic dish is an ancient process requiring patience and precision ... and, in the old days, many hands, as traditional cecina could measure up to 12 metres (39 feet) long! It also relies on the perfect combination of temperature, humidity and ventilation for sun drying – a process that thrives in Morelos, whose capital, Cuernavaca, is known as the 'City of Eternal Spring'.

Cecina can be trickier to recreate elsewhere, so I've adapted the process to use thin-sliced minute steaks, which work well to deliver the right texture and flavour. The simplicity of the dish highlights the meat's rich, salty flavour.

Ingredients

- 1 kg (2 lb 3 oz) minute steaks
- 150–200 g (5½–7 oz) table salt
- 200 g (7 oz) pork lard

To serve

- Tortillas de maiz page 314 →
- avocado slices
- Salsa borracha page 290 →

Method

Preheat the oven to 200°C (400°F) fan-forced.

Start by tenderising the steaks with a meat mallet until they are paper-thin and almost transparent. Generously salt both sides. Arrange the steaks on a perforated oven tray or wire rack over a roasting tin, to ensure they will bake evenly on both sides.

Transfer to the oven and bake for 20–30 minutes – the goal is to semi-dry the meat while keeping it soft. Remove from the oven and leave to cool, ensuring the steaks are draining well and free of liquid.

Once cooled, coat both sides of the meat with the lard. Keeping each piece separate, and leaving them flat, tightly wrap the steaks with plastic wrap. Leave in the fridge for at least 2 hours (and up to 1 week) – this step helps maintain the meat's salted flavour and flexible texture.

Unwrap and cook the cecinas in a hot comal or heavy-based frying pan for about 2 minutes on each side, until lightly charred and fragrant. Cut into pieces and serve in corn tortillas with avocado and salsa.

Paloma

Makes 1

I'm super excited to see palomas appearing on menus in Sydney. With their refreshing mix of tequila and grapefruit, they've become one of the most popular Mexican cocktails, starting to rival margaritas. They're even available in premix cans! While you might not find the same grapefruit sodas that are used in Mexico, such as Squirt or Fresca, there are plenty of good alternatives available – even sparkling water with a hint of grapefruit works. Add lime juice if you feel it needs powering up.

Method

Place some salt on a plate. Rub the lime wedge around the rim of a chilled glass, then press the rim of the glass into the salt.

Fill the glass with ice cubes, then add the tequila, grapefruit soda and lime juice and stir to combine. Enjoy immediately.

Ingredients

- flaked sea salt
- juice of 2 limes, plus 1 lime wedge
- handful of ice cubes
- 30 ml (1 fl oz) white tequila
- 200 ml (7 fl oz) grapefruit soda

Horchata

Serves 8

Mexican horchata is a refreshing and sweet beverage made primarily from rice, water and cinnamon. The addition of both condensed and evaporated milks gives it that creamy consistency and sweetness that makes it so yum. It's a popular drink throughout Mexico, and in Mexican restaurants worldwide, especially during hot weather.

This version is inspired by one served at a market stall at the Mercado de Azcapotzalco, a bustling market in Mexico City, where they add extra cinnamon to the mix and sprinkle more on top to serve. Other places are going fancier, adding crushed pecans or almonds, anise, coffee and even tequila. It seems like horchata is here to stay and I can't wait to see more additions for this delicious drink!

Method

Place the rice in a heatproof bowl or jar and add the boiled water. Stir, then cover and set aside to cool to room temperature. The rice will soften slightly.

Transfer the rice, soaking water and almonds or almond meal to a food processor and blend until the rice is finely chopped and almost dissolved.

Strain the liquid into a large bowl or jar, discarding any remaining bits of rice. Add the condensed milk, evaporated milk and cinnamon, stir well and refrigerate for 30 minutes.

Add the water to the horchata and mix together.

Serve in chilled glasses over ice, with a cinnamon stick, if you like.

Ingredients

- 50 g (1¾ oz) jasmine rice
- 1 litre (4 cups) just-boiled water
- 50 g (1¾ oz) blanched almonds or almond meal
- 75 g (2¾ oz) condensed milk
- 75 ml (2½ fl oz) evaporated milk
- 1 teaspoon ground cinnamon
- 500 ml (2 cups) chilled water
- ice cubes, to serve
- cinnamon sticks, to serve (optional)

Café de Olla

Pot coffee

Makes 1

Café de olla is one of Mexico's most iconic drinks. No matter where you are, it's always a good idea.

The key ingredients for a 'proper' café de olla are cinnamon, star anise and piloncillo (unrefined cane sugar). In some regions, they'll add orange peel, and, if you're lucky, a 'piquete' – a splash of rum, brandy, tequila, mezcal or other local spirit.

For me, café de olla is tied to memories of my mother's hometown, Agua Fria. Early mornings were filled with the aroma of coffee brewing in clay pots over wood or charcoal stoves – the air a fragrant, smoky, coffee embrace.

Even here in Sydney, café de olla holds a special place on my menu. Though it's vastly different from the typical 'flat white' that is so popular now, the adventurous souls brave enough to try it have never been disappointed.

Method

Let all the ingredients steep in 250 ml (1 cup) freshly boiled hot water for about 10 minutes.

Pour into a warmed mug and serve, adding a little more sugar, if you like.

Ingredients

- 1 shot of your favourite coffee
- 1 cinnamon stick
- 1 star anise
- 1 strip of lemon peel
- 1 teaspoon piloncillo (or to taste)

Platanos Fritos

Fried plantain

Serves 4

Unlike ice-cream vans in Australia, which pipe music to entice people out of their homes, Mexican street-food vendors selling platanos fritos emit a loud whistling sound, which comes from the dessert steamers. Still, the effect is the same, and people come running out for an early evening sugar hit! The platanos fritos cart drives through the streets looking for the best place to stop and wait for the neighbourhood to line up.

Crispy on the outside, soft and warm on the inside and often topped with a sprinkle of cinnamon or drizzle of syrup ... how I miss platanos fritos now I'm in Sydney!

Ingredients

- 250 ml (1 cup) vegetable oil
- 4 ripe plantains, peeled and halved lengthways
- 2 tablespoons condensed milk
- 80 g (2¾ oz) strawberry jam
- 1 tablespoon brown sugar

To serve

- chocolate or rainbow sprinkles
- marie (rich tea) biscuits
- vanilla ice cream (optional)

Method

Heat the oil in a large frying pan over medium–high heat. Add the plantain and cook, turning frequently, for 4–5 minutes, until lightly golden. Transfer to a plate lined with paper towel to drain.

Divide the plantain among four serving plates, drizzle with the condensed milk and top with the jam and sugar.

Finish with a scattering of sprinkles and serve with marie biscuits on the side and a scoop of vanilla ice cream, if you like.

MARIE

EL
Jalisco
Nayarit

Colima ✲✲✲ Michoacán ✲✲✲

EL OESTE

A night out in Tequila, Jalisco, can be quite the experience. As the sun dips below the horizon, banda and norteño music start up, the rhythm of the instruments pulsates through the streets and folk dancers in colourful costumes add to the atmosphere.

Tequila is famous for, well, tequila! The drink that gave the town its name has become an integral part of Mexico's culture. Despite agave fields stretching to the horizon and distilleries everywhere, Jalisco isn't just about tequila – it's also home to some great food.

Michoacán is the 'avocado capital of the world'. In Mexico we're not too proud to call avocados green gold, or 'el oro verde'. Michoacán is blessed with perfect avocado-growing conditions, with fertile volcanic soil and a temperate climate, plus farmers who follow old traditions. It's the only place on Earth where avocados grow all year round – these trees are overachievers, producing fruit in every season. Hass, the rockstar of avocado varieties, thrives here.

When I was young, I would go to my Aunt Luz's house in Michoacán for the summer holidays. Her neighbours would climb the avocado trees to get us the freshest and most beautiful fruit for breakfast. I was never allowed to climb those trees but I loved watching them do it. We would stand underneath with a bucket, ready to pick up the ripe avocados that fell dangerously near our heads. My cousins' classmate and neighbour Igor was the best climber, and it shocked me that he was able to climb up without shoes!

A traditional delicacy of Michoacán's Purépecha people are corundas (see page 154). Similar to tamales, they are distinguished by their triangular shape and rustic wrapping of fresh green corn leaves, rather than corn husks. They're also steamed like tamales, but using special Purépecha traditions to ward off any bad energy in the kitchen.

The birote is a characteristic bread of Jalisco, and is very different to the bolillo (bread rolls) commonly found in other parts of Mexico. Birotes are known for their exceptionally crusty exterior and dense, soft, chewy interior. Many bakeries in Guadalajara, Jalisco's capital, specialise in baking birote, their freshness a point of local pride. Some bakeries even add beer or lime juice to the dough! The local Torta ahogada (see page 146) has its own legendary place in Jalisco's food scene. If you haven't yet tried a 'drowned sandwich', imagine one of those perfect birote rolls filled with tender pork, doused in a chilli sauce to make the bread soft, with just the right amount of heat. Birotes are a large part of daily life in Jalisco, eaten at breakfast, lunch and dinner – I never tire of them.

Archaeologists believe the Mexicas (Aztecs) might have first settled in what is now Nayarit, Jalisco's northern neighbour. The state's long Pacific coastline offers a bounty of seafood, allowing you to feast on a brilliant array of dishes from grilled fish to ceviche-style Aguachile (see page 166) – prawns in a rich and smoky dark salsa. Filled with history and stories, the port of San Blas, midway along Nayarit's coastline, has inspired iconic songs that are sung across Mexico. One of the most popular snacks here is Balazos ('shrimp shots', see page 168), a great example of seafood freshness mixing with bold, tangy flavours.

Colima, a small state just south of Jalisco, was historically an important trading centre where indigenous peoples exchanged goods, including the Caxcan, who were known for their skills in cultivating maize, beans and squash. Today, Colima is famed for its coconut production – not just for coconut flesh, but an intriguing vinegar known as tuba, made from the sap of coconut trees. The sap is left to ferment into a sweet, tangy, vinegar-like liquid that adds flavour to the local slow-cooked tatemado stew (see page 160) and serves as a tenderising agent for the meat. The name 'tatemado' itself comes from the traditional method of cooking – meats and fresh vegetables are roasted over an open flame, imparting a hallmark smoky flavour to this traditional dish, which is often served at celebrations and community gatherings.

In this chapter you'll also find the Moorish (and more-ish!) sweet coconut bites, alfajores. For me, there's always something nostalgic about unwrapping an alfajor from its cellophane wrapper. It's like opening a tiny, edible gift from the past, carefully made under Jalisco traditions passed down over generations.

Tortas Ahogadas

Drowned sandwiches

Makes 4

Street vendors started selling these fabulously named sandwiches at lunchtime for hungry workers in Guadalajara, the capital of Jalisco, more than a century ago. They found the local Jalisco birote (bread), with its crisp crust and soft inside, was perfect for dipping into and soaking up a spicy sauce.

If you're in Jalisco, I highly recommend asking locals for their favourite tortas ahogadas spots. When I visited with my dad and my friend Juan Manuel, we spent several days tasting and finding the best tortas ahogadas. What a fun way to explore the city!

Here we're going to use sourdough French rolls instead of the birote.

Ingredients

- 4 sourdough French bread rolls
- 500 g (1 lb 2 oz) Frijoles negros refritos page 322 →
- 500 g (1 lb 2 oz) Carnitas page 334 →
- 1 small red onion, finely sliced and blanched for 3 minutes
- lime wedges, to serve

Tomato salsa

- 8 ripe roma (plum) tomatoes
- 1 white onion, chopped
- 2 garlic cloves, chopped
- 2 teaspoons table salt

Arbol salsa

- 5 dried arbol chillies, stems removed
- 1 dried guajillo chillies, stem removed
- 4 garlic cloves, chopped
- 2 teaspoons sesame seeds
- 3 black peppercorns
- 1 teaspoon dried Mexican oregano
- 1 teaspoon ground marjoram
- 2 teaspoons table salt
- pinch of ground cloves
- pinch of ground cumin
- 20 ml (¾ fl oz) white vinegar

Method

To make the tomato salsa, bring 1 litre (4 cups) water to the boil in a saucepan over medium heat. Add the tomatoes and simmer for 10–15 minutes, until soft and cooked through. Lift out the tomatoes and place in a food processor, reserving the cooking water. Add the onion, garlic, salt and 300 ml (10 fl oz) of the reserved cooking water. Blend until smooth and runny, adding more water if needed. Transfer the salsa to a bowl and clean out the food processor.

To make the arbol salsa, bring 1 litre (4 cups) water to the boil in a large saucepan over medium heat. Add the arbol and guajillo chillies and boil for about 10 minutes, until soft. Lift out the chillies, reserving the cooking water, and place in the food processor. Add the remaining arbol salsa ingredients and 200 ml (7 fl oz) of the reserved chilli cooking water to the food processor and blend until smooth.

Strain the arbol salsa into a bowl through a sieve to remove any solids. Use a spatula to push the mixture through and extract as much liquid as possible.

Cut the French rolls lengthways, without cutting all the way through. Spread each with a quarter of the refried beans and a quarter of the carnitas. Add about 75 ml (2½ fl oz) of the tomato salsa and close the rolls. To drown it or make a soupy torta, add as much arbol salsa as you like. Top with the blanched onion and serve immediately, with lime wedges for squeezing over.

Enchiladas de Picadillo Dulce

Sweet minced beef enchiladas

Serves 4

Whenever he saw it on a menu, Dad would always ask for picadillo dulce – sweet minced beef – and his face would light up when we made it at home. 'This picadillo is the best,' he'd declare, 'it's got just the right touch!' It became a bit of a tradition for Dad to always dive in for seconds – and maybe even thirds. Picadillo dulce makes a wonderful filling for these enchiladas, drizzled with a luxurious chocolate chilli salsa. This was a dish that always made him feel at home.

Ingredients

- 2 tablespoons vegetable oil
- 2 roma (plum) tomatoes, diced
- 1 teaspoon crushed garlic
- 250 g (9 oz) minced (ground) beef
- 250 g (9 oz) minced (ground) pork
- 1 carrot, cut into 1 cm (½ in) chunks
- 1 potato, cut into 1 cm (½ in) chunks
- 100 g (3½ oz) blanched almonds
- 50 g (1¾ oz) sultanas (golden raisins)

Chocolate chilli salsa

- 3 dried ancho chillies, stems removed
- 3 dried guajillo chillies, stems removed
- 90 g (3 oz) Mexican chocolate, such as Ibarra or Abuelita (see Note overleaf)
- 50 g (1¾ oz) piloncillo or soft brown sugar
- 1 teaspoon table salt
- 2 cinnamon sticks
- 5 allspice berries
- 2 teaspoons masa flour
- 2 tablespoons vegetable oil

Method

To make the chocolate chilli salsa, start by boiling the ancho and guajillo chillies in 1 litre (4 cups) water for 5 minutes. Set aside to cool.

In another pan, heat 500 ml (2 cups) water until it comes to a gentle boil. Stir in the chocolate and sugar, then remove from the heat. Set aside to dissolve.

Meanwhile, heat the oil in a frying pan over medium heat. Add the tomato and garlic and saute for 2–3 minutes, until soft. Add the beef and pork, and season well with salt. Cook, stirring, for about 5 minutes, until the meat has browned.

Stir in the carrot, potato and 100 ml (3½ fl oz) water. Cover and cook for about 10 minutes, until the vegetables are tender. Remove from the heat and stir in the almonds and sultanas. Cover the pan and set aside while you finish the chocolate chilli salsa.

Transfer the softened chillies to a food processor, reserving the chilli cooking water. Add the salt, cinnamon sticks, allspice and masa flour and blend with enough of the chilli cooking water to create a smooth sauce. Strain to remove any solids.

Heat the oil in a saucepan over medium heat and add the strained chilli sauce. Bring to a gentle boil, then stir in the melted chocolate mixture. Cook for about 5 minutes, stirring often, until the salsa thickens but remains pourable.

Recipe continues →

When ready to serve, heat the vegetable oil in a frying pan over medium heat. Lightly fry the tortillas in batches for a few seconds on each side. Dip each tortilla into the chocolate chilli salsa, then add 3 tablespoons of the meat filling. Roll up and arrange three enchiladas on each plate, side by side.

Drizzle with more chocolate chilli salsa and top with the onion, lettuce, crema, crumbled cheese and sliced radish. Serve immediately.

Note

You can buy Mexican chocolate online or from Latin American grocery shops.

To serve

- 200 ml (7 fl oz) vegetable oil
- 12 Tortillas de maiz page 314 →
- 1 white onion, finely diced
- ½ iceberg lettuce, shredded
- 200 ml (7 fl oz) crema
- 200 g (7 oz) queso fresco, Cotija or feta, crumbled
- 5 radishes, sliced

Pozole Rojo

Pork and hominy soup

Serves 6

I enjoyed a very special version of this soup at my friend Fernanda's house, who lives in a town called La Barca in Jalisco. It was simple, yet incredibly delicious – the broth rich and full of flavour, and the hominy cooked perfectly. I think that sums up how pozole should be: comforting and full of tradition.

There's nothing more Mexican than this pork and hominy soup, which comes in three traditional styles: green, white and red, just like the Mexican flag. Little wonder it's the favourite dish for Independence Day celebrations! My favourite is Pozole verde (see page 254), but this red version is the one that's most popular in Jalisco.

The word 'pozole' comes from the Nahuatl language and means 'boiled' or 'foam'. The hominy maize is white, round and large-grained – more puffy than regular corn. It looks like a flower when it's boiled and turns the cooking water foamy.

Method

Pour 2 litres (2 qts) water into a large stockpot. Add the pork, trotters, bay leaves, garlic bulb, one onion half and 1 tablespoon of the salt. Bring to the boil, then reduce the heat to low and simmer for 1 hour. Add the chicken and simmer for a further 30 minutes or until the meat is tender.

Meanwhile, place the guajillo and ancho chillies in a heatproof bowl, cover with boiling water and soak for 20 minutes, or until the chillies are soft. Transfer the chillies and 100 ml (3½ fl oz) of the chilli soaking water to a food processor. Add the oregano and the remaining garlic clove, onion half and salt. Blend until smooth. Strain the sauce into a bowl, discarding any solids.

Heat the oil in a large saucepan over medium heat. Add the strained chilli sauce and cook for about 7 minutes, or until it darkens slightly.

Using a slotted spoon, remove the bay leaves, onion and garlic bulb from the stockpot and discard. Remove the meat and set aside. Stir the chilli sauce and hominy through the stock. Simmer for 30 minutes, or until the hominy turns slightly red.

Ingredients

- 500 g (1 lb 2 oz) boneless pork shoulder, cut into 5 cm (2 in) chunks
- 4 pork trotters
- 3 bay leaves
- ½ garlic bulb, halved crossways, plus 1 extra clove
- 1 brown onion, cut in half
- 1½ tablespoons table salt
- 500 g (1 lb 2 oz) boneless, skinless chicken breasts
- 3 dried guajillo chillies, stems removed
- 2 dried ancho chillies, stems removed
- pinch of dried Mexican oregano
- 2 tablespoons vegetable oil
- 800 g (1 lb 12 oz) tinned hominy, drained and rinsed

Toppings

- ½ iceberg lettuce, shredded
- ½ small white onion, diced
- 4 radishes, finely sliced
- crushed dried arbol chilli
- pinch of dried Mexican oregano

Recipe continues →

Shred the chicken, pork and trotters with your fingers or two forks, discarding the skin and bones. Return the meat to the soup and heat through.

Divide the pozole among bowls and top each bowl with the lettuce, onion, radish, crushed chilli and oregano. Serve with lime wedges, and a side of tostadas topped with sour cream.

To serve

lime wedges

12 Tostadas page 318 →

200 g (7 oz) sour cream

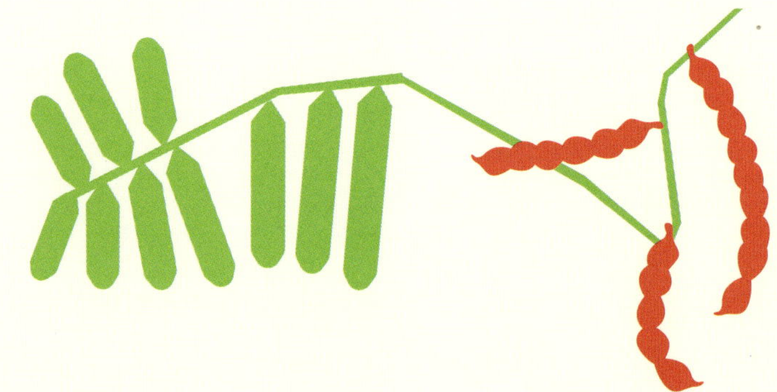

Corundas de Queso

Cheese triangle tamales

Makes 20

Rather than corn husks, these tamales from Michoacán are wrapped in fresh green corn leaves (hojas de milpa) and cooked using special Purépecha traditions that make them unique. It's said that corundas should always be steamed in a clay pot sealed with masa dough to prevent steam escaping. Folklore adds that fresh green corn leaves should be tied around the pot handle to ward off bad energy or gossip from the kitchen, so the corundas cook with nothing but good vibes. The Purépecha also believe that the person who made the corundas is the only one who can fill up the steamer, otherwise the corundas won't cook properly!

As fresh sweetcorn leaves can be very hard to find, the recipe below uses banana leaves instead.

Method

Place the lard and baking powder in a large bowl and whip as fast as possible with a wooden spoon – the lard needs to soften and look spongy. Don't stress if this takes a long time; it can take up to 15 minutes to achieve the right consistency.

Once the lard is ready, add the masa flour, salt and chicken stock and mix well until completely combined. To test if the dough is ready, drop a small ball of dough into a cup of cold water; if it floats to the top you're good to go!

You will need about 90 g (3 oz) dough and 25 g (1 oz) ricotta for each corunda. To create the triangle parcels, take a banana leaf and twist it into a triangular, cone-like shape, with the pointy, closed end at the bottom and an open pocket with two long ends of the banana leaf at the top. Fill the pocket with the dough and cheese, then fold down one leaf to enclose the filling, and then the other one to keep the triangular shape. (You can also make square parcels if this is too hard!) Repeat with the remaining banana leaves, dough and cheese.

Put the corundas in a steamer (or traditional clay pot) on top of each other, fitting as many as you can into the steamer – but be careful not to pack them in too tightly as they can burst. Place the steamer over a saucepan of simmering water and steam for 45 minutes.

The best way to check if the corundas are cooked is to remove one from the steamer, let it cool for 5 minutes, then unwrap the leaf. If the dough doesn't stick to the leaf and looks shiny and fluffy, your corundas are ready.

Leave them to cool for 15–20 minutes inside the steamer, then serve with the salsa and a drizzle of crema.

Ingredients

- 200 g (7 oz) pork lard
- 1 teaspoon baking powder
- 500 g (1 lb 2 oz) masa flour, sifted
- 2 teaspoons table salt
- 650 ml (22 fl oz) chicken stock, warmed
- 6 fresh banana leaves, cut into twenty 15 cm × 20 cm (6 in × 8 in) rectangles
- 500 g (1 lb 2 oz) ricotta
- Salsa con rajas de poblano, to serve page 303 →
- crema, for drizzling

MICHOACÁN'S MONARCH BUTTERFLIES

Monarch butterflies are among nature's most dazzling spectacles. These tiny creatures perform one of the most extraordinary migrations on the planet, fluttering thousands of kilometres from Canada and the USA to Mexico, where they land in the oyamel fir forests of Michoacán. The trees, also known as 'sacred firs', create a fairytale-like sanctuary for the delicate insects.

Every autumn these vivid orange-and-black butterflies fly up to 4500 kilometres (2800 miles) south to escape the northern cold. How do millions of monarchs manage to navigate from all over eastern and central North America to a small area in the mountains of central Mexico? They're apparently guided by an internal compass that uses the Sun and Earth's magnetic fields.

What's even more extraordinary is that the butterflies that arrive in Mexico have never been there before. Born in late summer, rather than early spring like their parents and grandparents, these lucky butterflies are known as the 'super generation'. They can live for up to eight months – a lifetime compared to the few short weeks their parents and grandparents lived – because as they overwinter in Mexico, their metabolism slows and they don't spend any energy reproducing. Once spring arrives, these butterflies mature and reproduce, starting the first new generation of butterflies that start migrating north to the monarchs' summer feeding and breeding grounds in Canada and the northern US.

The butterflies' winter refuge in Mexico is now a UNESCO World Heritage site. Known as the Monarch Butterfly Biosphere Reserve, the sanctuary spreads across Michoacán and the State of Mexico, and is about a three-hour drive from Mexico City. Once they arrive here in late October or early November, the butterflies roost for the winter, then in February and March they start breeding again and the annual cycle starts afresh.

Imagine standing in a forest with millions of butterflies clinging to the trees so the branches look as if they're made of molten gold. When the sun warms them up, the butterflies flutter like golden confetti. It's pure magic. If you visit on a sunny day, you'll see the monarchs take flight in massive, swirling clouds. On cooler or overcast days they'll often huddle together for warmth.

For the indigenous Purépecha people of the region, the butterflies are more than just a beautiful phenomenon, they are deeply symbolic. Their arrival coincides with Día de los Muertos – Day of the Dead – and many believe they carry the spirits of their ancestors.

There are several entry points to the sanctuary, but the most popular ones are El Rosario and Sierra Chincua. It's a bit of a hike to reach the butterfly colonies, and the forest trails can be steep, so pack your walking shoes and sense of adventure. An enchanting experience awaits.

Sopitos Colimenses

Colima-style sopes

Makes 20

Originally from the city of Villa de Alvarez in the state of Colima, sopitos are thick corn tortillas similar to sopes, but smaller. They also differ to the sopes from Mexico City in that they're served with a delicious minced beef topping, and a marvellous tomatillo sauce enriched with beef broth. No wonder they're such a beloved comfort food!

Ingredients

1 × quantity Tortilla de maiz dough page 314 →

cooking oil spray

100 g (3½ oz) pork lard or vegetable oil

Beef topping

2 garlic cloves, peeled

2 bay leaves

500 g (1 lb 2 oz) minced (ground) beef

Tomatillo sauce

5 tinned tomatillos, or fresh green bell peppers (capsicums), seeds and membranes removed

3 roma (plum) tomatoes

1 tablespoon dried Mexican oregano

1 teaspoon ground cumin

To serve

½ cabbage, shredded

100 g (3½ oz) queso fresco, Cotija or feta, crumbled

3 radishes, sliced

Method

To make the beef topping, bring 1.5 litres (6 cups) water to the boil in a large saucepan. Add the garlic and bay leaves. Divide the beef into four equal portions, season well with salt and roll into four meatballs. Drop the meatballs into the boiling water, ensuring they are fully submerged. Cook for 3 minutes, then reduce the heat to low and simmer for 30 minutes. Reserving the garlic and cooking broth, lift out the meatballs and set aside to cool.

To make the tomatillo sauce, simmer the tomatillos and tomatoes in the broth for about 20 minutes, until soft. Transfer the tomatoes, tomatillos and 100 ml (3½ fl oz) cooking broth to a blender, add the oregano, cumin and reserved garlic cloves and blend until smooth. Stir the mixture back into the pan of broth to create your sauce and season with salt. The broth is the star of the dish!

Meanwhile, place a plastic food bag over the bottom half of a tortilla press. Roll 3 tablespoons of the tortilla dough into a ball and place it in the middle of the press. Cover with another plastic food bag, then close the tortilla press and gently press to flatten the dough into a disc at least 1 cm (½ in) thick. If you don't have a tortilla press, flatten the dough into rounds using your hands. Repeat with the remaining dough to make 20 sopitos.

Lightly spray a comal or large heavy-based frying pan with cooking oil and place over medium–high heat. Cook the sopitos, in batches, for about 3 minutes each side, until lightly golden.

Fill a small bowl with cold water. Dip your fingers in the water, then pinch the edge of each sopito to form a rim.

Heat the lard in the same comal or frying pan. Working in batches, lightly fry the sopitos for 2 minutes, without flipping, until crispy underneath but soft on the inside.

Crumble the cooled meatballs with your hands, then scatter the meat over the sopitos. Serve immediately, topped with the cabbage, cheese, radish and as much of the beautiful tomatillo sauce as you like!

Tatemado Colimense

Colima-style pork

Serves 4

This traditional dish from Colima involves roasting meat and vegetables over an open flame, then slowly simmering them with a secret defining ingredient – local tuba vinegar made from the sap of the coconut tree. This vinegar adds flavour and serves as a tenderising agent.

If you can't get tuba vinegar, use coconut vinegar, or apple cider vinegar mixed with a spoonful of honey. I have also simplifed the cooking method, so it can be made easily on a stovetop.

Ingredients

- 3 dried guajillo chillies
- 3 dried pasilla chillies
- 1 cinnamon stick
- 4 garlic cloves, peeled
- 1 teaspoon ground cumin
- 3 tinned tomatillos
- 1 tablespoon freshly ground black pepper
- 4 bay leaves
- 1 tablespoon dried Mexican oregano
- 2 cloves
- 200 ml (7 fl oz) tuba vinegar
- 1 kg (2 lb 3 oz) boneless pork (shoulder and ribs), cut into 3 cm (1¼ in) cubes

Salad

- ½ iceberg lettuce, sliced
- 2 short cucumbers, finely sliced
- 1 small red onion, very finely sliced
- 2 fresh habanero chillies, finely sliced
- 4 radishes, sliced
- juice of 1 lime
- 1 teaspoon crushed dried Mexican oregano

Method

Remove the stems from the guajillo and pasilla chillies. Split the chillies, reserving the seeds.

Heat a comal or heavy-based frying pan over medium heat. Once hot, toast the chillies for 2 minutes, being careful not to burn them. Transfer to a large heatproof bowl, cover with 1 litre (4 cups) freshly boiled water and leave for 10 minutes to soften.

Toast the cinnamon stick in the pan until lightly browned on all sides, tossing frequently to avoid burning, then add to the bowl of soaking chillies. Toast the garlic cloves in the same way, then add to the chillies. Toast the cumin and reserved chilli seeds together for about 1 minute, stirring constantly, then add to the chillies. Lastly, toast the tomatillos, black pepper, bay leaves, oregano and cloves together, then add to the chillies.

Stir the vinegar into the bowl of soaking chillies, then set aside for about 30 minutes for all the spices to infuse into the soaking water.

Tip the mixture into a food processor and blend until smooth. Strain, then repeat the blending and straining until you have a smooth sauce. Season with salt to taste.

Pour the sauce into a large non-metallic bowl, add the pork and mix until well coated. Cover and leave the pork to marinate in the sauce for 30 minutes.

Transfer the meat and marinade to a saucepan, then cover and simmer over medium heat for 2 hours, until the pork is very tender.

Just before serving, make the salad. Toss the lettuce, cucumber and onion in a bowl, add the chilli and radish, drizzle with the lime juice and sprinkle with the oregano.

Ladle the tatemado into bowls and serve with the salad on the side.

Pescado Zarandeado

Grilled fish

Serves 4

There are many variations of this dish, but I think this version from Nayarit stands out for its simplicity and flavour. Traditionally, the fish would always be grilled over an open flame, giving it a smoky aroma and a charred finish – juicy inside but with a crisp crust.

I've cooked this dish in Sydney at my friend Claudio's house on his perfect wood-fired grill, but you can make it on the stove using a comal or large heavy-based frying pan, or under a hot grill. The results aren't quite as authentically Mexican, but the fish will still taste fabulous!

Ingredients

- 120 g (4½ oz) whole-egg mayonnaise
- 2 teaspoons crushed garlic
- 1 teaspoon freshly ground black pepper
- 2 teaspoons soy sauce
- 1 tablespoon Valentina hot sauce, Huichol or sriracha chilli sauce, plus extra to serve
- 1 teaspoon sour cream
- 1 teaspoon American mustard
- 4 × 200 g (7 oz) skinless firm white fish fillets, such as barramundi, cod or snapper, about 2 cm (¾ in) thick
- olive oil spray
- lime wedges, to serve

Method

In a bowl, mix together the mayonnaise, garlic, pepper, soy sauce, hot sauce, sour cream and American mustard. Mix well to make a smooth marinade.

Using a sharp knife, cut a few shallow slashes along the top of each fish fillet to help the marinade penetrate the flesh. Season the fish on both sides with salt and pepper.

Lay the fish flat in a large shallow dish and pour the marinade over to evenly coat. Cover and leave to marinate in the fridge for at least 15 minutes, or up to 1 hour, to absorb all the flavours.

Preheat a grill (broiler) to medium–high.

Line a baking tray with foil and spray with olive oil spray. Transfer the fish to the tray and grill (broil) for 5–6 minutes, until the fillets are cooked through and have a nicely golden crust. The flesh should be flaky and tender.

Serve immediately with lime wedges, and an extra drizzle of hot sauce, if you like.

MEXCALTITÁN

Often referred to as the 'Venice of Mexico', this tiny island town lies in the state of Nayarit in the municipality of Santiago Ixcuintla. Barely 400 metres (1,310 ft) across, Mexcaltitán is surrounded by marshlands and the waters of the Rio San Pedro. Its unique charm and historical significance have made it one of Mexico's Pueblos Mágicos – 'Magical Towns'.

Steeped in legend, Mexcaltitán is even believed by some historians to be the mythical Aztlan, the ancestral home of the Aztecs – the starting point of the Aztecs' migration to the Valley of Mexico, where they eventually founded Tenochtitlan (modern-day Mexico City). The name Mexcaltitán is thought by some to mean 'House of the Mexicas', reinforcing the Aztec connection. And the island's unique layout – concentric streets that become flooded canals during the rainy season – echoes the description of the mythical Aztec homeland.

Today this circular island is home to a small population that relies on fishing for sustenance and their livelihoods. Prawn (shrimp) fishing in particular is a major activity, and the island is celebrated for its delicious prawn dishes. During the rainy season, when the streets often flood, the locals use boats to navigate their island, hence the Venice comparison.

Mexcaltitán's simple and tranquil lifestyle is in stark contrast to the hustle and bustle of general Mexican urban life, offering visitors a peaceful retreat and a glimpse into a traditional way of living that's deeply connected to nature.

To reach Mexcaltitán, you'll usually travel by boat from La Batanga, a small dock about 20 minutes away. The journey through lush mangroves adds to the magical experience. Once on the island, you can explore its quaint streets, admire the colourful houses, and visit museums that showcase local artefacts and Aztlan legends.

Mexcaltitán offers a unique blend of history, mythology and natural beauty. It's a great place to connect with Mexico's cultural roots in a stunning landscape – and the local food scene is to die for!

Aguachile Negro

Chilli prawns with black salsa

Serves 6

This is a unique and bold twist on the classic aguachile – one of Mexico's most popular seafood dishes – featuring a rich, dark sauce made with lots of spices. I learnt to make this with my good friend Fabián in Sydney. We had a lot of fun recreating those deep, smoky flavours to go with the fresh prawns.

Method

Using a small knife, cut halfway through the back of each prawn lengthways and open it out like a pair of butterfly wings. Place the prawns in a large non-metallic bowl. Finely chop two of the cucumbers and add to the prawns with the onion, salt and pepper.

Roughly chop the remaining cucumber and place in a blender. Add the lime juice and coriander and blend until smooth. Pour the mixture over the prawns and stir to combine. Cover and set aside in the fridge for 30 minutes for the flavours to come together.

Pour the salsa negra over the prawns and gently mix through. Cover and leave for another 20 minutes so the prawns 'cook' in the sauce.

Serve the prawns in a large bowl for guests to help themselves, with the avocado and salted crackers or totopos on the side.

In true tradition, make sure you have a cold beer on hand!

Ingredients

- 1 kg (2 lb 3 oz) raw small prawns (shrimp), peeled and deveined
- 3 short cucumbers
- 1 red onion, finely sliced
- 1 teaspoon table salt
- pinch of freshly ground black pepper
- juice of 2 limes
- 1 small bunch of coriander (cilantro), finely chopped
- 250 ml (1 cup) Salsa negra page 298 →
- 2 avocados, sliced
- salted crackers or Totopos, to serve page 318 →

Balazos

Shrimp shots

Makes 6

A serene and peaceful coastal town in Nayarit, San Blas is a 'Pueblo Mágico', one of the many Mexican towns recognised for their beauty, history and legends. A popular snack in San Blas are these spicy little seafood shots – perfect for whetting your appetite before diving into the difficult task of deciding what to eat next.

Method

Pour some chamoy sauce onto a small plate. Dip the rims of six chilled shot glasses into the sauce, then coat the rims with Tajin seasoning for a spicy, tangy touch.

Place an oyster and half a prawn in each glass. Squeeze the juice of ½ lime into each glass, then to each add ½ teaspoon of salsa de siete chillies and 1 teaspoon of salsa negra.

Sprinkle in a pinch of salt for added flavour, then fill up the glasses with Clamato.

Stir or shake (make sure your hand is covering the glass!) the shot glasses to mix all the flavours together. Top each shot glass with a slice of cucumber dusted with Tajin for extra crunch.

Drink straightaway, just like a tequila shot, savouring the mix of tangy, spicy, savoury flavours.

Ingredients

- Salsa chamoy (store-bought or homemade) page 295 →
- Tajin seasoning
- 6 fresh oysters
- 3 large cooked, peeled prawns (shrimp), cut in half lengthways
- juice of 3 limes
- 1 tablespoon Salsa de siete chiles page 306 →
- 2 tablespoons Salsa negra page 298 →
- 300 ml (10 fl oz) Clamato
- 6 cucumber slices

Gazpacho

Fruit salad cocktail

Serves 4

Gazpacho is a great example of just how diverse Mexican cuisine can be. When a Mexican girl named Edevi came to work with me in 2016 for a few months after arriving in Australia, one of her favourite requests was the sweet, savoury, spicy and tangy fruit cocktail salad known – confusingly – as 'gazpacho'. At first, it didn't make any sense to me. Back in Mexico City, when I thought of a fruit cocktail, I imagined it topped with whipped cream and lots of honey. But gazpacho? It had chilli and onion in it!

It made me realise how much our food varies from one region to another. Gazpachos from Michoacán, unlike the escamochas (fruit salads) I grew up with, are packed with bold flavours that somehow all work together. Below is the traditional recipe, but you can also add watermelon, melon or cucumber, if you fancy.

Ingredients

- 1 mango, finely diced
- 1 jicama, finely diced (see Note)
- 200 g (7 oz) pineapple flesh, finely diced
- 1 white onion, finely diced
- 1 fresh jalapeno chilli, seeds removed, finely diced
- 1 teaspoon table salt
- 1 teaspoon Tajin seasoning, plus extra to serve
- 300 ml (10 fl oz) orange juice
- 100 g (3½ oz) queso fresco, Cotija or feta
- Valentina hot sauce
- juice of 1 lime

Method

Place the mango in a large bowl with the jicama, pineapple, onion and chilli. Add the salt, Tajin and orange juice and mix gently but thoroughly so everything is evenly coated with the juice and seasonings.

Pile some of the fruit mixture into four tall glasses. Crumble some cheese over, sprinkle with more Tajin seasoning and drizzle with Valentina hot sauce. Repeat the layers until the glasses are full, finishing with cheese and a final drizzle of Valentina hot sauce.

Squeeze the lime juice over the top for extra zing, and serve.

Note

Also known as the Mexican bean yam, jicama is a crunchy, tuberous root vegetable that is peeled and eaten raw in salads or as a street snack. If you can't get hold of any, you could use a crunchy fresh cucumber in this salad instead, after removing any seeds.

Cantarito

Little pot

Makes 1

I love this drink so much – it's one of the stars on the bar menu in my tamaleria in Sydney. Made with tequila and fresh citrus, this fun, refreshing drink from Jalisco takes its name from the charming clay cup it is traditionally served in, which not only looks cool, but also keeps your iced drink well chilled.

I remember so fondly spending hours at Cantaritos El Güero – a famous cantarito shop in Jalisco on the highway between Guadalajara and Tequila – with my dad and my friend El Oso. We were laughing, dancing and singing along with the crowd and the musicians, who were playing everything from banda to mariachi to norteño. The music was loud, the atmosphere full of joy, and everyone felt part of the same party. That's a truly Mexican experience!

Method

Mix all the ingredients, except the ice cubes, together in a cocktail shaker.

Toss some ice cubes into a chilled glass (or a clay cup, if you have one!), pour in the cocktail and enjoy straightaway.

Ingredients

- 50 ml (1¾ fl oz) tequila (blanco or reposado)
- 2 orange slices
- juice of 1 orange
- ½ lime, sliced
- juice of 1 lime
- 1 teaspoon caster (superfine) sugar or agave syrup
- 250 ml (1 cup) grapefruit soda
- ice cubes

Alfajores de Coco

Coconut bites

Makes 12

'Alfajor' comes from the Arabic word 'al-hasú', meaning 'stuffed' or 'filled'. When the Spanish colonised Mexico in the 16th century, they brought with them their culinary traditions, including alfajores – which had been gifted to the Spanish much earlier by their Moorish rulers. In Colima, on Mexico's central western coast, the tropical climate and local produce inspired a version using coconut, sugar and a pinch of cinnamon.

Unlike the alfajores of South America, which are often sandwich cookies filled with dulce de leche, Colima's coconut alfajores are a type of solid candy made by layering different coloured mixtures in a mould.

Ingredients

- 300 g (10½ oz) desiccated coconut
- 400 g (14 oz) caster (superfine) sugar
- 2 tablespoons cornflour (corn starch)
- 1 cinnamon stick
- pink food colouring

Method

Line a baking tray with baking paper.

Place the desiccated coconut in a large heatproof bowl.

Combine the sugar, cornflour, cinnamon stick and 400 ml (14 fl oz) water in a saucepan. Set over medium heat and stir constantly until the mixture comes to the boil.

Very carefully pour the hot sugar mixture over the coconut and stir well with a spoon until you have a firm paste. Scoop out 200 g (7 oz) of the mixture into another bowl and add a few drops of pink food colouring, mixing it in evenly. Return the pink coconut mixture to the plain coconut and gently mix through.

While the mixture is still warm and working quickly, place a 5 cm (2 in) cookie cutter on the prepared tray, scoop 60 g (2 oz) of the coconut mixture into the centre of the cutter and press to evenly spread the mixture. Gently remove the cutter, then repeat with the remaining coconut mixture.

Refrigerate for 2 hours to set.

Store the alfarojes in an airtight container in the fridge for up to 1 week.

EL
Hidalgo
Tlaxcala

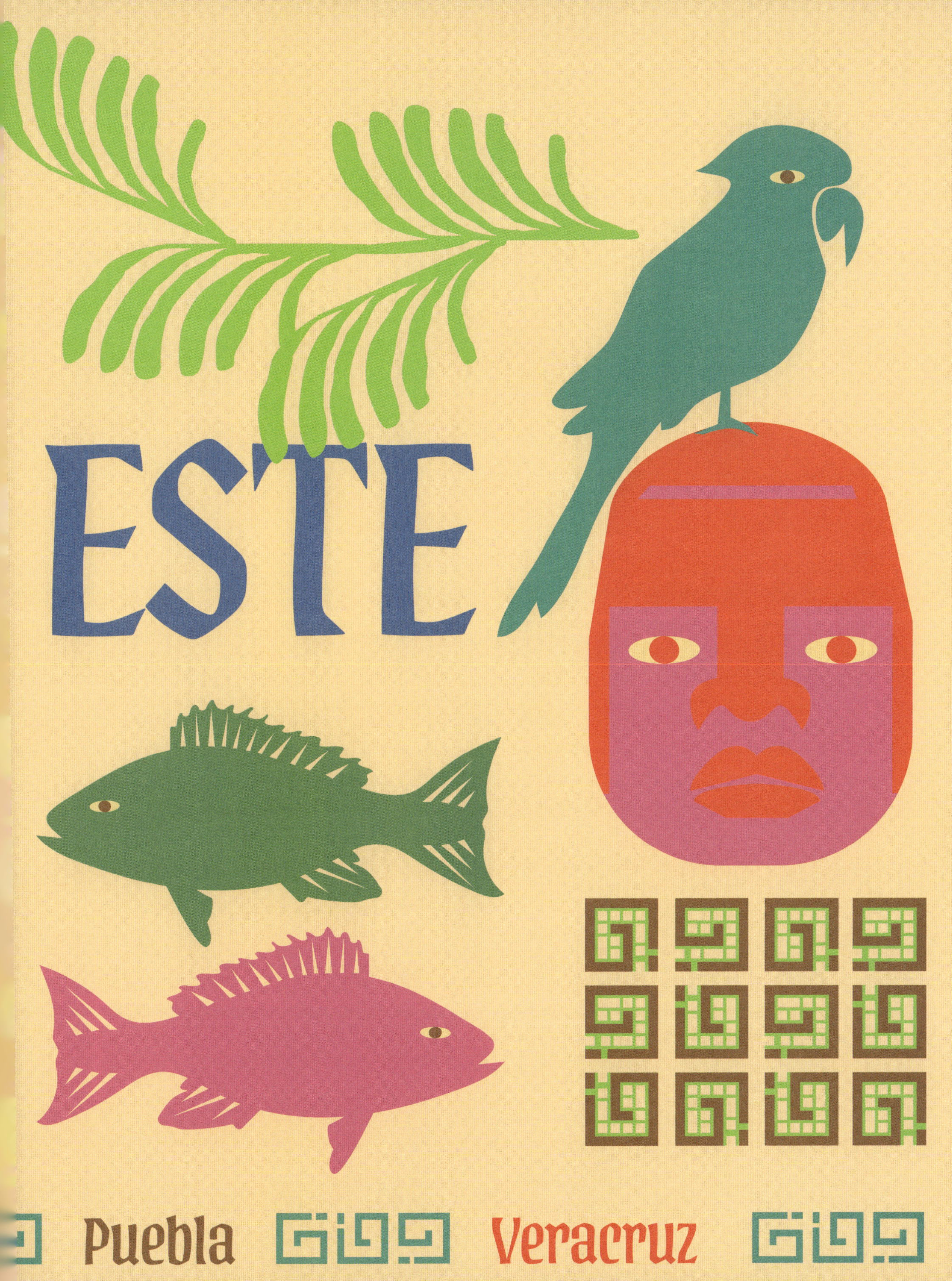
ESTE
Puebla
Veracruz

EL ESTE

Mexico's east is a vibrant patchwork of history, tradition and mouth-watering food. Stretching from Puebla to Veracruz, including Hidalgo and Tlaxcala, this is a hub of both indigenous and colonial culinary influences, where ancient techniques are still used alongside modern innovations.

The food here tells the story of diverse peoples, from the Nahua, Otomi, Totonac and Huastec groups, to the Spanish colonists in the 1500s, to the Cornish miners from southern England who brought their practical pasties along with their mining skills. Local tropical fruits were supplemented by citrus and pineapples introduced by the Spanish, as well as European herbs such as bay leaves, coriander (cilantro), thyme and parsley, while plantain was introduced by African slaves.

Puebla is home to some of Mexico's most famous dishes, including mole poblano. Known for its deep, smoky, chocolatey taste, mole is at the heart of Pueblan cuisine – and every mole tells a story. If you're in Puebla, it would be a crime not to sample Chiles en nogada (see page 182), as well as some of the region's dulces poblanos, such as Camotitos (see page 208). Pueblan sweets are not simply sugar bombs: they often feature local fruits, nuts and spices that bring a unique depth to their flavours.

Hidalgo is famous for barbacoa, an ancestral dish in which a whole lamb is wrapped in agave leaves and slow-cooked in an underground earth oven. The meat is tender, juicy and full of unique and incomparably rich, smoky flavours, and is usually eaten with salsas and tortillas (see page 192). It's the kind of meal that brings people together, because barbacoa always provides enough food to feed the whole neighbourhood. Hidalgo's barbacoa is more than just a dish; it's an essential part of the region's culture, often made over the weekend and for family gatherings and festive celebrations – and naturally it requires accompanying music and plenty of cold beers! In the cities, barbacoa stalls are particularly popular on weekend mornings with Mexicans looking for a good hangover cure.

Despite being small in size, the state of Tlaxcala packs a punch when it comes to food. The state's name comes from the Nahuatl word 'tlaxcalli', meaning 'tortilla' or 'corn bread'. It's thought that the process of nixtamalisation – where corn kernels are soaked and cooked in an alkaline solution, then washed and hulled to improve their nutritional value and flavour, before being dried and ground into masa flour for making tlaxcalli, tortillas, quesadillas and gorditas and the like – originated from this region. What ingenuity the ancient Mesoamerican communities had – they turned corn into a nutritious staple that has remained the backbone of the Mexican diet for centuries. You can still enjoy the ancient Mesoamerican dish Tlaxcales (see page 206) in this region, a simple dessert made from corn and sugar, and moulded into a triangular shape.

Veracruz is arguably one of Mexico's most beautiful states. Its coastline stretches for hundreds of kilometres, with seafood playing a huge role in the region's cuisine. Veracruz's Arroz a la tumbada (see page 202) is a must-try. I recommend enjoying it with a traditional Torito de cacahuate (see page 210) to sip on.

The eastern states of Puebla, Hidalgo, Tlaxcala and Veracruz all have something special to offer, but what makes them truly unique is the way their food reflects both the land and its people. There's a sense of deep pride and respect for the ingredients and the culture. In this region, food isn't just about flavour and fuelling the body, it's about tradition. It's about celebrating the history, the people and the stories that have shaped its towns and villages over centuries.

For me, it's a reminder of what it means to be from Mexico. I come from a place where food isn't just sustenance but a way to connect with others, to share stories, and to honour those who came before us. My family and I would often go to Veracruz, where we'd sit by the sea and enjoy eating fresh fish, listening to the sound of the waves in the warmth of the sun. They are memories that, much like the food of this region, will stay with me forever.

Arroz a la Poblana

Puebla-style rice

Serves 4

Poblano rice was one of my Grandma Tete's favourite dishes, so of course I had the best teacher to show me how to cook this delicious recipe from Puebla! Arroz a la poblana is still well-loved at our family reunions. When I visit Mexico, it's a dish my friends always ask me to cook, especially my dear friend Edgar, so I guess you could say it has become one of my 'family signature specials'!

Here I'll share two ways to make it – because there are so many versions and nothing beats creating your own. First I'll give you the traditional recipe, to honour its roots and give this dish the respect it deserves. My family always makes it with sour cream and cheese on top, which adds an amazing flavour and texture; you'll find this variation at the end, so you can pick and choose as the mood takes you.

Ingredients

- 4 fresh or tinned poblano chillies
- 2 tablespoons vegetable oil
- 2 garlic cloves, peeled but left whole
- 500 g (2½ cups) long-grain white rice or jasmine rice
- 150 g (¾ cup) tinned corn kernels, drained

Method

If using fresh chillies, preheat a barbecue grill or use a stovetop gas flame to char the chillies, turning occasionally, until the skins are blackened and blistered. Using tongs, immediately transfer the chillies to a large zip-lock bag and let them sweat for 5–10 minutes – this will make peeling them much easier. Once the chillies are cool enough to handle, peel away the skins and seeds and discard.

Roughly chop three of the chillies and blend in a food processor with 1 litre (4 cups) water, until smooth. Cut the remaining chilli into thin strips and set aside.

Heat the oil in a large saucepan over medium heat. Add the garlic and cook for 2 minutes on each side, taking care it doesn't burn, then remove and discard the garlic. Add the rice to the pan and cook for 5 minutes, stirring occasionally to ensure it doesn't burn.

Once the rice is golden, stir in the blended chilli mixture and corn kernels. Cover the pan, reduce the heat to low and leave to simmer for about 25 minutes, until the liquid is absorbed and the rice is perfectly cooked.

Remove the lid and arrange the reserved poblano chilli strips over the rice. Let the rice rest, uncovered, for 15 minutes before serving.

Variation

For my family's version, blend 150 g (5½ oz) sour cream with the chilli mixture before adding it to the rice. Once the rice is cooked, sprinkle 200 g (7 oz) grated manchego over the top, then cover and leave to melt before serving.

Chiles en Nogada

Stuffed chillies with creamy pecan sauce

Makes 12

This iconic celebratory dish is often eating during September, Mexico's independence month – because its vibrant green, white and red colours mirror those of the national flag.

The picadillo filling can be made up to three days ahead and stored in an airtight container in the fridge. If you can't get plantain for the filling, just use banana.

Method

Start by making the picadillo filling. Pour 1 litre (4 cups) water into a saucepan, add the tomatoes and bring to the boil. Leave to boil for 1 minute, then lift out using tongs or a slotted spoon. Leave to cool a little, then peel off the skins and puree the flesh (without adding any water).

Heat the lard in a large saucepan over medium heat. Saute the onion and garlic for 2–3 minutes, until fragrant. Add all the meat, seasoning well with salt and pepper. Cook, stirring, for 5–10 minutes, until cooked through.

Stir in the pureed tomato and simmer for about 5 minutes to develop its flavour.

Add the sultanas, thyme, oregano, cinnamon and clove, and cook, stirring, for 10 minutes. Fold the almonds through, along with the peach, pear and plantain. Simmer for a further 10 minutes, until the fruits have softened. Set aside to cool completely.

To prepare the poblano chillies, preheat a barbecue grill or use a stovetop gas flame to char the chillies, turning occasionally, until the skins are blackened and blistered. Using tongs, immediately transfer the chillies to a large zip-lock bag and let them sweat for 5–10 minutes – this will make peeling them much easier. Once the chillies are cool enough to handle, peel away and discard the skins. Carefully slit each chilli open and remove the seeds, keeping the chillies intact for stuffing.

Very gently stuff each chilli with about 4 tablespoons of the cold picadillo filling.

Place the flour in a wide shallow bowl.

Make a batter by whisking the egg whites to stiff peaks using hand-held electric beaters, then gently folding the yolks through.

Ingredients

- 12 fresh poblano chillies
- 500 g (3⅓ cups) plain (all-purpose) flour
- 6 eggs, separated
- vegetable oil, for shallow-frying
- 200 g (7 oz) pomegranate seeds
- handful of flat-leaf parsley leaves

Picadillo filling

- 4 roma (plum) tomatoes
- 2 tablespoons pork lard or vegetable oil
- 1 white onion, finely chopped
- 1 garlic clove, finely chopped
- 500 g (1 lb 2 oz) minced (ground) pork
- 500 g (1 lb 2 oz) minced (ground) beef
- 30 g (1 oz) sultanas (golden raisins)
- pinch of dried thyme
- pinch of dried Mexican oregano
- pinch of ground cinnamon
- pinch of ground cloves
- 200 g (7 oz) flaked blanched almonds
- 3 peaches, cut into 1 cm (½ in) dice
- 2 pears, cut into 1 cm (½ in) dice
- ½ ripe plantain (or 1 banana), peeled and cut into 1 cm (½ in) dice

Nogada

- 50 g (1¾ oz) blanched almonds
- 300 g (10½ oz) shelled pecans, peeled and chopped (see Note overleaf)
- 190 g (6½ oz) cream cheese
- 1 tablespoon sherry
- 1 tablespoon white sugar
- pinch of table salt

Recipe continues →

Pour enough oil to half-cover the chillies into a deep heavy-based frying pan. Heat the oil to 180°C (350°F).

Working in batches, lightly toss the stuffed chillies in the flour, then quickly dip them in the batter. Immediately transfer to the hot oil and shallow-fry for 2 minutes on each side, until golden. Drain on paper towel and leave to cool.

While the chillies are cooling, place all the nogada ingredients in a food processor and blend until you have a smooth, velvety sauce.

Chiles en nogada are served at room temperature. Place the fried chillies on a serving platter, spoon a generous amount of nogada sauce over each one and garnish with the pomegranate seeds and a few parsley leaves – the colours of the Mexican flag!

The fried chillies will keep in an airtight container in the fridge for 4 days.

Note

It's very important to remove the skin from the pecans before using them in the nogada, as the skin changes the colour and adds a bitter flavour – nogada should be white, with a nutty consistency. To remove the skin, soak the pecans in boiling water for 5 minutes, then drain and allow to cool for 2 mintues. Transfer the pecans to a clean tea towel, wrap them up and gently rub to carefully remove the skin. Use a small knife to remove any remaining bits of skin still stuck to the pecans.

Mole Poblano

Puebla-style mole

Serves 4

Mole poblano is one of Mexico's most iconic recipes, now often considered the national dish. The story of mole poblano is as colourful as the food itself. Legend tells us it originated in the state of Puebla in the 17th century, when nuns in the Convent of Santa Rosa were asked to prepare dinner for a visiting archbishop. In a stroke of brilliance, they gathered up their neighbourhood's abundant ingredients to cook an unforgettable feast, throwing everything delicious into a pot of sauce, including dried chillies, spices, bread, nuts and chocolate. The archbishop loved it – of course! – and mole poblano has been a favourite of the region ever since.

Ingredients

- 4 chicken marylands, skin on
- 4 bay leaves
- 1 tablespoon table salt

Poblano mole

- 60 g (2 oz) pork lard or vegetable oil
- 30 g (1 oz) dried ancho chillies, stems removed
- 30 g (1 oz) dried guajillo chillies, stems removed
- 50 g (1¾ oz) dried mulato chillies, stems removed
- 30 g (1 oz) unsalted peanuts
- 30 g (1 oz) unsalted natural almonds
- 20 g (¾ oz) sultanas (golden raisins)
- 1 ripe plantain (or banana), peeled and sliced
- 1 white onion, finely chopped
- 2 garlic cloves, chopped
- 5 allspice berries
- 1 teaspoon anise seeds
- 1 teaspoon cloves
- 2 cinnamon sticks
- 1 Tortilla de maiz page 314 →
- 30 g (1 oz) sesame seeds, toasted, plus extra to serve
- 20 g (¾ oz) marie (rich tea) biscuits, crushed
- 20 g (¾ oz) dried breadcrumbs
- 90 g (3 oz) bar of Mexican chocolate, such as Ibarra or Abuelita (see Note overleaf)
- 30 g (1 oz) piloncillo or soft brown sugar

Method

Put the chicken in a large saucepan with the bay leaves, salt and 4 litres (4 qts) water. Bring to the boil, then reduce the heat and simmer for 30 minutes, or until the chicken is cooked through. Lift out the chicken and set aside, reserving the broth.

For the mole sauce, heat half the pork lard in a frying pan over medium heat. Working in batches, fry each chilli variety separately for 3 minutes at a time, turning the chillies often and taking care they don't burn. Remove from the pan and set aside to cool.

In the same pan, again working with each ingredient separately, lightly toast the peanuts, almonds, sultanas, plantain, onion, garlic, allspice, anise, cloves and cinnamon sticks for about 5 minutes, until golden and fragrant, again taking care not to scorch them. (Toasting all the spices separately is part of the fun of making mole, but you can toast them all at the same time if you need to.)

Finally, scorch the corn tortilla in the pan for about 5 minutes on each side, until a few char marks appear, turning once.

Tear the toasted tortilla into chunks and place in a food processor with the chillies and all the toasted ingredients. Start blending together with 250 ml (1 cup) of the reserved chicken broth. If the mixture is too thick to process smoothly, add a bit more broth. Finally, blend in the sesame seeds, crushed biscuits and breadcrumbs to make a rich, smooth paste, adding more chicken broth as needed.

Recipe continues →

Heat the remaining pork lard in a large saucepan over low heat. Add the mole sauce and gently cook for 1 hour, stirring often to prevent sticking, and gradually stirring in another 2 litres (2 qts) of the reserved chicken broth.

Break in the bar of chocolate and add the sugar, stirring until dissolved completely. Continue cooking for another 30 minutes, until the mole sauce is thick, silky and deeply aromatic. The mole is ready when the oil from the chillies starts to rise to the surface and begins to bubble. This indicates that the flavours have blended well and the sauce is reaching the right consistency. As it continues cooking, the bubbling will reduce, and the oil will fully mix with the rest of the sauce, meaning the mole has reached its perfect cooking point. At that moment, it should have a smooth texture and a deep flavour.

For the last 10 minutes of cooking, add the chicken to the sauce to heat through.

Serve the chicken and mole sauce, topped with toasted sesame seeds, and with rice, refried beans and warm tortillas on the side.

The chicken mole will keep in the fridge in an airtight container for 4 days.

Note

You can buy Mexican chocolate online or from Latin American grocery shops.

To serve

steamed white rice or Arroz Mexicano page 327 →
Frijoles negros refritos page 322 →
Tortillas de maiz page 314 →

Tacos de Canasta

Basket tacos

Makes 20

Tacos de canasta always take me straight back to my time as a student in Mexico City, where these popular street-food snacks were often sold by vendors on bicycles. Seeing a bicycle bearing baskets ('canastas') of hot, steamed, perfectly organised tacos was the highlight of those busy days living in Mexico City.

The last time I travelled back there with my dad, we stopped at a street corner and shared some of those simple but filling tacos. As we ate, we shared stories from our college days: different generations, same tacos, same nostalgia. It was a beautiful moment, showing how food can bridge time and connect people.

I recommend using store-bought tortillas here, instead of making them yourself, as they need to be strong enough to hold the heavy filling, which is then covered with salsa.

Ingredients

- 30 g (1 oz) dried cascabel chillies, stems removed
- ½ white onion
- 1 teaspoon minced garlic
- 2 teaspoons table salt
- 20 store-bought corn tortillas, 11 cm (4¼ in) in diameter
- 1 × quantity Frijoles negros refritos page 322 →
- Salsa verde, to serve page 286 →

Method

Place the dried chillies in a small saucepan with the onion, garlic and 300 ml (10 fl oz) water. Bring to the boil, then reduce the heat and simmer for 10 minutes. Set aside to cool slightly.

Tip the mixture into a blender, add the salt and blend until you have a runny, dark orange sauce. Transfer to a bowl.

Meanwhile, heat a comal or heavy-based frying pan over medium–high heat. In batches, heat the tortillas, flipping frequently, until soft and warmed through, placing them in a tortilla warmer or wrapping them in a tea towel to keep them warm.

One by one, dip the warm tortillas in the cascabel chilli sauce to coat on both sides.

Place the soaked tortillas on a chopping board and spoon about 1 tablespoon of the refried beans onto each tortilla. Fold the tortillas in half and press the edges together with your fingertips.

Using the same pan, fry the tortillas over medium heat for 1–2 minutes each side, until nicely coloured, dry and lightly crisp.

Serve immediately, with salsa verde.

Mole de Amaranto

Amaranth mole

Serves 4

I first tried this mole in Puebla at the Feria de Atlixco – a small cultural fair in Atlixco that showcases, among other things, the city's moles. I often went there with my brother, Julio, who would drive all the way from Mexico City, some two hours away, and we always loved to order several different types of moles.

After lots of sampling, we decided their amaranth mole was one of the best, so I'm excited to share this version with you. Amaranth is an important staple ingredient in Mexico and was used by warriors to increase their strength.

Ingredients

- 4 chicken marylands, skin on
- 4 bay leaves
- ½ white onion
- 1 tablespoon table salt

Amaranth mole

- 2 tablespoons vegetable oil
- 1 roma (plum) tomato
- 1 garlic clove, peeled
- ¼ white onion
- 400 g (14 oz) tinned tomatillos, drained
- 1 dried ancho chilli, stem removed
- 1 dried pasilla chilli, stem removed
- 1 dried guajillo chilli, stem removed
- 30 g (1 oz) unsalted peanuts
- 100 g (3½ oz) puffed amaranth
- 50 g (1¾ oz) Mexican chocolate, such as Ibarra or Abuelita
- 2 cloves, freshly ground
- ½ teaspoon freshly ground black pepper
- ½ teaspoon ground cumin
- ½ teaspoon dried Mexican oregano
- 15 g (½ oz) dried breadcrumbs

To serve

- steamed white rice
- toasted sesame seeds

Method

Put the chicken in a large saucepan with the bay leaves, onion, salt and 2 litres (2 qts) water. Bring to the boil, then reduce the heat and simmer for 30 minutes, or until the chicken is cooked through. Lift out the chicken and set aside, reserving the broth.

For the mole, heat the oil in a large saucepan over medium heat and cook the whole tomato, garlic, onion and tomatillos for 7–10 minutes, turning now and then, until deeply browned and aromatic. Using tongs or a slotted spoon, transfer the ingredients to a bowl. Fry all the dried chillies in the oil for 3 minutes, being careful not to burn them, then transfer to the bowl.

In the same pan, lightly toast the peanuts and amaranth for a few minutes, until fragrant.

Return all the fried chillies and vegetables to the pan. Break in the bar of chocolate, then stir in the remaining spices, oregano, breadcrumbs and 500 ml (2 cups) of the reserved chicken broth. Reduce the heat to low, then cover and simmer over low heat for about 20 minutes, until the flavours have come together.

Transfer the mole to a food processor and blend until smooth, adding more chicken broth if needed.

Return the mole to the pan and add the chicken. Cover and simmer for about 10 minutes, until the chicken is heated through.

Serve the chicken and mole sauce on a bed of steamed white rice, and topped with toasted sesame seeds.

The chicken mole will keep in an airtight container in the fridge for 4 days.

Tacos de Barbacoa

Slow-cooked lamb tacos

Serves 4

This slow-cooked lamb dish is now on the menu at my restaurant, La Tamaleria, served with consomme, as is traditional with barbacoa. My customers also really enjoy it with a cold beer! It's so popular we also offer the slow-cooked meat frozen for takeaways and home delivery.

Agave leaves are hard to find outside of Mexico, so I've also given banana leaves as an option here instead. Although the flavour is not quite the same, you won't be disappointed with the result.

Ingredients

- 1 kg (2 lb 3 oz) boneless lamb (a mix of leg, shoulder and shank), chopped into 5 cm (2 in) chunks
- 80 g (2¾ oz) table salt
- 1 teaspoon minced garlic
- 1 large agave leaf or banana leaf (see Note)

To serve

- 16 Tortillas de maiz, warmed page 314 →
- lime wedges, to serve
- ½ white onion, diced
- 1 bunch of coriander (cilantro), leaves chopped
- 200 g (7 oz) Guacamole page 299 →
- 300 ml (10 fl oz) Salsa borracha page 290 →

Method

Place the lamb in a bowl and rub with 3 tablespoons of the salt and the garlic.

Pour 2 litres (2 qts) water into a large saucepan and add the remaining salt. Place a steamer basket on top and bring to a simmer.

Cut the agave leaf or banana leaf into four 15 cm (6 in) squares. Divide the meat among the leaves. Bring together the corners of each leaf and secure with kitchen string to make four pouches.

Place the pouches in the steamer and put the lid on. Steam for 45 minutes, adding up to 1 litre (4 cups) more water to the saucepan if it starts to dry out.

Carefully remove the parcels from the steamer. Let them cool a little, then unwrap and place the meat on a chopping board. Gently pull the lamb apart using two forks.

Top each tortilla with some lamb, onion, coriander, guacamole and salsa, and serve with lime wedges.

The cooked lamb meat will keep in an airtight container in the fridge for 4 days.

Note

You'll find banana leaves in Southeast Asian grocery stores. You can use fresh or frozen banana leaves in this recipe.

MOLES

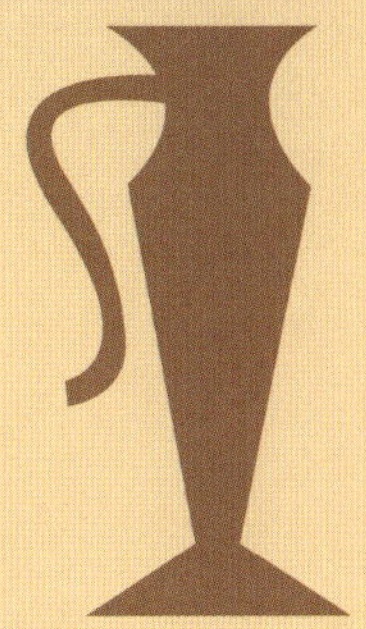

My home country's intriguing dark, savoury sauce with chilli and chocolate has captivated the world's imagination. Who on earth would put chocolate in a sauce for chicken, or turkey?

Mole is truly so much more than a recipe, it's a symbol of Mexican heritage, deeply embodying the country's rich history, culture and diversity. The evolution of mole is intertwined with Mexico's journey from its indigenous roots through to the colonial era and into the modern age. Just about every area of Mexico has its own mole – and each one tells a story.

The indigenous peoples of Mexico, including the Aztecs and the Maya, ingeniously used local ingredients, such as fresh or roasted chillies, spices, ground seeds and cacao to create thick sauces that were packed with flavour and nutrients.

After the Spanish arrived in the 1500s, exotic new ingredients, such as almonds, cinnamon and even sugar, were stirred into the moles and the sauce continued to evolve, with different regions adding their own unique touches to create a huge varieties: pink (see page 252); guava (see page 90); white (see page 196); soft red (see page 257); and green. Some use more chocolate, others focus on the heat of the chillies, some add their local fruits and herbs, others different nuts.

Mole is not a dish to rush. It requires time and attention to detail. The flavours have to be balanced, and the sauce has to be perfectly smooth.

The ingredients are always carefully roasted in a comal or heavy-based frying pan to bring out all their flavours. A traditional corn tortilla is often crumbled into the mix to help create the authentic smoky notes. Traditional mole makers will often use a metate (a flat stone mortar and pestle) to grind the ingredients – it helps release the oils and aromas from the seeds and chillies, and is also considered to add a magical flavour of volcanic stone. While modern blenders can certainly speed up the process, as with so many things in the Mexican kitchen, most chefs still prefer the old time-honoured ways.

After grinding or blending, the ingredients are stirred into chicken stock or chilli water and slowly simmered to build up the flavours and allow the mole time to develop its characteristic velvety thickness. The sauce is usually served with chicken, turkey or pork.

Mole Blanco

White mole

Serves 4

A hidden gem of Mexican cuisine, mole blanco may not be as famous or as common as its deeper, darker cousins, but it's a real treat when it appears on restaurant menus. Nicknamed 'bride's mole' for its beautiful white colour, legend says it originated in a convent in Puebla, although nobody knows for sure. It has a softer flavour than the darker moles and a nutty, creamy texture, and is considered the most elegant of the mole sauces.

Ingredients

- 1 kg (2 lb 3 oz) skinless chicken breasts
- 4 bay leaves
- ½ white onion
- 1 tablespoon table salt

White mole

- 3 fresh guero chillies
- 100 g (3½ oz) butter
- ½ white onion, finely chopped
- 4 garlic cloves, minced
- pinch of anise seeds
- 150 ml (5 fl oz) dry sherry
- 70 g (2½ oz) sesame seeds
- 70 g (2½ oz) blanched almonds
- 70 g (2½ oz) pine nuts
- 1 golden delicious apple, peeled and diced
- 1 ripe banana, peeled and roughly chopped
- 2–3 tablespoons white sugar
- pinch of table salt

To serve

- steamed white rice
- Tortillas de maiz page 314 →
- flaked blanched almonds

Method

Put the chicken in a large saucepan with the bay leaves, onion, salt and 2 litres (2 qts) water. Bring to the boil, then reduce the heat and simmer for 30 minutes, or until the chicken is cooked through. Lift out the chicken and set aside, reserving the broth.

To make the mole, boil the chillies in a separate saucepan for 5 minutes to soften them. Drain the chillies, then chop and set aside.

Melt the butter in a large saucepan over medium heat and saute the onion and garlic for 2–3 minutes, until soft. Add the chopped chillies and anise seeds and cook, stirring, for 1 minute. Pour in the sherry and let it bubble for a couple of minutes.

Heat a comal or heavy-based frying pan over medium heat and toast the sesame seeds, almonds and pine nuts, keeping your eye on them the whole time to ensure they don't burn, until lightly golden. Tip them over the onion and chilli mixture and stir together.

Transfer the mixture to a food processor, along with the apple and banana. Add the sugar and salt and pour in 500 ml (2 cups) of the warm reserved chicken broth. Blend until you have a smooth, creamy paste that's packed with flavour.

Pour the mixture back into the saucepan, stirring in more chicken broth if needed to achieve a thick but pourable sauce. Bring to a simmer over medium heat, then cook for about 15 minutes, stirring constantly as it thickens up and all the flavours blend together.

Add the chicken and simmer for about 10 minutes, until heated through.

Serve the chicken and mole with steamed white rice and tortillas, topped with a few flaked blanched almonds.

The chicken mole will keep in the fridge in an airtight container for 4 days.

Pastes

Meat and potato pasties

Makes 15

When miners from Cornwall, a county at the southwestern tip of England, arrived in the town of Real del Monte, Hidalgo, in 1824 to work in the silver mines, they brought their skills and traditions with them. They also brought their Cornish pasty – a simple but ingenious pie of meat and vegetables, encased in firm baked pastry, that provided them with a portable, hearty meal that could endure long hours underground.

As the Cornish miners integrated into Real del Monte, so did their pasties. The robust shortcrust pastry dough didn't change, being designed to withstand handling with sooty fingers – but the fillings began to feature local ingredients. Beans, chorizo and even pineapple went into uniquely Mexican interpretations of the traditional dish.

For me, the Mexican paste is a bridge to my family's shared memories. Every time I visit my aunt and cousins in Hidalgo's capital city, Pachuca, a trip to the small mountain town of Real Del Monte is a must. My cousin Lucy, always the family planner, takes charge of gathering everyone for our reunions, as the minivan that takes us to Real del Monte departs right outside Lucy's house. We usually hire the whole bus for the 40-minute trip, singing, laughing, talking and sharing stories and family memories the whole way. Our go-to spot when we get to Real del Monte is a humble yet magical shop called 'Los Portales', tucked away just by the minivan stop. My favourite is the potato-filled paste, which carries the legacy of the original Cornish recipe, closely followed by the pineapple pastes that evoke memories of childhood trips to Hidalgo's capital, Pachuca, with my mother and siblings, our hands permanently sticky with the syrupy filling.

Every visit to Real del Monte feels like a homecoming – not only the familiar streets and faces, but also the comforting smell of fresh pastes being baked.

Ingredients

- 500 g (3⅓ cups) plain (all-purpose) flour, plus extra for dusting
- 1 teaspoon caster (superfine) sugar
- 1 teaspoon table salt
- 100 g (3½ oz) chilled pork lard, diced
- 100 g (3½ oz) chilled unsalted butter, diced
- 190 ml (6½ fl oz) chilled water
- 1 egg, whisked

Paste filling

- 3 tablespoons vegetable oil
- 1 small white onion, finely chopped
- 3 garlic cloves, finely chopped
- 250 g (9 oz) potatoes, cut into 1 cm (½ in) dice
- 150 g (5½ oz) minced (ground) pork
- 150 g (5½ oz) minced (ground) beef
- 2 teaspoons table salt
- ½ teaspoon freshly ground black pepper

Method

To make the pastry, place the flour, sugar and salt in a large bowl and mix together using a spatula. Add the lard and butter, cutting them into the flour mixture with a knife until the mixture resembles coarse sand or breadcrumbs. Avoid using your hands to mix the ingredients – you want to keep the dough as cold as possible, as this will give you the best pastry.

Gradually add the cold water, incorporating it into the mixture little by little with a spatula. Continue mixing gently until the dough just comes together. Do not overmix or knead.

Roughly shape the dough into a ball, place in a container, then cover and chill in the fridge for 30 minutes.

To make the filling, heat the oil in a large frying pan over medium heat and saute the onion and garlic for about 3 minutes, until soft and fragrant. Stir in the potato, ensuring the cubes are evenly coated in the oil, and cook for 5–7 minutes, until tender.

Add the meat to the pan, breaking it up with a wooden spoon as it browns. Sprinkle in the salt and pepper, mixing thoroughly. Reduce the heat to medium–low. Cook, stirring occasionally, for 10 minutes, until the meat is fully cooked and all the liquid has evaporated. Any moisture in the filling will make the pastry soggy during baking, so strain the filling if necessary. Set aside to cool completely.

Preheat the oven to 200°C (400°F) fan-forced. Line a large baking tray with baking paper.

Lightly flour your work surface. Without overworking the dough, lightly roll it out to a thickness of about 5 mm (¼ in). Use a 15 cm (6 in) round cutter to cut out 15 circles.

Spoon 2 tablespoons of meat filling into the centre of each dough round. Fold the dough over the filling in a half-moon shape, pressing the edges together to seal. Pinch and crimp the edges with your fingers, working along the seam to ensure the pastry is completely sealed. Transfer to the lined baking tray. Lightly glaze the tops with the whisked egg, to give them a golden, shiny finish.

Bake for 45 minutes, or until the pastry is lightly golden and fully cooked. Allow to cool slightly before serving.

The pastes will keep in an airtight container in the fridge for 4 days.

Arroz a la Tumbada

Seafood rice

Serves 4

My amigo Gil was a big fan of 'pueblear' – exploring small towns, meeting new people and soaking up the stories of every place. On one of our journeys we were cruising along the coast of Veracruz, chatting and enjoying the view, when heavy rain forced us to make an unplanned stop in the closest town, which happened to be Alvarado. As soon as we arrived, the warmth of its people was obvious, and a small restaurant was recommended where we could try arroz a la tumbada. 'Es un clasico,' they said, 'no se lo pueden perder!' We couldn't resist trying this classic that could 'never be forgotten', and were soon seated in a little family-run spot overlooking the water.

The dish arrived in all its vibrant glory, loaded with prawns, crabs, squid and rice perfectly cooked in a rich, tomato-based broth. The epazote gave it that unmistakable touch of Veracruz, while jalapeno chillies added kick. We squeezed our lime wedges over our dish and dug in. Gil, always one to fully immerse himself in the moment, declared it the best arroz a la tumbada he'd ever had and, honestly, I couldn't disagree.

Here's how to enjoy a taste of Veracruz at home.

Ingredients

- 100 g (3½ oz) butter
- 1 teaspoon vegetable oil
- 250 g (1¼ cups) long-grain white rice
- 12 whole prawns (shrimp)
- 1 tablespoon table salt
- 2 tomatoes, roughly chopped
- 1 large white onion, roughly chopped
- 2 garlic cloves, peeled
- 2 crabs, cleaned and cut in half down the middle (or 4 small crabs)
- 200 g (7 oz) pipis or small clams, purged
- 1 bunch of coriander (cilantro), chopped
- 1 teaspoon dried epazote
- 300 g (10½ oz) firm white fish fillets, such as barramundi, cod or snapper, cut into 1 cm (½ in) cubes
- pinch of dried Mexican oregano
- 4 fresh red or green jalapeno chillies

To serve

- 2 avocados, sliced
- lime wedges

Method

Heat the butter and oil in a large saucepan over medium heat. Add the rice and cook for 5 minutes, stirring occasionally, until golden and evenly toasted. Remove from the heat.

Meanwhile, peel and devein the prawns, reserving the heads and shells. Put the heads and shells in another large saucepan with the salt and 4 litres (4 qts) water. Bring to the boil, then strain, discarding the shells and reserving the prawn stock. Allow to cool slightly.

Blend the tomatoes, onion and garlic in a food processor with 350 ml (12 fl oz) of the reserved prawn stock until smooth. Pour the mixture into the pan of toasted rice, season to taste and stir over medium heat to combine. Add the crabs, reduce the heat to low, then cover and cook for about 5 minutes.

Add the peeled prawns, pipis, coriander and epazote. Pour in another 300 ml (10 fl oz) of the prawn stock, then cover and cook gently for 10 minutes. Add the fish, oregano and the whole jalapenos and season well. If needed, add more prawn stock to ensure the rice cooks through properly. Cover and cook for an additional 10 minutes.

Serve hot, topped with slices of fresh avocado and lime wedges.

Arroz a la tumbada will keep in the fridge in an airtight container for 2 days.

Molotes

Fried masa pockets

Makes 15–20

Some say these satisfyingly crunchy golden pockets – classic street fare from Veracruz – evolved as a way to turn leftovers into pure magic.

My Aunt Luz taught me how to make molotes when I was little. Although I was probably more in her way than helpful, she had a knack for making you feel like the most important guest every time you visited, and her molotes were a big part of that charm.

She'd patiently show me how to press the masa dough into little discs, just the right thickness, and then stuff them with fillings. 'The secret,' she'd say with a wink, 'is not to overfill them. Otherwise, they'll fight in the fryer.' Of course, I overfilled mine, and sure enough, my molotes burst open in the oil like a little volcano of chicken filling.

When we sat down to eat, Aunt Luz had already made a fresh salsa with secret ingredients from her own pantry.

Ingredients

- 1 × quantity Tortilla de maiz dough page 314 →
- vegetable oil, for deep-frying

Chicken salsa filling

- 3 tomatoes, roughly chopped
- ½ white onion, roughly chopped
- 1 garlic clove, peeled
- 350 ml (12 fl oz) chicken stock
- 1 tablespoon table salt
- pinch of ground cumin
- 3 tablespoons vegetable oil
- 1 small bunch of thyme, leaves picked
- 350 g (12½ oz) finely shredded cooked chicken

Toppings

- 1 small iceberg lettuce, shredded
- 150 ml (5 fl oz) crema
- 200 g (7 oz) queso fresco, Cotija or feta, crumbled
- Salsa roja page 286 →

Method

To make the chicken salsa filling, place the tomato, onion, garlic, chicken stock, salt and cumin in a food processor and blend to a chunky salsa.

Heat the oil in a frying pan over medium heat. Add the salsa and cook, stirring frequently, for 7 minutes, or until reduced and thick. Stir in the thyme leaves and cook for a further 5 minutes, then remove from the heat and leave to cool to room temperature. Stir through the shredded chicken and set aside to cool completely.

Roll 50 g (1¾ oz) of the tortilla dough (a piece about the size of an apricot) into a ball. Using your hands, gently flatten the ball and add 1 tablespoon of the chicken salsa filling. Fold the dough over the filling to enclose, then form the dough into an oval shape with pointy ends. Repeat with the remaining dough and filling to make 15–20 molotes.

Meanwhile, heat about 10 cm (4 in) vegetable oil in a large heavy-based saucepan over medium–high heat to 180°C (350°F) on a kitchen thermometer.

Working in small batches, fry the molotes for 4–5 minutes, or until puffed up and lightly golden, draining each batch on paper towel.

Divide the molotes among shallow bowls and serve topped with the lettuce, crema, cheese and salsa.

The molotes are delicious hot or cold.

Tlaxcales

Corn breads

Makes 10

Tlaxcales are an ancient Mesoamerican bread from the eastern Mexican state of Tlaxcala. The state takes its name from the Nahuatl word 'Tlaxcallan', which means 'The place of the tortilla or corn bread'.

Despite their rich cultural significance, tlaxcales risk fading into obscurity, so I'm celebrating them here! You can enjoy this versatile snack in lots of ways. If you're after something savoury, try them topped with spicy salsa, sour cream and cheese. For a sweet treat, slice them open, spread with butter, then add a sprinkling of sugar or your favourite jam and serve with Mexican hot chocolate!

Ingredients

- 500 g (2½ cups) fresh corn kernels
- 300 g (10½ oz) yellow or white masa flour
- 120 g (4½ oz) butter, softened
- 100 g (3½ oz) piloncillo or brown sugar
- 1 tablespoon ground cinnamon
- vegetable oil, for pan-frying

Method

Whiz the corn kernels in a blender until they form a smooth corn paste. Transfer to a large bowl. Add the masa flour, butter, sugar and cinnamon and mix with your hands until combined. Knead into a firm dough that you can easily shape with your hands.

Divide the dough into 10 equal portions and shape each portion into a triangle about 1 cm (½ in) thick.

Heat a little vegetable oil in a comal or heavy-based frying pan over low heat. Working in batches, cook the tlaxcales for 5 minutes on each side, until golden brown all over.

Leave to cool slightly before serving.

The tlaxcales will keep in an airtight container in the fridge for 4 days.

Camotitos de Puebla

Puebla-style sweet potato candies

Makes 20

My mum loves these so much that we'd sometimes drive all the way to Puebla, two hours away, just to buy them fresh. No matter the distance, it was always worth it to bring home a box of these sweet potato treats, fresh and perfectly irresistible.

Sweet potatoes are used in a lot of dishes in this region, but these candies are the most famous and most popular way to enjoy them. This candy recipe has its roots in the colonial era, but sweet potatoes have been a key part of local agriculture for millennia.

Ingredients

- 300 g (10½ oz) white sugar
- 1 teaspoon natural vanilla extract
- 1 kg (2 lb 3 oz) boiled and mashed white sweet potato
- pink, yellow and green food colouring
- 100 g (3½ oz) cornflour (cornstarch), for coating

Method

Begin by making a caramel base. Put the sugar and vanilla in a large saucepan with 100 ml (3½ fl oz) water. Stir over medium heat for 5–7 minutes, until it starts bubbling and turns into a syrup. Add the mashed sweet potato and stir continuously for 10–15 minutes, until the mixture thickens into a paste with a dry, jam-like consistency.

Divide the mixture equally between three bowls. Add a couple of drops of pink food colouring to one portion, yellow food colouring to another portion and green food colouring to the third portion, mixing in each food colouring thoroughly and evenly. Transfer to the fridge and leave to cool for about 30 minutes, until firm.

Cut waxed baking paper into 20 rectangles, measuring about 10 cm × 20 cm (4 in × 8 in). Spread the cornflour on a plate. Shape 2 tablespoons of the sweet potato mixture into a small cigar or sausage (dip your fingers in water first if the mixture is too sticky), then roll in the cornflour until fully coated, using a pastry brush to gently remove any excess. Repeat with the remaining mixture.

Wrap each sweet potato candy in a piece of waxed paper, twisting the ends to secure it. These sweets are perfect for sharing and make beautiful gifts.

The candies will keep in an airtight container in the fridge for 1 week.

Torito de Cacahuate

Peanut torito

Serves 6

Toritos aren't just a drink, they're part of a whole vibe. And no one embodies that vibe better than my sister, Ana. Every year Ana would pack her sequins, heels and unstoppable attitude and head to the Veracruz Carnival with her dance crew. When she came back, she'd pour toritos at the kitchen table and regale us with tales of the trip – the float that got stuck mid-parade so they had to dance on the spot for almost an hour, her friend's insistence on trying a new salsa move that took out two innocent bystanders ... We'd sip our toritos and laugh until our sides hurt.

For me, toritos are always tied to Ana lighting up the room with her stories, so this sweet, creamy drink somehow tastes like adventure. 'This one's for dessert,' she'd say with a grin, pouring us all another round.

Method

Pour the milk, condensed milk and evaporated milk into a blender. Add the vanilla, peanut butter and sugar and blend until smooth and creamy.

Pour into a large jug or punch bowl and stir in the crushed peanuts. Slowly add the sparkling water and white rum, stirring gently.

Serve chilled or over ice, with a few extra crushed peanuts on top, if you like.

Ingredients

- 1 litre (4 cups) milk
- 395 g (14 oz) tinned sweetened condensed milk
- 375 ml (12½ fl oz) tinned evaporated milk
- 2 teaspoons natural vanilla extract
- 270 g (1 cup) peanut butter
- 50 g (1¾ oz) soft brown sugar
- 150 g (1 cup) unsalted crushed peanuts, plus extra to serve (optional)
- 600 ml (20½ fl oz) chilled sparkling water
- 700 ml (23½ fl oz) white rum
- ice cubes, to serve (optional)

EL
Tabasco
Campeche

SURESTE
Yucatán
Quintana Roo

EL SURESTE

Spanning the states of Yucatán, Quintana Roo, Campeche and Tabasco, southeast Mexico is a melting pot of rich indigenous history and bold flavours. Past and present come together here on a plate, with vibrant dishes that showcase land, sea and centuries of tradition.

One weekend, my friend Luis and I headed to the Yucatán capital of Mérida for one of our 'food exploration' getaways. Mérida welcomed us with open arms and delicious smells wafting from every corner. Fragrant spices, the earthy aromas of achiote, and a faint citrus tang in the air promised a feast like no other.

The people of Yucatán have a culinary legacy that's deeply tied to the Maya civilisation. Their traditional cooking methods include pib, where food is slow-cooked in an underground oven lined with hot stones. If you're lucky enough to see this in action, it can make you feel very connected to ancient times. And when you taste Cochinita pibil (see page 216) – meltingly tender pork slow-cooked in this way – all its smoky, tender perfection is infused with the history of the region.

Yucatán isn't just about slow-cooking, though. It's also home to zesty, tangy Sopa de lima (see page 228) and the popular Papadzules (see page 230) – soft corn tortillas filled with hard-boiled eggs and topped with a traditional rich pepita (pumpkin seed) sauce.

A surprising addition to local pantries is Edam cheese, which arrived in Yucatán after a Dutch shipwreck on the Caribbean coast. When wheels of the red-wax-coated cheese rolled up onto the local beaches from the wreckage, they made it into local kitchens and became a cornerstone of many Yucatán dishes. Try the extraordinary hollowed-out whole Edam stuffed with a celebratory spiced pork filling (see page 239) for a true meeting of kitchen cultures!

The bright heat of habanero chilli pops up in a huge number of dishes in this region, from salsas to marinades, leaving its fiery signature on your tastebuds. It's one of the spiciest chillies in Mexico, sitting right up there on the Scoville scale!

One of the most distinctive ingredients in Yucatecan cuisine is recado negro (see page 218). This unique paste, proudly rooted in ancient Mayan traditions, is made by burning chillies and spices to impart a smoky flavour and deep black colour. It's a labour-intensive process that can fill the kitchen with smoke and cause irritated eyes and coughing!

Achiote is everywhere in the local cuisine of Tabasco, making everything from meat to rice pop with flavour. An earthy spice that comes from the seeds of the annatto tree, achiote is the secret ingredient that gives the region's food its rich warmth and slightly peppery flavour – and in the case of their bite-sized tamales known as Chanchamitos (see page 236), their bold red colouring.

While the idea of stuffing plantains (see page 232) isn't unique to the Tabasco region, given the abundance of this staple tropical fruit in so many Latin American households, it's become a particularly beloved side dish in Tabasco and is often served at family gatherings or festive meals. I first ate stuffed plantain from a roadside stall, crisp and hot and oozing with melted cheese. Unforgettable.

Campeche offers a unique mix of influences, blending Mayan, Spanish and Afro–Mexican elements with a distinct coastal vibe that sets it apart. The food is as colourful and lively as the region's traditions, offering dishes that feel simultaneously comforting and exotic. Pan de cazon (see page 224), a layered 'Mayan lasagne' of fish, tortillas and a rich tomato sauce, is just one of the unforgettable meals you'll enjoy here. There's even a 1980s-style coconut shrimp (see page 226)!

The indigenous communities across these states, especially the Maya, have left an indelible mark on the culinary landscapes. Their techniques – grinding maize on the metate, fermenting cacao for drinks and smoking meats – are seen all around, preserving ancient traditions as a part of everyday modern life.

Tacos de Cochinita Pibil

Pulled-pork tacos

Makes 10

Cochinita pibil – 'real' pulled pork from the Yucatán peninsula – is one of Mexico's most popular dishes. It's the most famous of all the taco fillings, and one of the bestsellers at my tamaleria. Originally it would have been made with pheasant, deer or peccary (a sort of wild boar), until the Spanish arrived and introduced pork.

Ingredients

- 100 g (5½ oz) achiote paste
- 50 ml (1¾ fl oz) white vinegar
- 50 ml (1¾ fl oz) bitter orange juice (or normal orange juice)
- 1 tablespoon table salt
- 1 kg (2 lb 3 oz) boneless pork shoulder or leg, cut into 5 cm (2 in) chunks
- 20 Tortillas de maiz, 11 cm (4¼ in) in diameter page 314 →
- lime wedges, to serve

Topping

- 1 red onion, finely sliced
- 1 tablespoon dried Mexican oregano
- 1 teaspoon lemon juice
- pinch of table salt
- 1 teaspoon white vinegar

Method

In a small bowl, mix together the achiote paste, vinegar, orange juice and salt to make a thick paste.

Place the pork in a large non-metallic bowl and rub the achiote marinade into the meat. Cover and leave in the fridge to marinate for at least 3 hours.

Preheat the oven to 220°C (430°F) fan-forced.

Place the marinated pork in a roasting tin in a single layer. Cover with foil and bake for 1 hour.

Remove the foil from the tin, reduce the oven temperature to 150°C (300°F) and roast for a further 15 minutes.

Meanwhile, make the topping. Bring a small saucepan of water to the boil, add the onion and blanch for 1 minute. Drain and immediately plunge the onion into a bowl of cold water to stop the cooking process. Drain again and combine the onion in a bowl with the oregano, lemon juice, salt and vinegar.

Using two forks, gently shred the pork. Divide the pulled pork among 10 double-thickness warm tortillas and add the onion topping. Serve immediately, with lime wedges.

Relleno Negro

Stuffed meatballs in black sauce

Serves 4

Relleno negro is one of the most popular dishes for the Day of the Dead holiday in Yucatán. I first tried it during a trip to Mérida, the Yucatán capital, with my friend Luis. We're both food enthusiasts who'll try anything once, no matter how unusual or unfamiliar. Wandering through the central market, we found ourselves surrounded by dishes we'd never seen before, each one more intriguing than the last.

It was the smoky aroma and dark, almost mysterious, appearance of relleno negro that drew us in. Made with recado negro, a unique burnt black chilli sauce, the layers of smoky flavours were unforgettable – and we were hooked! Albondigas rellena (stuffed meatballs) filled with hard-boiled egg are another key component of this dish, bearing witness to the influence of Arab and Spanish cuisines on Yucatán's rich culinary heritage. While turkey was commonly used, chicken is a good replacement nowadays.

It's impossible to single out a 'star' ingredient in relleno negro; each component plays a fundamental role in elevating this delicious dish.

You'll need to start the recado negro a day ahead, but if you don't want to take on the challenge of making it from scratch, pre-made chilmole paste is available from most Latin American stores. Using 80 g (2¾ oz) of the paste here will bring the same bold flavours to your cooking.

Method

Start by making the recado negro. In batches, carefully toast the puya chillies in a hot comal or heavy-based frying pan over medium heat for 10 minutes, turning them now and then, and making sure they incinerate completely. Meanwhile, mix the salt and 500 ml (2 cups) water in a jug.

Add the cloves, allspice berries, bay leaves and salted water to the pan and gently warm through. Transfer to a bowl, then cover and leave for 24 hours, or at least overnight, to allow the chillies to lose their bitter, ashy taste, and to reach the right consistency.

The next day, toast the tomatoes, onion and garlic cloves in a hot comal or heavy-based frying pan, turning often, for about 5–7 minutes, until charred and well roasted. Set the tomatoes and half an onion aside for the meatballs.

To finish making the recado negro, put the roasted garlic cloves and remaining onion half in a food processor. Drain the chilli mixture and add to the processor with the peppercorns and cumin seeds. Blend to a smooth paste and set aside.

Ingredients

- 2 tomatoes
- 1 onion, halved
- 3 garlic cloves, peeled
- 500 g (1 lb 2 oz) boneless, skinless chicken breasts
- 3 allspice berries
- 1 teaspoon dried epazote
- 1 tablespoon cornflour (corn starch)
- 1 dried guajillo chilli
- 1 teaspoon ground black pepper

Recado negro

- 30 g (1 oz) dried puya chillies (chile seco)
- 2 tablespoons table salt
- 4 cloves
- 4 allspice berries
- 20 g (¾ oz) dried bay leaves (about 10 leaves)
- 3 roasted garlic cloves (from above)
- ½ roasted onion (from above)
- 4 black peppercorns
- 1 tablespoon cumin seeds

Recipe continues →

Put the chicken in a saucepan with the allspice berries and 1 litre (4 cups) water. Bring to the boil, then reduce the heat and simmer for 30 minutes, until cooked through. Lift out the chicken, reserving the broth, and shred the meat. Return the chicken to the broth and stir in 150 g (5½ oz) of the recado negro. Keep warm.

To make the meatballs, finly chop the reserved roasted tomatoes and remaining onion half and place in a bowl. Add the pork and salt and mix together with your hands, then roll into four meatballs. Gently flatten each meatball in the palm of your hand and add a hard-boiled egg, then fold the meat around the egg to enclose it and roll again to form a large meatball.

Add the meatballs and epazote to the pan of chicken and broth. Simmer over low heat for about 20 minutes, until the meatballs are cooked through. Lift out the meatballs and chicken.

Stir the cornflour with 3 tablespoons cold water to make a smooth slurry, then add it to the broth. Remove the stem and seeds from the dried guajillo chilli, then finely chop and add it to the broth, along with the black pepper. Simmer, stirring constantly to avoid lumps, for 10 minutes, until the sauce thickens a little.

Spoon a meatball and some shredded chicken into each bowl. Spoon the rich recado negro sauce over the top and serve with tortillas and habanero chilli on the side.

Any leftover meatballs, chicken and sauce will keep in an airtight container in the fridge for 4 days.

Any leftover recado negro will keep in an airtight container in the fridge for 2 weeks.

Stuffed meatballs

- 2 roasted tomatoes (from the previous page)
- ½ roasted onion (from the previous page)
- 400 g (14 oz) minced (ground) pork
- 1 tablespoon table salt
- 4 hard-boiled eggs, peeled

To serve

- Tortillas de maiz page 314 →
- fresh red habanero chillies, sliced

Pibipollo

Yucatecan baked chicken tamal

Serves 4

I tried pibipollo in Yucatán with Gina, the owner of the Mexican hot sauce company La Meridana, who took me to her favourite restaurant to experience it, proud to show off the amazing quality of the local habanero chillies. This dish is like a giant baked tamal, with achiote and spice-infused chicken or pork bundled up in masa dough and wrapped in banana leaves. It is traditionally cooked underground, but you can easily bake it at home to create those smoky, comforting flavours. That way you get a true taste of Yucatán without digging up your backyard!

Method

Start by poaching the chicken. In a food processor, blend the onion, garlic, tomato and achiote paste until smooth. Transfer to a large saucepan and add the allspice berries, cumin, cloves, oregano, epazote and salt. Pour in 1 litre (4 cups) water and bring to the boil. Add the chicken, then reduce the heat and simmer for 30 minutes, until the chicken is tender. Remove from the heat.

Lift out the chicken, remove and discard the skin and bones, then shred the meat with two forks and set aside. Measure out 250 ml (1 cup) of the chicken broth, discarding the rest of the broth in the pan. Strain the reserved broth, then pour it back into the pan. Add the masa flour to the broth, stirring constantly to avoid lumps. Now your broth is ready.

Preheat the oven to 180°C (350°F) fan-forced.

Dig out a 24 cm × 15 cm (9½ in × 6 in) baking tray and cut off a piece of foil that's double the length of the tray. Lay half the foil over the tray, with the other half overhanging. Lay a banana leaf over the foil on the tray. Next, lay the second banana leaf in the other direction, to create a cross shape.

Ingredients

- 2 fresh banana leaves
- 500 g (1 lb 2 oz) Tortilla de maiz dough page 314 →
- 200 g (7 oz) pork lard
- 1 white onion, sliced
- 3 roma (plum) tomatoes, sliced
- 1 fresh habanero chilli, sliced

To poach the chicken

- ½ white onion, roughly chopped
- 1 garlic clove, peeled
- 2 roma (plum) tomatoes, roughly chopped
- 1 teaspoon achiote paste
- 2 allspice berries
- 1 teaspoon ground cumin
- 1 teaspoon ground cloves
- 1 teaspoon dried Mexican oregano
- 1 teaspoon dried epazote (or add an extra 1 teaspoon dried Mexican oregano)
- 2 teaspoons table salt
- 4 chicken marylands, skin on
- 50 g (1¾ oz) masa flour

Recipe continues →

Place the tortilla dough in a bowl and beat in the lard using a wooden spoon until fully combined and soft. Spread half the tortilla dough over the banana leaf. Add 125 ml (½ cup) of the reserved broth, along with the shredded chicken, sliced onion, tomato and habanero chilli. Add a little more broth, then top with the remaining dough and press to seal everything inside. Drizzle the remaining broth over the top to stop it drying out.

Fold the banana leaves over the dough to completely enclose the tamal, hugging it like a blanket, then fold the foil over the entire pibipollo, making sure it is fully enclosed.

Transfer to the oven and bake for about 1½ hours.

To check your pibipollo is ready, carefully lift up the foil and banana leaf, using tongs or oven mitts – it will be extremely hot. The dough should be cooked through and not sticky.

Once cooked, serve immediately.

Any leftover pibipollo will keep in an airtight container in the fridge for 4 days.

Pan de Cazon

Shark and tortilla stack

Serves 2

This is the kind of meal that tells a story – of fishermen hauling in fresh cazon (dogfish), of epazote growing wild, and of Yucatán kitchens filled with the scent of chargrilled habanero chillies. Pan de Cazon is pure comfort food with a tropical twist – it's a love letter to the coastal traditions of Yucatán, particularly the city of Campeche. Often called the 'Mayan lasagne', it's made with layers of tortillas, black beans and shredded fish, and served with a rich, smoky tomato sauce.

Ingredients

- 1 tablespoon vegetable oil
- ½ white onion, diced
- 1 garlic clove, chopped
- 1 teaspoon tomato paste (concentrated puree)
- 10 g (¼ oz) dried epazote

To poach the fish

- 500 g (1 lb 2 oz) skinless dogfish or a similar white fish fillet, such as gummy shark (see Note)
- 2 garlic cloves, peeled
- 1 teaspoon table salt
- 1 teaspoon dried Mexican oregano
- 2 pinches of dried epazote

Tomato sauce

- 4 roma (plum) tomatoes
- 1 teaspoon table salt
- ½ white onion, chopped
- 10 g (¼ oz) dried epazote

To serve

- 8 Tortillas de maiz, warmed page 314 →
- 400 g (14 oz) Frijoles negros refritos page 322 →
- avocado slices
- 2 fresh habanero chillies, chargrilled

Method

To poach the fish, place it in a large deep frying pan with the garlic, salt, oregano, epazote and 1 litre (4 cups) water. Simmer for 7 minutes, or until tender, then drain. When cool enough to handle, flake the flesh and set aside.

To make the tomato sauce, bring a saucepan of water to the boil. Carefully add the tomatoes and cook for about 1 minute, until their skins loosen. Drain and leave to cool slightly, then peel the tomatoes and place in a food processor. Add the salt, onion, epazote and 250 ml (1 cup) water and blend until smooth. Transfer to a saucepan and simmer over low heat for 10–15 minutes, until reduced and slightly thickened.

Meanwhile, heat the vegetable oil in a saucepan and saute the onion and garlic for 2–3 minutes, until fragrant. Add the flaked fish, tomato paste, epazote and 3 tablespoons of the tomato sauce. Simmer for 2–3 minutes, until heated through.

To serve, spread 2–3 tablespoons of the remaining tomato sauce on a large plate and top with a warm tortilla. Spread with a layer of refried beans, then a layer of the fish mixture. Repeat the layers to create a stack with four tortillas. Top with more tomato sauce.

Garnish with sliced avocado and the chargrilled habaneros and serve immediately.

The fish will keep in an airtight container in the fridge for 2 days, and the tomato sauce for 4 days.

Note

You can also use any firm white-fleshed fish such as barramundi or cod – whatever is local and sustainably sourced in your area.

Camarones al Coco

Coconut shrimp

Serves 2–4

It was the 1980s, and Don Carmino Buenfil, owner of the popular '303' restaurant in Campeche, had a passion for trying new dishes on his travels. On one of his trips, he tasted a shrimp recipe that inspired him to create something similar, using the abundant fresh prawns from the Gulf of Mexico, but with a Campechano twist – serving them in a coconut shell with a mango and habanero salsa, to highlight the region's fabulous local produce.

The dish he came up with impressed then-Governor Eugenio Echeverría Castellot, who enthusiastically shared it with influential figures at formal dinners. Word spread, and the crispy sweet camarones al coco has been a favourite in restaurants and homes along the coast ever since.

To really get into the vibe, use half a coconut shell as a serving bowl for the mango habanero sauce!

Method

Season the prawns well with salt and pepper, then lightly coat them in the flour, shaking off any excess.

Using a fork, beat the eggs with the orange juice in a bowl. In another bowl, mix the desiccated coconut and breadcrumbs.

Dip each prawn in the egg mixture, then coat thoroughly in the coconut breadcrumbs, pressing on the prawns gently to help the crumbs stick. Place the breaded prawns on a tray and freeze for 15 minutes to help the crumb coating stay intact during frying.

Heat about 10 cm (4 in) vegetable oil in a deep frying pan over medium–high heat to 180°C (350°F) on a kitchen thermometer. Deep-fry the prawns in small batches for about 4 minutes, or until golden brown. Drain briefly on paper towel.

Arrange some lettuce leaves on a serving platter and top with the onion and lime slices. Place a small bowl of the mango habanero sauce in the centre and scatter the prawns around it.

Serve immediately, with steamed white rice.

Ingredients

- 500 g (1 lb 2 oz) raw prawns (shrimp), peeled and deveined
- plain (all-purpose) flour, for coating
- 2 eggs
- 100 ml (3½ fl oz) orange juice
- 250 g (9 oz) desiccated coconut
- 100 g (3½ oz) dried breadcrumbs or panko crumbs
- vegetable oil, for deep-frying

To serve

- cos (romaine) lettuce leaves
- 1 red onion, finely sliced
- 1 lime, finely sliced
- Salsa de Habanero con Mango page 310 →
- steamed white rice

Sopa de Lima

Lime soup

Serves 4

I first tasted sopa de lima not in Yucatán, where it originated, but in a charming little restaurant in Mexico City that specialised in regional dishes. The tangy lime broth was a refreshing balance of spice and citrusy zing, the chicken was tender and juicy, and crispy tortilla strips added a satisfying crunch. Sopa de lima has such a zesty kick it's often served as a hangover remedy!

Method

Toast the onion, banana chilli and garlic cloves in a hot comal or heavy-based frying pan, turning often, for about 5–7 minutes, until charred and well roasted. Set aside to cool slightly.

Roughly chop the roasted onion, banana chilli and garlic and place in a large saucepan. Add the chicken, along with the allspice berries, bay leaves, salt, achiote paste and 2 litres (2 qts) water. Bring to the boil, then reduce the heat and simmer for 30 minutes, or until the chicken is tender. Lift out the chicken, reserving the broth, then shred the meat and set aside. Strain the broth, discarding the aromatics, and return it to the saucepan.

Heat the oil in a large saucepan and saute the tomato and bell pepper over medium heat for a few minutes, until soft. Add them to the broth, along with the lime juice and pepper. Bring the soup back to a gentle simmer.

Meanwhile, bring a small saucepan of water to the boil, add the finely sliced red onion and blanch for 10 seconds. Drain and plunge into a bowl of cold water to stop the cooking process. Drain again and set aside.

Set out your soup toppings: shredded chicken, fried tortilla strips, lime slices, coriander, the blanched onion and avocado slices.

Divide the shredded chicken among four serving bowls. Add a ladleful of soup, a handful of fried tortilla strips and the lime slices. Let the lime slices infuse briefly – no more than 2 minutes – to make the soup tangy but not sour.

Fish the lime slices out and top up each bowl with more of the soup. Garnish each bowl with the coriander, onion and avocado and serve immediately, with an extra squeeze of lime juice if you like.

The broth and shredded chicken will keep in separate airtight containers in the fridge for 4 days.

Ingredients

- ½ white onion
- 1 fresh banana chilli, stem removed
- 2 garlic cloves, peeled
- 4 chicken marylands, skin on
- 3 allspice berries
- 2 bay leaves
- 1 tablespoon table salt
- 1 teaspoon achiote paste
- 1 tablespoon vegetable oil
- 2 roma (plum) tomatoes, cut into quarters, seeds removed
- 1 green bell pepper (capsicum), cut into 4 cm (1½ in) chunks
- juice of 2 limes, plus extra to serve (optional)
- pinch of freshly ground black pepper

To serve

- 1 red onion, finely sliced
- 4 Tortillas de maiz, cut into strips and fried page 314 →
- 1 lime, finely sliced
- 1 bunch of coriander (cilantro), finely chopped
- 1 avocado, sliced

Papadzules

Pepita sauce enchiladas

Serves 4

The first time I tasted papadzules was with my friend Luis. We sat down at a local Yucatán restaurant and, as soon as they brought the plate to the table, the aroma of the pepita sauce hit us. The dish was warm and comforting, and so was the restaurant with its lively folk music!

Ingredients

- 12 hard-boiled eggs
- table salt
- 1 teaspoon dried epazote or Mexican oregano
- 3 roma (plum) tomatoes
- 1 white onion, ½ roughly chopped, ½ finely sliced
- 1 garlic clove, peeled
- 1 tablespoon vegetable oil
- 1 fresh habanero chilli, stem removed, sliced
- 100 g (3½ oz) pepitas (pumpkin seeds)
- 12 Tortillas de maiz, warmed page 314 →

Method

Peel all the eggs. Cut four eggs in half lengthways and set aside for serving. Place the remaining eight eggs in a large bowl and roughly mash with a fork, so they have a chunky consistency. Season with a pinch of salt.

Pour 1 litre (4 cups) water into a saucepan and add the epazote. Bring to the boil, then keep at a rolling boil for 5 minutes, to infuse the water. Set aside.

Bring another saucepan of water to the boil. Carefully add the tomatoes, then boil for about 1 minute, until their skins loosen. Drain and leave until cool enough to handle, then peel the tomatoes and blend them in a food processor with 100 ml (3½ fl oz) of the epazote water, the roughly chopped onion, garlic and 1 teaspoon of salt.

Heat the oil in a saucepan and add the tomato mixture and sliced habanero. Warm the sauce over medium heat until it comes to the boil, then set aside.

Using a blender or molcajete, grind the pepitas and 1 teaspoon salt into a paste, mixing in enough of the warm epazote-infused water to give you a smooth, creamy sauce.

Dip each tortilla into the warm pepita sauce, ensuring they're well coated. Fill the tortillas with the mashed egg, then roll them up and divide among four serving plates. Pour more pepita sauce over the top, as if serving enchiladas.

Top the papadzules with two hard-boiled egg halves, a drizzle of the tomato sauce and a few slices of onion. Serve immediately.

Any leftover pepita sauce or tomato sauce will keep in separate airtight containers in the fridge for 4 days.

Platanos Rellenos de Carne

Beef-stuffed plantain gorditas

Makes 10

I was visiting the Tabasco region with friends when we stopped at a little food stand on the side of the road. Platanos rellenos were handed to us fresh from the deep-fryer – crispy on the outside, and oozing with juicy beef filling. What an irresistible and unforgettable combination.

For a vegetarian option, stuff the plantains with diced mozzarella or Oaxaca cheese instead of meat.

Ingredients

- 1 kg (2 lb 3 oz) ripe plantains, peeled and chopped into large chunks
- 150 g (1 cup) plain (all-purpose) flour, plus extra for dusting
- vegetable oil, for deep-frying

Beef filling

- 1 tablespoon vegetable oil
- 1 garlic clove, finely chopped
- 250 g (9½ oz) minced (ground) beef
- 1 roma (plum) tomato, chopped
- ½ white onion, finely chopped
- ½ green bell pepper (capsicum), finely chopped
- ½ teaspoon table salt

To serve

- crema
- crumbled queso fresco, Cotija or feta

Method

Start by making the filling. Heat the vegetable oil in a large saucepan over medium heat and saute the garlic for 1–2 minutes, until fragrant. Add the beef and cook, breaking it up with a wooden spoon, for 5–10 minutes, until browned.

Stir in the tomato, onion, bell pepper and salt. Cook, stirring occasionally, for 15–20 minutes, until the mixture is well combined and the moisture has evaporated. The filling should be as dry as possible for stuffing the plantain gorditas.

Meanwhile, bring a large saucepan of water to the boil. Add the plantain and cook for about 20 minutes, until soft. Drain, then place the plantain in a large bowl and mash. Allow to cool, then mix in the flour and bring together to form a dough.

With lightly floured hands, roll about 100 g (3½ oz) of the plantain dough into a ball and gently flatten it into a thick cup shape, no bigger than the size of your hand. Place about 40 g (1¼ oz) of the meat filling in the centre, then gather the dough over the filling to enclose and roll into a large ball. With slightly cupped hands, very gently flatten the ball, exerting pressure only around the edge of the gordita, so that the filling stays in the centre. Repeat with the remaining dough and filling.

Meanwhile, heat about 10 cm (4 in) vegetable oil in a large heavy-based saucepan to 200°C (400°F) on a kitchen thermometer.

Working in batches, fry the plantain gorditas for about 5 minutes, until golden and crispy, and briefly drain on paper towel.

Serve immediately, topped with a drizzle of crema and crumbled cheese.

TAMALES

There are more than 500 types of tamales in Mexico, with every region adding its own local spin. When you're talking tamales, you're talking a whole world of flavours and fillings!

An integral part of Mexico's heritage, tamales have always been a cherished part of my life. When I was a child, my family's kitchen would often be filled with the comforting warmth of masa dough steaming to perfection. Making tamales was a labour of love that brought us all together, especially during the holiday season and on special occasions.

As I grew older, my appreciation for this iconic dish deepened, and I started to explore the history and incredible variety of Mexican tamales, each with its own unique flavour and cultural significance.

Ancient civilisations, including the Aztecs and Mayans, created tamales as handy portable meals for warriors and travellers. Made from corn masa, they're typically filled with meats, cheeses, fruits and vegetables, then wrapped in corn husks or banana leaves and steamed.

In some regions, tamales are wrapped in acelga (Swiss chard) leaves instead of corn husks, adding a subtle earthiness and vibrant colour, and reminding us how adaptable local cooks can be.

Some traditional fillings are often quite adventurous. In Oaxaca and Puebla, for example, you'll find tamales filled with chapulines (grasshoppers), toasted and seasoned beforehand to enhance their flavour. They're crispy and crunchy and my son has developed quite a taste for them!

In the southern states of Mexico, especially Oaxaca and Guerrero, you'll find tamales de frijol and tamales de mole. The former has black beans mixed into the masa, while the latter are filled with a surprising rich dark mole sauce.

In northern Mexico, especially Sinaloa and Chihuahua, tamales de carne are common, filled with meats seasoned with local spices. Tamales de elote (corn tamales) are also popular in these regions, made from sweetcorn and mainly eaten as a dessert.

Tamales are often enjoyed during festive holidays, where the act of making them together becomes part of the celebration. Families might have their own secret recipes passed down through the generations, like an ancient, well-guarded cookbook.

My great-aunt Chita would come to our house with all her kitchen utensils to make tamales. Her hands worked expertly, mixing the masa and filling them perfectly. The kitchen would come alive with laughter and stories. Memories of those experiences now seem magical.

Today, living in Australia, tamales have become my signature dish. I love introducing them to people because they embody the essence of Mexican cuisine – an incredible fusion of history, culture and love. I may not be in Mexico anymore, but tamales will always evoke memories of family and the warmth of home.

Chanchamitos

Tabasco-style pork tamales

Makes 20

The name of this dish comes from the Mayan word 'ch'an', which means 'small', so these are cute, bite-sized tamales. Don't let their size fool you – they pack a punch with their filling of seasoned pork and achiote.

Method

To make the filling, put the pork in a large saucepan with the bay leaves, half an onion, 1 tablespoon of the salt and 2 litres (2 qts) water. Bring to the boil, then reduce the heat to medium and cook for about 45 minutes, until the pork is tender and cooked through. Lift out the pork and cut into 2 cm (¾ in) cubes.

In a separate pan of water, boil the dried chillies for about 5 minutes, until soft. Drain, reserving the cooking water. Cut the stems off the chillies and set the chillies aside.

Heat a comal or heavy-based frying pan and toast the tomatoes, garlic and remaining onion half over medium–high heat for 5–7 minutes, or until soft and charred all over. Tip into a food processor. Add the softened chillies, cumin, oregano and epazote, and blend with about 150 ml (5 fl oz) of the reserved chilli cooking water to make a smooth sauce.

Heat the oil in a large frying pan, add the blended chilli sauce and the remaining 1 tablespoon salt. Simmer for about 5 minutes, until the sauce thickens slightly. Add the chopped pork and mix in gently so it is fully coated.

Soften the corn husks in a large bowl of warm water for about 5 minutes, then drain to remove any excess water.

To make the tamales, place the lard and baking powder in a large bowl and whip the mixture as fast as possible using a wooden spoon – the lard needs to soften and look spongy. Don't stress if this takes a long time; it can take up to 15 minutes to achieve the right consistency.

Once the lard is ready, add the masa flour, salt, achiote paste and warm chicken stock and mix well until completely combined. (Depending on the brand of masa flour you've used, you may need to add a little more water to achieve the right consistency.) To test if the dough is ready, drop a small ball of dough into a cup of cold water; if it floats to the top you're good to go! (If the dough doesn't float, mix the dough a little longer until it does float.)

Ingredients

- 40 dried sweetcorn husks (see Note overleaf)
- 1 red onion, finely chopped, to serve

Pork filling

- 1 × 500 g (1 lb 2 oz) piece of boneless pork shoulder or leg
- 3 bay leaves
- 1 white onion, halved
- 2 tablespoons table salt
- 1 dried guajillo chilli
- 1 dried mulato chilli
- 2 tomatoes
- 2 garlic cloves, peeled
- 1 teaspoon ground cumin
- 1 tablespoon dried Mexican oregano
- 1 tablespoon dried or chopped fresh epazote
- 1 tablespoon vegetable oil

Tamales masa

- 200 g (7 oz) pork lard
- 1 teaspoon baking powder
- 500 g (1 lb 2 oz) masa flour, sifted
- 2 teaspoons table salt
- 1 teaspoon achiote paste
- 650 ml (22 fl oz) chicken stock, warmed

Recipe continues →

Spread 40 g (1½ oz) of the dough in the middle of a damp sweetcorn husk, leaving a 4 cm (1½ in) border around the edge. Add 50 g (1¾ oz) of the pork filling, then cover with another 20 g (¾ oz) of the dough.

Place another sweetcorn husk over the filling, then wrap up the tamale by overlapping the sides and folding over the top and bottom ends towards the centre to enclose the filling. Secure with kitchen string and set aside. Repeat with the remaining husks and ingredients to make 20 tamales.

Stand the tamales upright in a large steamer. Fit as many tamales as you can into the steamer, but be careful not to pack them in too tightly or they may burst, leaving you with empty tamales. Place the steamer over a saucepan of simmering water and steam for 45 minutes.

The best way to check if your tamales are cooked is to remove one from the steamer, let it cool for 5 minutes and then unwrap the husk. If the dough doesn't stick to the husk and looks shiny and fluffy, then your tamales are ready.

Let the tamales cool for 15–20 minutes inside the steamer, before serving with the finely chopped red onion as a garnish.

The tamales are best served freshly steamed, but will keep for 3–4 days in an airtight container in the fridge.

You can make the pork filling up to 2 days ahead.

Note

You can buy dried sweetcorn husks from Latin American supermarkets or online. It's better to buy more than you need, as they are unpredictable and can sometimes be small or break. They can be frozen, or kept in an airtight container in the pantry.

Queso Relleno

Stuffed cheese ball

Serves 12

Edam cheese arrived on the Yucatán Peninsula after a Dutch ship ran aground on the Caribbean coast while sailing from Suriname to the Dutch colony of Curaçao. The curious wheels of Edam cheese that were salvaged from the wreckage quickly became a beloved ingredient in the local kitchens. The fusion of Dutch cheese with traditional Mayan flavours is a perfect example of how Mexican cuisine has always been open to new influences and how culinary traditions evolve and adapt.

Ingredients

1 × 2 kg (4 lb 6 oz) ball of Edam cheese, in its red wax casing

Pork filling

- 5 hard-boiled eggs
- 4 roma (plum) tomatoes, diced
- 1 green bell pepper (capsicum), diced
- 2 garlic cloves, peeled
- ½ white onion
- 2 tablespoons vegetable oil
- 1 kg (2 lb 3 oz) minced (ground) pork
- 2 teaspoons table salt
- 1 teaspoon freshly ground black pepper
- 1 teaspoon sweet paprika
- 1 teaspoon apple cider vinegar

Kol sauce

- 250 ml (1 cup) pork broth (from the filling)
- 100 g (⅔ cup) plain (all-purpose) flour
- 1 teaspoon table salt
- 1 teaspoon apple cider vinegar

Salsa topping

- 2 tablespoons vegetable oil
- 1 white onion, diced
- 4 roma (plum) tomatoes, diced
- 100 g (3½ oz) pitted whole green olives, halved
- 100 g (3½ oz) raisins
- 100 g (3½ oz) flaked blanched almonds
- 500 ml (2 cups) tomato passata (pureed tomatoes)

Method

Using a sharp knife, carefully cut out a 5 cm (2 in) square from the top of the cheese ball, leaving the red wax on, and reserving the square 'lid' for sealing it back up later. Using a spoon, carefully start scooping out the cheese from inside (this will take a while – use that yummy cheese for other dishes such as quesadillas). You need to hollow out the ball of cheese while maintaining its shape, so it becomes like a bowl with 2 cm (¾ in) thick sides. Once you've hollowed it out, use a sharp knife to remove the red wax casing.

To make the pork filling, peel the eggs and separate them into yolks and whites, taking care to keep the yolks whole. Finely dice the whites and set the yolks aside on a plate.

Place the tomato, bell pepper, garlic and onion in a food processor. Pour in 500 ml (2 cups) water and blend until smooth.

Heat the oil in a large saucepan over medium heat. Add the blended tomato mixture and cook until it begins to simmer. Before it comes to the boil, add the pork. Stir in the salt, pepper, paprika, vinegar and 500 ml (2 cups) water, then simmer for about 5 minutes, stirring occasionally.

Strain the mixture, reserving the pork and the broth separately. Place the pork in a bowl, add the diced egg whites and stir together well; this is your pork filling.

To make the kol sauce, pour 125 ml (½ cup) of the reserved pork broth into a clean saucepan. Mix the flour with another 125 ml (½ cup) of the reserved pork broth until smooth, then add to the pan, along with the salt and vinegar, stirring until combined. Gently warm the broth over medium–low heat, then let it simmer gently for 10 minutes, stirring occasionally, until it thickens.

Recipe continues →

To make the salsa topping, heat the oil in a saucepan and saute the onion and tomato over medium heat for about 5 minutes, until softened. Add the olives, raisins, almonds, passata and 200 ml (7 fl oz) water and simmer for about 10 minutes, until everything is cooked through and you have a chunky salsa. Season to taste and set aside.

Now that you have all the recipe elements ready, it's time to start filling the Edam ball!

Spoon the pork filling into the cheese ball, adding the whole egg yolks as you go. Top with the reserved square lid of cheese to enclose the filling.

Carefully wrap the stuffed cheese ball in foil, then place in a large steamer basket. Place the steamer over a large saucepan of simmering water and steam for about 40 minutes, or until the cheese is soft enough to slice.

Carefully remove the cheese ball from the steamer and unwrap the foil. Using a large sharp knife, carefully slice the stuffed cheese into wedges while it's still warm.

Serve the warm cheese wedges in separate bowls, with the kol sauce and the salsa.

Any leftover stuffed cheese will keep in an airtight container in the fridge for 4 days. The kol sauce and salsa will keep refrigerated in separate airtight containers for up to 1 week.

Poc Chuc

Citrus-marinated pork with two salsas

Serves 2

Back in 2009, there was a small community of Mexicans living in Sydney's inner west. This is how I met Roberto, who is originally from Mérida in Yucatán, and we have been very good friends ever since. When Roberto's mum visited Sydney, she treated us to her incredible poc chuc. We went shopping with her for the ingredients and it was an enlightening experience. She was so particular about finding the freshest cuts of pork and the juiciest limes, explaining to us how every ingredient plays a key role in the dish. Watching her cook felt like taking a masterclass. And the result? Unforgettable flavours that transported us straight to Yucatán.

Ingredients

- juice of 1 orange
- juice of 2 limes
- 2 garlic cloves, finely chopped
- 1 teaspoon freshly ground black pepper
- table salt
- 500 g (1 lb 2 oz) pork steaks

Charred onion salsa

- 1 red onion, cut into 3 cm (1¼ in) chunks
- ½ white onion, cut into 3 cm (1¼ in) chunks
- juice of 1 orange
- juice of 2 limes
- ½ bunch of coriander (cilantro), chopped

Chiltomate salsa

- 4 roma (plum) tomatoes, quartered
- 2 fresh habanero chillies, sliced
- ½ bunch of coriander (cilantro), chopped

To serve

- Frijoles negros refritos page 322 →
- 1 avocado, sliced
- 2 cucumbers, sliced

Method

Start by marinating the pork. Pour the orange and lime juice into a non-metallic bowl. Add the garlic, pepper and 1 teaspoon salt and whisk well. Add the pork and stir to coat, then leave to marinate in the fridge for at least 1 hour, and up to 24 hours.

To make the charred onion salsa, char the red and white onion chunks in a hot comal or heavy-based frying pan for about 5 minutes, until nicely browned. Transfer to a bowl and add the orange and lime juice. Stir in the coriander and a pinch of salt.

To make the chiltomate salsa, char the tomato and habanero chilli in the hot comal or frying pan for about 10 minutes, until they're nicely charred. Roughly mash the charred tomato in a bowl – it should be rustic and chunky – and add the charred chilli. Stir in the coriander and a pinch of salt.

Reheat the comal or frying pan over medium heat and cook the pork, along with the marinade, for 15–20 minutes, turning now and then, until beautifully golden and cooked through on both sides.

Serve the pork topped with the two salsas, refried black beans, avocado and cucumber.

The salsas will keep in the fridge in separate airtight containers for up to 1 week.

Marquesitas

Crispy crepe rolls

Makes 6

In the 1930s an ice cream seller in the Yucatán capital of Mérida called Leopoldo Mena invented these crispy snacks to sell in the cooler months. His original filling was grated Edam cheese, but over time, sweet cajeta, chocolate and jam became even bigger hits.

Whenever I think of marquesitas, I'm reminded of my friends Pamela and Robbie's wedding in Cancun. It was a night of great food and unforgettable moments – one of which was the arrival of the marquesita cart halfway through the celebrations.

A queue quickly formed as everyone waited to customise their marquesita. The classic fillings of queso de bola and cajeta were on offer, alongside Nutella and hazelnut butter. I went for the traditional combo of Edam and cajeta – equal parts sweet and savoury, with the marquesita's signature crunch in every bite.

The guests' reactions were priceless: wide eyes and delighted laughs. It was a moment when food brought everyone together, and a reminder that, in Mexico, even at a big fancy wedding, a humble street cart can steal the show!

Ingredients

- 50 g (1¾ oz) unsalted butter, at room temperature, plus extra for pan-frying
- 100 g (3½ oz) caster (superfine) sugar
- 100 ml (3½ fl oz) milk
- 120 g (4½ oz) plain (all-purpose) flour
- 1 teaspoon natural vanilla extract
- pinch of table salt

Fillings

- 100 g (3½ oz) grated Edam or other Dutch cheese
- 220 g (8 oz) Nutella
- 200 g (7 oz) chopped strawberries

Method

In a bowl, cream together the butter and sugar with a wooden spoon until smooth. Add the milk and mix well. Gradually beat in the flour, vanilla and salt, mixing until you have a smooth, slightly runny batter, similar to pancake batter.

Heat a crepe pan, frying pan or a marquesita iron over medium heat and lightly grease with a little butter. Pour a small ladleful of batter onto the centre of the pan, spreading it thinly and evenly. Cook for about 2 minutes, until the edges lift slightly and the underside is golden brown, then flip it over to cook the other side for about 1 minute.

Transfer the crepe to a plate and, while the marquesita is still hot, add your filling: grated cheese, Nutella or chopped strawberries. (In the photo opposite, we've used all three!) Quickly roll up the marquesita – it will harden as it cools, creating that signature crunch, and repeat with the remaining batter and fillings.

The marquesitas are best enjoyed straight away.

Ponche

Punch

Serves 6

This warm fruity punch is perfect for a festive gathering. In Mexico, it's a popular choice for posadas (pinata parties) in December when winter hits, helping revellers stay wonderfully warm while enjoying the party. You could also throw in a splash of tequila or white rum just before serving to give it a cheeky kick! If you happen to have some tejocote (the tiny, tart fruit from Veracruz), definitely add that too, as it's a very traditional ingredient. It's difficult to find outside of Mexico, so I've used guava here.

You could also enjoy this punch chilled in summer. Once you've simmered the spices and fruits, pour the infused liquid into a jug and chill in the fridge for several hours, until completely cold, stirring in the guava and orange just before serving.

You'll find fresh sugar cane and tamarind in larger Asian supermarkets.

Ingredients

- 80 g (⅓ cup) brown sugar
- 4 cinnamon sticks
- 3 star anise
- 20 g (¾ oz) dried hibiscus flowers
- 6 sugar cane sticks, cut into 8 cm–10 cm (3¼ in–4 in) lengths, then split lengthways into quarters
- 60 g (2 oz) tamarind paste
- 1 pear, finely diced
- 1 apple, finely diced
- 4 prunes, finely diced
- 6 fresh or tinned guavas, cut in half
- 1 orange, sliced

Method

Put the sugar, cinnamon sticks, star anise and hibiscus in a saucepan with 2 litres (2 qts) water and bring to the boil. Add the remaining ingredients except the guava and orange. Let it simmer for about 7 minutes, until the sugar cane sticks are soft and have soaked up all the flavours. Set aside to cool a little, then transfer to a jug.

Just before serving, stir in the guava and orange. (Don't add the guava too early, or it will break down too much. You want to keep the fruit intact.)

If you're using fresh guava, taste and add a little more sugar if they're tart. (Tinned guava will likely be in syrup, making them much sweeter.)

Serve hot, in warmed mugs.

EL
SUR
Guerrero

OESTE

aca  Chiapas 

EL SUROESTE

Oaxaca, Guerrero and Chiapas are an excitingly vibrant trio of Mexican states.

Oaxaca is often referred to as 'the land of legends': it's a cultural treasure trove, and its food is just as complex as its culture. Cooking is communal here, and every step, from grinding roasted cacao beans on a metate, to charring tortillas on the comal to turn into the traditional drink, Tascalate (see page 282), is an act of tradition and reverence. The Zapotecs and Mixtecs – the region's indigenous groups from before the Spanish, even before the Aztecs – infuse their cooking practices with ritualistic importance. Beyond the kitchen, the startling landscape provides an endless backdrop of inspiration, where artistry and food blend into the daily rhythms of life. With a patchwork of different microclimates, the produce here is incredibly varied – you'll find things in Oaxaca's street markets that you won't get to eat anywhere else.

My son, Julio, became hooked on the local Tlayudas (see page 266), a favourite Oaxacan street food dish that consists of an oversized corn tortilla smothered with lard, refried beans and cheese and maybe topped with salsa. Julio's preferred topping combo included beef, chorizo, crickets and insect salsa. Flavours only found in Oaxaca!

Something else only found in this amazing state is the tlayuda press, a massive, heavy contraption made for pressing these oversized snacks. It looks more like a mini coffee table than a tortilla press.

Oaxaca is famous for being the land of the seven moles, with Mole coloradito (see page 257) a treasured staple. Its roots burrow deep into pre-Hispanic times, combining indigenous ingredients such as chillies, cacao and tomatoes with Spanish influences such as almonds and spices. Over time, it's become a household favourite. Unlike its darker mole siblings, mole coloradito doesn't overwhelm the tastebuds, it is lighter and more approachable. It's a sort of family-friendly mole, and it's relatively easy to prepare, too!

Mole is such an important part of Oaxaca's food culture that it even has its own festival, with local chefs and food lovers from all over gathering to showcase the region's rich mole tradition at the 'fiesta del mole'.

Guerrero holds a special place in my heart. It's the homeland of my father's family and I go there whenever I'm in Mexico. Visiting Guerrero feels like stepping into a storybook – and cooking here is as integral to identity as the spoken word. It's a region steeped in history, with a deep connection to its land and sea. Indigenous communities like the Nahuas and Mixtecs have long used innovative techniques to prepare meals that honour both nature and tradition. Guerrero's cultural essence is clearly visible in its bustling markets, coastal villages and mountain towns.

Every Thursday is pozole day in Guerrero's crowded streets. Every pozoleria serves a quart of mezcal at the table while you wait for your pozole blanco or pozole verde (see page 254). Chiles capones (see page 260) are one of the classic snacks to accompany pozole, and I always start my feast with one of them. Don't save them just for pozole, though – I think they go well with just about anything!

In Chiapas, Sopa de pan (see page 274) perfectly blends 'new' Spanish ingredients such as saffron, brought in during colonial times, with local vegetables, chicken and eggs. The Tzotzil, Tzeltal and Lacandon Maya communities uphold cooking practices that are not just functional but spiritual. From shaping clay cooking vessels to elaborate rituals surrounding food, Chiapas is a living synergy of tradition and creativity.

What unites these regions is the ingenuity of their people. Cooking techniques in this part of Mexico are a masterclass in resourcefulness, shaped by landscapes that demand adaptability. The use of natural elements – such as open flames, earth-based ovens, and steaming – reflect the peoples' harmony with their environment. The food that is created here is not just about making dinner – it's a living, breathing heritage that reminds us of where we come from and the stories we carry forward.

Mole Rosa

Pink mole

Serves 4

Made with beetroot and usually served with chicken, turkey or pork, this mole from Guerrero is famed for its beautiful rose colour and sweet–spicy flavour. I tasted it for the first time while watching the baile de la iguana (iguana dance) with my cousin Oscar, and now the two are intertwined in a lasting memory of Guerrero for me.

Ingredients

- 4 chicken marylands, skin on
- ½ white onion
- 4 bay leaves
- 1 tablespoon table salt

Mole rosa

- 1 medium beetroot (beet), peeled
- 30 g (1 oz) sesame seeds
- 30 g (1 oz) pine nuts
- 50 g (⅓ cup) unsalted skinless peanuts
- 50 g (⅓ cup) flaked blanched almonds
- 5 pecans, peeled (see Note on page 184)
- 1 small cinnamon stick
- 3 tablespoons pork lard or vegetable oil
- 40 g (¼ cup) dried cranberries
- 2 tablespoons dried breadcrumbs
- ½ white onion, roughly chopped
- 1 garlic clove, peeled
- 2 allspice berries
- 1 clove
- pinch of ground star anise
- 200 ml (7 fl oz) white wine
- 1 teaspoon table salt
- 1 teaspoon ground white pepper

To serve

- steamed white rice
- Tortillas de maiz page 314 →

Method

Put the chicken in a large saucepan with the onion, bay leaves, salt and 4 litres (4 qts) water. Bring to the boil, then reduce the heat and simmer for 30 minutes, or until the chicken is cooked through. Lift out the chicken and set aside, reserving the broth.

To make the mole, cook the beetroot in 1 litre (4 cups) boiling water for about 15 minutes, or until tender. Drain and set aside.

Lightly toast the sesame seeds, pine nuts, peanuts, almonds, pecans and cinnamon stick, one ingredient at a time, in a dry frying pan over medium heat, keeping your eye on them so they don't burn.

Transfer the toasted ingredients to a food processor. Add the beetroot and 200 ml (7 fl oz) of the reserved chicken broth and blend until smooth. Pass the pink sauce through a strainer.

In a large saucepan, heat the lard over low heat. When hot, add the pink sauce and bring to a simmer, stirring occasionally.

Rinse out the food processor, then blend the cranberries, breadcrumbs, onion, garlic, allspice, clove and star anise with another 1 litre (4 cups) of the chicken broth until smooth. Strain for a silkier texture, then slowly stir into the simmering pink sauce. Stir in the wine, salt and white pepper.

Simmer the mole over low heat for 15–20 minutes, until the sauce thickens and the flavours meld together. Add the chicken to the sauce and simmer for another 10 minutes to heat through.

Serve the chicken and pink mole with steamed white rice and corn tortillas. Add a pink flower to the plate for a gourmet touch if you like!

The mole rosa will keep in an airtight container in the fridge for 4 days.

Pozole Verde

Green pozole

Serves 6

In Guerrero, every Thursday is pozole day! Pozole blanco (see page 120) is a specialty of Guerrero and has been in my life for as long as I can remember. It is considered the base of all pozoles, with the addition of green or red chillies the difference between the other two main pozoles: verde and rojo (see page 151). While pozole blanco is widely consumed in Guerrero, pozole verde is the king of pozoles, and is the one most Guerrerenses go for.

On my last trip to Guerrero with my dad, my Aunt Silvia and Uncle Oscar took us for a drive around the town of Tixtla, where my paternal grandfather was born. The pozolerias always have a range of fruity mezcals available, so of course a few of those came to the table while we waited for our pozoles. If you order pozole in Guerrero, get the small bowl – trust me, it's way bigger than you think! Pozoles are hearty and filling, with sides and snacks arriving before the soup. The meal always starts with 'botana' – tostadas with sour cream and cheese – and a quart of mezcal, so you need to be super hungry!

Ingredients

- 1 kg (2 lb 3 oz) boneless pork shoulder
- 1 kg (2 lb 3 oz) skinless, boneless chicken breasts
- 4 bay leaves
- ½ white onion
- 1 garlic clove, peeled
- 200 g (7 oz) chicharron or pork crackling (see Note overleaf), plus extra to serve
- 1 tablespoon table salt
- 800 g (1 lb 12 oz) tinned hominy, drained and rinsed

Pozole verde sauce

- 2 tablespoons pork lard
- 5 tinned tomatillos
- 1 fresh poblano chilli, seeds and membranes removed, chopped
- 3 fresh jalapeno chillies, seeds and membranes removed, chopped
- ½ white onion, cut into chunks
- 3 garlic cloves, chopped
- ½ bunch of spinach, roughly chopped
- 1 bunch of coriander (cilantro), roughly chopped
- 1 teaspoon dried epazote
- 150 g (5½ oz) roasted pepitas (pumpkin seeds)
- 5 iceberg lettuce leaves, roughly chopped
- 1 teaspoon dried Mexican oregano

Method

Take your largest stockpot and toss in the pork shoulder, chicken, bay leaves, onion, garlic, chicharron or pork crackling, salt and 4 litres (4 qts) water.

Bring to the boil, then reduce the heat and simmer for about 45 minutes, skimming off any foam that rises to the surface. When all the meat is cooked through, lift it out, shred using two forks and set aside. Strain the broth, discarding the aromatics, and keep warm over low heat.

To make the pozole verde sauce, heat the lard in a large saucepan over medium heat. Add the tomatillos, chillies, onion and garlic. Saute for about 10 minutes, until golden. Add the spinach, coriander and epazote, and cook, giving it all a good mix as you go, until the greens wilt. Stir in the roasted pepitas and cook for another 2 minutes. Toss in the lettuce and oregano and leave to soften. Remove from the heat.

Allow the mixture to cool a little, then blend the whole lot in a food processor with enough of the meat broth to achieve a smooth and creamy sauce.

Recipe continues →

Pour the blended sauce back into the saucepan and cook over medium heat for 30 minutes, stirring constantly so the sauce doesn't stick or burn. Taste for seasoning and add salt as needed.

Meanwhile, add the hominy to the warm stockpot of pork broth and simmer for 15 minutes, until the hominy grains pop open. Add the pozole verde sauce, stir well, and let it all bubble together for 15 minutes. Add a little water if it's too thick – it's your pozole, so make it how you like!

To serve, spoon a generous helping of hominy, shredded meat and soup into each bowl.

Load up with your favourite toppings and serve immediately, with your chosen sides.

The broth and poached meats will keep in separate airtight containers in the fridge for 4 days.

Note

You can buy pork crackling in the supermarket, in the chips (crisps) aisle.

Topping options

- Mexican oregano
- diced white onion
- sliced avocado
- lime wedges
- radish slices
- toasted dried arbol chillies
- haloumi or queso ranchero, crumbled
- sardine fillets (optional, but very authentic)

To serve

Tostadas page 318 →

sour cream and queso fresco, Cotija or feta, crumbled

Chiles capones page 260 →

Pickled pork trotters page 262 →

Salsa verde page 286 →

Mole Coloradito

Soft red mole

Serves 4

Mole coloradito is one of the seven famous moles of Oaxaca. In my opinion, it's the easiest to make, so it's a perfect starting point for the beginner mole cook – not every mole has to be a culinary marathon! Its name comes from the reddish-brown colour of the sauce ('colorado' means 'red' in Spanish).

On one trip to Oaxaca I had the chance to try all seven moles from the area. All different, all delicious – and all so Mexican!

Ingredients

- 1 kg (2 lb 3 oz) chicken drumsticks, skin removed
- ½ white onion
- 4 bay leaves
- 1 tablespoon table salt

Mole coloradito

- 20 g (¾ oz) flaked blanched almonds
- 40 g (1½ oz) sesame seeds
- 40 g (1½ oz) raisins
- 1 cinnamon stick
- 5 allspice berries
- 3 cloves
- 2 garlic cloves, peeled
- 3 roma (plum) tomatoes
- 3 tinned tomatillos, or 3 fresh green bell peppers (capsicums), stems and seeds removed
- ½ white onion, cut into big chunks
- 1 teaspoon table salt
- 3 dried ancho chillies, stems and seeds removed
- 2 dried guajillo chillies, stems and seeds removed
- 20 g (¾ oz) dried breadcrumbs
- 1 teaspoon pork lard
- 25 g (1 oz) brown sugar

To serve

- steamed white rice
- Tortillas de maiz page 314 →
- Frijoles negros refritos page 322 →

Method

Put the chicken in a large saucepan with the onion, bay leaves, salt and 3 litres (3 qts) water. Bring to the boil, then reduce the heat and simmer for 30 minutes, or until the chicken is cooked through. Lift out the chicken and set aside, leaving the broth in the pan over very low heat.

Meanwhile, make the mole. Heat a comal or heavy-based frying pan over medium heat. Lightly toast the almonds until fragrant and golden, keeping your eye on them so they don't burn, then transfer to a bowl. Lightly toast the sesame seeds, then the raisins – and then, in separate batches, the cinnamon stick, allspice berries, cloves and garlic, adding them all to the bowl.

Add the tomatoes, tomatillos and onion to the pan. Sprinkle with the salt and cook, stirring now and then, for 5–10 minutes, to let the juices run out.

Pour 500 ml (2 cups) of the reserved hot chicken broth into a heatproof bowl. Add all the dried chillies and soak them in the hot broth for about 10 minutes, until they're soft and pliable.

Place the softened chillies and their soaking liquid in a blender. Add the breadcrumbs, brown sugar, toasted ingredients and tomatillo mixture. Blend until you have a smooth and rich paste, adding a splash more chicken broth to help the blender if needed. The sauce should be thick but pourable.

Recipe continues →

Heat the pork lard in a large saucepan over medium heat. Add the blended chilli mixture and the remaining chicken broth. Cook for about 40 minutes, stirring often to prevent sticking or burning. The mole should thicken slightly as the flavours meld together. Stir through the brown sugar.

For the last 10 minutes of cooking, add the chicken so it heats through.

Serve the mole with steamed white rice, tortillas and refried black beans.

The mole coloradito will keep in an airtight container in the fridge for 4 days.

Chiles Capones

Cheese-stuffed chillies

Makes 8

These are one of the classic snacks to accompany pozole, especially in Guerrero. Whenever I sit down at a pozoleria, I start the feast with one of these beauties. It's a bit of a gamble as to whether it will be spicy or not, but it's always an exciting way to dive into the array of snacks that go with the meal.

These spicy little treats are a staple on the region's tables and go well with just about any dish. I have a fond memory of eating them at my aunt Tía Gloria's house. I dropped by unannounced one afternoon and they were eating taquitos (small crispy stuffed tortillas) with chiles capones. They were smoky, creamy and melted in the mouth. Pure bliss!

Ingredients

- 8 fresh jalapeno chillies (preferably green)
- 200 g (7 oz) ricotta
- 1 white onion, finely diced
- 1 tablespoon dried Mexican oregano
- 1 teaspoon table salt

Method

Preheat a barbecue grill or use a stovetop gas flame to char the chillies, turning occasionally, until the skins are blackened and blistered. Using tongs, immediately transfer the chillies to a large zip-lock bag and let them sweat for 5–10 minutes – this will make peeling them much easier. Once the chillies are cool enough to handle, trim the stems, leaving the base attached to the chillies, then peel away and discard the skins. Carefully slit each chilli open lengthways and remove the seeds, keeping the chilli intact for stuffing. Dry with paper towel.

Put the ricotta, onion, oregano and salt in a bowl. Beat together with a fork until well combined.

Stuff the chillies with the ricotta filling and they're ready to serve!

The chiles capones will keep in an airtight container in the fridge for 4 days.

Fiambre

Mixed meat platter

Serves 4

What makes this dish so special is the vibrant dressing: a zingy mix of vinegar, spices and chillies.

When I was little, visiting Uncle Juan's house in Guerrero always meant a feast, with fiambre as the star dish. I would avoid the pig trotters, sticking to the beef and chicken. Uncle Juan used to joke, 'One day, you'll fight over those trotters,' and I'd laugh, thinking, never!

Fast forward, and now my son Julio and I argue over who gets the last one. Those trotters, with their irresistible gelatinous texture and tangy flavour, are my favourite part.

This recipe has a lot of different elements, but don't be alarmed. You don't have to cook the beef, trotters and chicken all at the same time. You can prepare them in stages, then pull it all together at the end.

The cooked beef, trotters, chicken and dressing will keep in the fridge in separate airtight containers for 4 days. The dish needs to be served hot – the trotters are best steamed to bring their temperature back up, but the chicken and beef can simply be warmed in a pan until heated through.

Method

Marinate the beef: Put the chillies and tomatoes in a saucepan with 250 ml (1 cup) water. Bring to the boil and boil for 5 minutes, then remove from the heat and leave in the water to cool.

Remove the stems from the chillies, then tip the cooled mixture (including the cooking water) into a food processor. Add the bay leaf, onion, garlic, salt, white pepper and vinegar. Blend until very smooth.

Transfer to a large bowl and add the beef, tossing to coat all over. Cover and marinate in the fridge for at least 2 hours.

Heat the lard in a large saucepan over low heat. Add the beef with its marinade and cook, stirring often, for 30 minutes, until the meat is fully cooked and tender.

Prepare the trotter: Put the trotter in a large saucepan with 1 litre (4 cups) water. Bring to the boil and boil for 5 minutes, then drain.

Put the trotter in a pressure cooker with the bay leaves, onion, garlic, 1 tablespoon salt and 2 litres (2 qts) water (see Note). Seal the lid on, bring up to pressure, then cook for 45 minutes, until the trotter is soft and tender. Release the pressure using the quick-release method recommended by the manufacturer.

Ingredients

Marinated beef

- 2 dried guajillo chillies
- 1 roma (plum) tomato
- 1 bay leaf
- ¼ onion, roughly chopped
- 1 teaspoon crushed garlic
- ½ teaspoon table salt
- ½ teaspoon ground white pepper
- 1½ teaspoons white vinegar
- 500 g (1 lb 2 oz) chuck steak, cut into 4 cm (1½ in) chunks
- 1 tablespoon pork lard or vegetable oil

Pork trotter

- 1 pork trotter, cut in half lengthways
- 2 bay leaves
- ½ onion
- 2 garlic cloves, peeled
- table salt
- 1 tablespoon white vinegar
- 1 teaspoon dried Mexican oregano
- 1 teaspoon ground white pepper

Strain the liquid, place the trotter in a bowl and leave to cool for 20 minutes. Add the vinegar, oregano, white pepper and another 1 teaspoon salt and toss gently to coat.

Marinate the chicken: In a food processor, blend together the onion, garlic, bay leaves, vinegar, salt, white pepper and 300 ml (10 fl oz) water to make a thick marinade.

Heat the oil in a large saucepan over medium heat, then brown the chicken for 5–7 minutes, turning often. Add the marinade and simmer gently for 30 minutes, until the chicken is cooked through.

Make the dressing: Combine the ingredients and 125 ml (½ cup) water in a saucepan and cook, stirring, over low heat, until the sugar has dissolved.

Assemble and serve: Arrange the shredded lettuce on a serving platter. Add a good amount of the dressing, then top with the beef, chicken, pork trotter and crumbled chorizo.

Serve hot, with baguette slices or tortillas and pickled chillies, and with the remaining dressing on the side.

Note

If you don't have a pressure cooker, simply bring the ingredients to the boil in a large saucepan, then cover and cook over medium heat for about 3 hours, until the trotter is cooked.

Marinated chicken

- 1 onion, roughly chopped
- 2 teaspoons crushed garlic
- 2 bay leaves
- 1 tablespoon white vinegar
- 1 teaspoon table salt
- 1 teaspoon ground white pepper
- 1 tablespoon vegetable oil
- 4 chicken drumsticks, skin removed

Agrito dressing

- 125 ml (½ cup) white vinegar
- 1 teaspoon brown sugar
- ¼ teaspoon table salt
- ¼ teaspoon freshly ground black pepper
- juice of 1 lime

To serve

- ½ iceberg lettuce, shredded
- 250 g (9 oz) Mexican-style fresh chorizo, crumbled and cooked
- sliced baguette or Tortillas de maiz page 314 →
- Chiles en vinagre page 330 →

Tlayudas

Mexican corn pizzas

Makes 12

Tlayudas are the heart and soul of Oaxacan street food – crunchy, oversized tortillas, loaded with all the good stuff! I ate tlayudas in Oaxaca with my son, Julio, who got hooked on a combo of beef, chorizo, crickets and insect salsa ... surely a flavour adventure that only Oaxaca can deliver.

Oaxaca also brings its own unique tools to the kitchen – including the gigantic tlayuda press which turns out tortillas about 35–40 cm (14–16 in) in diameter. But don't worry, we're making regular tortilla-sized tlayudas here.

Method

To make the tlayuda bases, use the same method for making the corn tortillas on page 314, but cook them for about 2 minutes longer in the comal or frying pan so they have a crunchier consistency.

Make sure the lard is at room temperature and the refried beans and cecina are heated.

Heat the vegetable oil in a frying pan over medium heat, add the chorizo and cook for 3–4 minutes, until lightly browned and cooked through.

To assemble each tlayuda, spread some lard over the cooked tlayuda base to cover the surface. Add 3 tablespoons of refried beans to each one, a handful of shredded cheese, some cecina, a spoonful of crumbled chorizo, then top with sliced tomato, avocado and onion – almost like making a pizza. Serve with the salsa on the side.

Untopped tlayuda bases will keep in the pantry in a sealed bag or plastic wrap for 3 days.

Ingredients

12 Tortillas de maiz page 314 →

200 g (7 oz) pork lard, softened

400 g (14 oz) Frijoles negros refritos, warmed page 322 →

1 × quantity Cecina, warmed page 132 →

2 teaspoons vegetable oil

500 g (1 lb 2 oz) Mexican-style fresh chorizo, skin removed, crumbled

800 g (1 lb 12 oz) Oaxaca cheese or mozzarella, shredded

4 roma (plum) tomatoes, seeds removed, sliced

4 avocados, sliced

1 white onion, sliced

Salsa macha, to serve page 294 →

Quesadillas de Flor de Calabaza

Zucchini flower quesadillas

Makes 10

Zucchini flower quesadillas are an absolute treat across Mexico, but they hit a whole new level of amazing in Oaxaca. Their zucchini flowers are huge and super fresh, and the Oaxacan cheese is always freshly made and authentically traditional.

When my friend Ana María took me on a tour of Oaxaca's villages, we tried these quesadillas just about everywhere, served with a roasted salsa.

The recipe below uses an oval tortilla press to shape the quesadillas. If you don't have one of these, don't worry. Just use a regular tortilla press and roll 50 g (1¾ oz) balls of dough instead, and reduce the amount of filling accordingly. And if you don't have a tortilla press, simply flatten them by hand as thinly as possible, using a rolling pin or even a wine bottle!

Ingredients

- 3 tablespoons vegetable oil
- ½ white onion, diced
- 100 g (3½ oz) fresh zucchini (courgette) flowers, stamens removed
- 1 teaspoon table salt
- ¾ × quantity Tortilla de maiz dough, made with blue corn masa flour page 314 →
- 500 g (1 lb 2 oz) Oaxaca cheese or firm mozzarella, grated
- Salsa roja, to serve page 286 →

Method

Heat the oil in a frying pan over medium heat and saute the onion for 3 minutes. Add the zucchini flowers and salt and gently stir. Set aside.

Divide the dough into 10 even portions, about 70 g (2½ oz) each. Shape the portions into ovals. Place a plastic food bag over the bottom half of an oval tortilla press and place a portion of dough in the middle. Cover with another plastic food bag, then close the lid and gently press to flatten the dough into a 26 cm × 11 cm (10¼ in × 4¼ in) oval. Open the tortilla press and remove the top plastic bag.

Heat a comal or heavy-based frying pan over medium–high heat. Place 50 g (1¾ oz) of the cheese and about 1 tablespoon of the zucchini flower mixture along the length of the tortilla in the middle, then fold the tortilla in half lengthways. Flip the tortilla onto your hand, remove the bottom plastic bag and place in the pan. Cook, flipping frequently, until the cheese has melted and the quesadilla is slightly crisp. Repeat with the remaining ingredients to make 10 quesadillas.

Serve hot, with the salsa roja!

Any leftover quesadillas will keep in an airtight container in the fridge for 4 days. Just heat them up in a pan for 2–3 minutes each side until the cheese melts.

Tamales de Cambray

Chiapas-style tamales

Makes 10

Tamales de cambray are a beloved classic from Chiapas. The version below is made with corn dough stuffed with poached chicken, prunes, red bell pepper and almonds, and wrapped in banana leaves instead of corn husks (although you can use corn husks if you prefer). Bursting with flavour and texture, these tamales are perfect for a special gathering.

Ingredients

- 1 kg (2 lb 3 oz) boneless, skinless chicken breasts
- 2 bay leaves
- ½ onion
- table salt
- 500 ml (2 cups) Mole poblano page 185 →
- 200 g (7 oz) pork lard
- 1 teaspoon baking powder
- 500 g (1 lb 2 oz) masa flour, sifted
- 1 teaspoon achiote paste
- 4 banana leaves, cut into 15 cm (6 in) squares
- 1 red bell pepper (capsicum), cut into 10 slices
- 200 g (7 oz) flaked blanched almonds
- 10 prunes, cut in half, stones removed

Method

Put the chicken in a large saucepan with the bay leaves, onion, 1 tablespoon salt and 2 litres (2 qts) water. Bring to the boil, then reduce the heat and simmer for about 30 minutes, until the chicken is tender and cooked through. Lift out the chicken, reserving the broth. Shred the chicken using two forks, let it cool in a bowl, then mix with the mole poblano to coat.

Place the lard and baking powder in a large bowl and whip the mixture as fast as possible with a wooden spoon – the lard needs to soften and look spongy. Don't stress if this takes a long time; it can take up to 15 minutes to achieve the right consistency. Once the lard is ready, add the masa flour, 2 teaspoons salt, the achiote paste and 650 ml (22 fl oz) of the warm chicken broth and mix well. To test if the dough is ready, drop a small ball of dough into a cup of cold water; if it floats to the top you're good to go!

Spread 80 g (2¾ oz) of the dough in the middle of a banana leaf square, leaving a 4 cm (1½ in) border around each edge. Add 50 g (1¾ oz) of the chicken mole, 1 slice of red bell pepper, 1 tablespoon flaked almonds and 2 prune halves. Cover with another 20 g (¾ oz) of dough. Wrap the banana leaf around the filling and secure with kitchen string. Repeat to make 10 tamales.

Place the tamales in a large steamer, stacking them on top of each other. Fit as many tamales as you can into the steamer, but be careful not to pack them in too tightly as they can burst. Place the steamer over a saucepan of simmering water and steam for 45 minutes.

The best way to check if your tamales are cooked is to remove one from the steamer, let it cool for 5 minutes and then unwrap. If the dough doesn't stick to the banana leaf and looks shiny and fluffy, then your tamales are ready.

Let the tamales cool for 15–20 minutes inside the steamer before serving.

The tamales will keep in an airtight container in the fridge for 4 days.

Cochito al Horno

Baked marinated pork

Serves 4

This dish is all about comfort and tradition. Slow-cooked to perfection, the pork becomes incredibly tender – a true taste of Chiapas.

Cochito always makes me think of my friend Angie. When she was in Australia, she used to tell me how much she missed the food from her hometown, especially this dish, and we'd laugh about how often she'd find herself craving it. Now that Angie's back home in Chiapas with her Australian husband, I'm pretty sure cochito will be a regular on their dinner table. I wonder what foods her husband is craving?

Ingredients

- 2 fresh tomatillos, or 2 roughly chopped green bell peppers (capsicums)
- ½ white onion, cut into chunks
- 1 garlic clove, peeled
- 2 dried ancho chillies, stems and seeds removed
- 4 dried guajillo chillies, stems and seeds removed
- 2 bay leaves
- 2 teaspoons white vinegar
- 1 teaspoon dried thyme
- 1 teaspoon ground cloves
- 1 teaspoon table salt
- 1 teaspoon freshly ground black pepper
- 1 tablespoon pork lard or vegetable oil
- 1 kg (2 lb 3 oz) boneless pork shoulder, cut into 3 cm (1¼ in) chunks

To serve

- steamed white rice
- Frijoles negros refritos page 322 →
- Salsa borracha page 290 →

Method

Preheat the oven to 160°C (320°F) fan-forced.

Put the tomatillos, onion, garlic and dried chillies in a food processor with the bay leaves, vinegar, thyme, clove, salt, pepper and lard. Add 1 litre (4 cups) water and blend together.

Pour the sauce into a bowl. Add the pork and gently mix to coat all over. Transfer to a large baking dish and bake for 2 hours, or until the pork is tender and slightly dry.

Serve warm, with steamed white rice, refried beans and salsa.

The cochito will keep in an airtight container in the fridge for 4 days.

Sopa de Pan

Bread soup

Serves 4

This recipe has deep colonial roots, blending Spanish ingredients, such as saffron, with local produce from Chiapas. Bread soaks up the saffron-infused broth, fried plantain adds a sweet–savoury twist, and layers of vegetables, chicken and hard-boiled eggs tie it all together.

This is a rich, thick, bread-pudding-meets-soup dish that very much feels as if you're eating your way through Chiapas history, one bite at a time!

Ingredients

- 2 carrots, sliced on an angle
- 2 potatoes, sliced on an angle
- 20 g (¾ oz) green beans, trimmed
- 1 tablespoon sultanas (golden raisins)
- 3 tablespoons vegetable oil
- 1 ripe plantain, peeled and sliced on an angle
- 2 teaspoons pork lard, plus extra for greasing
- 2 roma (plum) tomatoes, sliced on an angle
- ½ onion, chopped
- 2 zucchini (courgettes), sliced on an angle
- 1 cinnamon stick
- 1 teaspoon dried Mexican oregano
- 1 teaspoon freshly ground black pepper
- 1 teaspoon chicken stock powder
- pinch of saffron threads
- 1 French baguette, cut into 1 cm (½ in) thick slices
- 4 hard-boiled eggs, peeled and sliced

For the broth

- 600 g (1 lb 5 oz) skinless boneless chicken breasts
- 1 garlic clove, peeled
- 4 bay leaves
- ½ onion
- 1 tablespoon table salt

Method

To make the broth, put the chicken in a large saucepan with the garlic, bay leaves, onion, salt and 2 litres (2 qts) water. Bring to the boil, then reduce the heat and simmer for about 30 minutes, until the chicken is cooked through. Lift out the chicken, leaving the broth in the pan over very low heat. Shred the chicken and set aside.

Meanwhile, simmer the carrot, potato, green beans and sultanas in a saucepan of water for about 10 minutes, until tender. Drain.

Heat the vegetable oil in a frying pan over medium heat and fry the plantain on both sides for about 3 minutes, until lightly golden. Remove to a plate.

Heat the lard in the same pan. Add the tomato and onion and saute for 5–10 minutes, until softened. Spoon this mixture into the pan of chicken broth and bring to a gentle boil. Add the zucchini, cinnamon stick, oregano, pepper, stock powder and saffron and keep warm at a low simmer.

Meanwhile, toast the baguette slices until crisp and lightly golden.

Now for the layering! Lightly grease a deep serving dish with a thin layer of lard. Build up layers of toasted bread, shredded chicken, vegetables, plantain and egg. Keep layering until everything is used up, saving some egg slices for the top.

Pour the saffron-infused broth over the layers, letting the bread soak it all up. The 'soup' won't be too soupy – it's meant to be thick and hearty. Top with the remaining egg and it's ready to take to the table and ladle out into bowls.

This is a dish that's best enjoyed immediately, as the bread will become soggy as it absorbs all the broth.

CACAO

One of the world's most revered ingredients – described by the Maya as 'food of the gods' – started off as a tiny cacao bean in the rainforests of ancient Mesoamerica. But cacao (*Theobroma cacao*) has been central to the cultures of this region for thousands of years, long before it was turned into the 'chocolate' we know today.

There is evidence that the Olmecs, who lived around Veracruz and Tabasco from 1200 BCE to 400 BCE, might have domesticated the cacao tree – but it was the Maya who really kicked things off. They turned those beans into a thick, bitter drink called 'xocolatl', spiced it up with flavourings such as chilli and annatto, and drank it for their sacred ceremonies.

Cacao was so important to the Maya that they also used it as currency. A single cacao bean was worth as much as a tortilla or an egg, and it became a major bartering chip in local trade and commerce.

The Mexica (Aztecs), who rose to power after the Maya, took cacao to another level, turning the sacred drink into a daily beverage for the elites. Their version of xocolatl was made with cacao, ground maize, vanilla and sometimes a little chilli. Unlike the Maya, who regarded cacao as the food *of* the gods, the Mexica believed cacao was a gift to them *from* the gods, and that the god of wisdom and life, Quetzalcoatl, brought the cacao tree to Earth. The Mexica would also offer cacao to the gods during their religious rituals.

When the Spanish arrived in the 16th century, they were intrigued by this exotic drink, but, unused to its dark bitterness, they sweetened it by adding sugar and honey. This was the start of the chocolate we are familiar with. The Spanish excitedly took this amazing new ingredient to Europe, where it quickly became a hit – but they also brought along cacao seeds, and soon the plant was being cultivated in tropical regions all around the world.

During colonial times, cacao became one of Mexico's most valuable exports and an important part of the country's economy. While the Spanish exploited the local population to work on large plantations around Veracruz, Tabasco and Oaxaca, the cacao bean itself remained integral to the region's identity. The cacao bean wasn't just a product for export, but something all Mexicans had become deeply connected to, from the rural farmers who grew it, to the cooks who used it in traditional dishes such as mole.

Even after thousands of years, our fascination and love for this magical tiny bean remains.

Churros

Mexican doughnuts

Makes 15

In winter, city cafes will put out signs to entice customers to enjoy these crunchy, pillowy-centred doughnuts with a warming bowl of melted chocolate to dip them in. When I was growing up, we had a favourite churros place three blocks from my grandma's house. A large churros machine churned out lengths of dough that went into huge vats of bubbling oil, deep-frying the little doughnuts to achieve that distinctive crunch.

Ingredients

- 1 litre (4 cups) vegetable oil
- 250 g (1⅔ cups) plain (all-purpose) flour
- 100 g (3½ oz) caster (superfine) sugar
- 2 teaspoons ground cinnamon
- 1 teaspoon table salt

Chocolate dipping sauce

- 2 × 90 g (3 oz) bars of Mexican chocolate (see Note), broken into chunks
- pinch of ground cinnamon
- 60–70 g (2–2½ fl oz) thickened or pouring cream

Method

Heat the oil in a large heavy-based saucepan to 180°C (350°F).

Meanwhile, place the flour in a large heatproof bowl, and combine the sugar and cinnamon on a plate.

Heat 250 ml (1 cup) water in a small saucepan to 60°C (140°F) on a kitchen thermometer. Stir in the salt.

Pour the warm salty water into the flour and use a wooden spoon to mix until you have a sticky dough. Cool for 5 minutes, then transfer to a piping bag fitted with a 1 cm (½ in) star nozzle.

Working in batches, pipe 10 cm (4 in) lengths of the dough into the hot oil and fry for 2 minutes, or until brown and crisp. Using a slotted spoon, lift the churros onto a plate lined with paper towel to drain. Roll the hot churros in the cinnamon sugar to coat.

Meanwhile, make the dipping sauce. Melt the chocolate in a heatproof bowl placed over a pan of simmering water (don't let the base of the bowl sit in the water). Stir in the cinnamon and enough cream to make a dipping sauce.

Serve the warm churros with the dipping sauce.

Note

You can buy Mexican chocolate online or from Latin American grocery stores.

Chilate

Rice and cacao water

Serves 4

Known for its warm and humid climate, the Costa Chica ('Short Coast') along Mexico's Pacific Coast from Guerrero to neighbouring Oaxaca has long been a fertile area for growing cacao. This popular drink, with its earthy, smoky taste, came about thanks to a fusion of indigenous and African cultures in Costa Chica. Local cacao was mixed with rice – a crop introduced to Mexico during the colonial period by enslaved Africans – then ground to a paste with piloncillo added as a sweetener and dissolved in water to make a rich, foamy drink. Today, chilateras (the women who sell this drink in Costa Chica) will pour their chilate from a jicara, holding it as high up as possible, making the drink foam up as much as they can!

I have only tried chilled chilate from the shops or freshly served over ice from street stalls, but you can also drink it hot.

Ingredients

- 120 g (4½ oz) piloncillo, grated, or soft brown sugar
- 150 g (¾ cup) jasmine rice
- 2 teaspoons ground cinnamon
- 50 g (1¾ oz) cacao powder
- ice cubes, to serve

Method

Combine the sugar, rice, cinnamon, cacao and 1 litre (4 cups) water in a large bowl and leave to soak for at least 1 hour, until the rice has softened.

Transfer to a food processor and blitz until the rice has completely broken down and everything is well combined – ideally, you want this to be foamy.

Strain the mixture until smooth. Pour into a cocktail shaker with ice and give it an extra shake, then serve in chilled glasses over ice.

The chilate will keep in a sealed jar in the fridge for up to 5 days. Give it a quick shake in a cocktail shaker with ice before serving.

Tascalate

Tortilla water

Serves 1–2

Tascalate is a traditional, centuries-old ceremonial drink from the highlands of Chiapas. It was originally made by the indigenous Zoque people by grinding roasted maize with cacao, achiote and spices. The name 'tascalate' comes from the Nahuatl term for 'corn dough'. It was drunk during important rituals and was also believed to have medicinal properties.

Now it's a popular drink on a hot day, with its unique blend of sweet and savoury ingredients – richness from cacao, slight earthiness from achiote, and with a hint of sweetness from the sugar.

Method

Toast the tortilla in a hot comal or frying pan for about 3 minutes, until crispy.

Crumble the toasted tortilla into a blender. Add the chocolate powder and pour in the milk, then blitz to bring it all together.

Add the achiote paste, coffee and sugar. Blend again until smooth, making sure the tortilla is fully broken down. Strain the mixture to ensure the liquid is smooth, then return to the blender, along with the ice cubes, and blend again.

Pour into glasses and serve.

The tascalate will keep in a sealed jar in the fridge for up to 8 hours.

Ingredients

- 1 Tortilla de maiz page 314 →
- 1 teaspoon Mexican chocolate powder or cacao powder
- 250 ml (1 cup) milk
- 1 teaspoon achiote paste
- 1 teaspoon instant coffee
- 1 teaspoon soft brown sugar
- 4 ice cubes

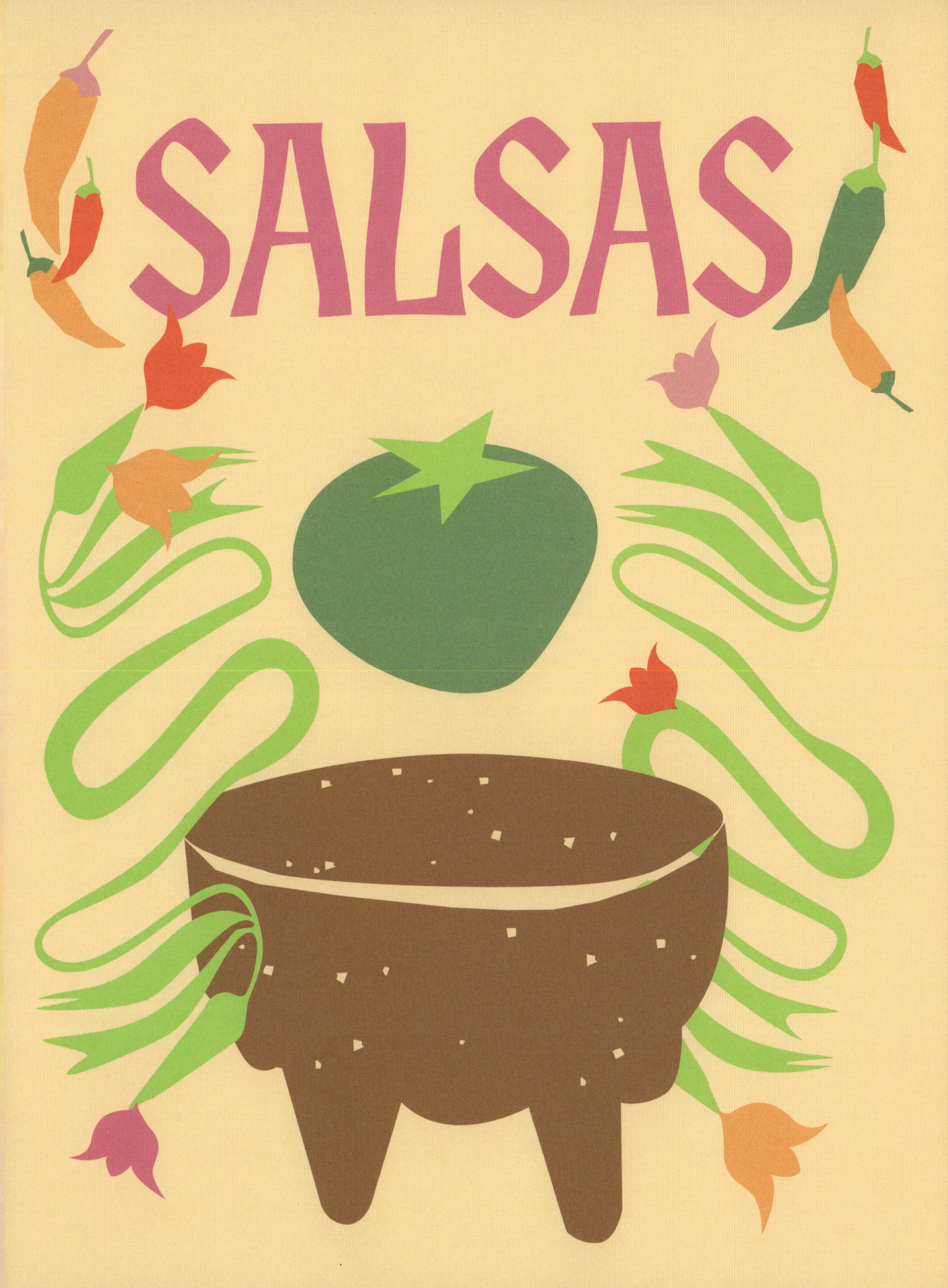
SALSAS

Green salsa

Salsa Verde

Makes about 250 ml (1 cup)

Enough for 10 tacos

Ingredients

- 300 g (10½ oz) fresh or tinned tomatillos
- 10 fresh green chillies, such as jalapeno, serrano or long chillies, roughly chopped
- ½ white onion, roughly chopped
- ½ garlic clove, finely chopped
- 1 teaspoon table salt
- 1 small bunch of coriander (cilantro) leaves, finely chopped

Method

If you are lucky enough to find fresh tomatillos, remove the husks and thoroughly wash the fruit. If using tinned tomatillos, drain and rinse them. Roughly chop the tomatillos.

Heat a dry comal or large heavy-based frying pan over medium–high heat. Add the tomatillos, chilli and onion and cook, stirring frequently, for about 5–7 minutes, until charred on all sides.

Using a blender or molcajete, blend or pound the charred tomatillo mixture with the garlic, salt and 250 ml (1 cup) water, until you have a chunky salsa.

Stir through the coriander and transfer to a serving bowl.

The salsa verde will keep in an airtight container in the fridge for up to 1 week.

Red salsa

Salsa Roja

Makes about 250 ml (1 cup)

Enough for 10 tacos

Ingredients

- 4 large tomatoes, chopped
- ½ white onion, roughly chopped
- 3 dried arbol or pequin chillies
- ½ garlic clove, finely chopped
- 1 teaspoon table salt
- 1 small bunch of (1 oz) coriander (cilantro) leaves, finely chopped
- 3 tablespoons vegetable oil (if making a cooked salsa)

Method

Heat a dry comal or heavy-based frying pan over medium–high heat. Add the tomato and onion and cook, stirring frequently, for about 7 minutes, until slightly charred.

Place the dried chillies in a small saucepan. Cover with 250 ml (1 cup) water and bring to the boil. Cook for 5–8 minutes, until the chillies are soft. Set aside to cool for 5 minutes, then remove the stems.

Using a blender or molcajete, blend or pound the charred tomato and onion with the garlic, salt, chillies and 1 teaspoon of their cooking water, until you have a chunky salsa. Stir through the coriander and transfer to a serving bowl.

I prefer to serve salsa roja fresh, but it can also be cooked. To cook the salsa, heat the oil in a small saucepan over medium–high heat. Add the salsa and cook, stirring, for 7 minutes, or until heated through and slightly reduced. The salsa is ready when the colour changes to a dark orange. Set aside to cool before serving.

I recommend eating this salsa on the day it's made, as the tomato is delicate and will start to collapse into a liquidy mess after a few hours.

Chipotle salsa

Salsa de Chipotle

Makes about 750 ml (3 cups)

Enough for 25 tacos

Ingredients

- 50 g (1¾ oz) chipotle chillies in adobo sauce
- 4 tomatoes, roughly chopped
- ½ white onion, roughly chopped
- 1 garlic clove, peeled
- 1 teaspoon table salt
- 2 tablespoons vegetable oil

Method

Put the chipotle chillies, tomato, onion, garlic and salt in a blender and blend until you have a smooth, runny salsa.

Heat the oil in a frying pan over medium heat. Add the salsa and cook, stirring, for 5 minutes. Transfer to a bowl and set aside to cool.

The salsa will keep in an airtight container in the fridge for up to 5 days.

Chipotle mayonnaise

Mayonesa de Chipotle

Makes about 350 g (12½ oz)

Ingredients

- 150 g (5½ oz) whole-egg mayonnaise
- 30 g (1 oz) sour cream
- 50 g (1¾ oz) chipotle chillies in adobo sauce
- juice of ½ lime
- 1 teaspoon table salt
- pinch of freshly ground black pepper

Method

Place all the ingredients in a blender and pour in 100 ml (3½ fl oz) water and blend until smooth.

The chipotle chillies bring that smoky heat, the mayo and sour cream deliver the creamy goodness and a little lime juice adds that zing.

The chipotle mayo will keep in an airtight container in the fridge for up to 1 week.

Fresh salsa

Pico de Gallo

Makes about 450 g (2½ cups)

Serves 4

Ingredients

- ½ white onion, finely diced
- 4 fresh green jalapeno, serrano or Thai chillies, finely chopped
- handful of coriander (cilantro) leaves, finely chopped
- juice of 2 limes
- 1 teaspoon table salt
- 3 tomatoes, cut into 1 cm (½ in) dice

Method

Place the onion, chilli and coriander in a bowl, add the lime juice and salt and gently stir until the salt is fully incorporated.

Stir through the tomato and serve immediately.

Pico de gallo is best eaten on the day it is made.

Drunken salsa

Salsa Borracha

Makes about 500 ml (2 cups)

Enough for 15 tacos

Ingredients

- 1 tablespoon vegetable oil
- 10 fresh green chillies, such as jalapeno, serrano or cayenne, finely chopped
- 3 tomatoes, diced
- ½ white onion, diced
- 1 garlic clove, finely chopped
- 100 g (3½ oz) coriander (cilantro) leaves, finely chopped
- 2 teaspoons table salt
- 330 ml (11 fl oz) bottle of Mexican lager

Method

Heat the oil in a heavy-based frying pan over medium heat. Add the chilli, tomato, onion, garlic, coriander and salt and cook, stirring frequently, for about 7 minutes, until you have a thick salsa.

Stir in the beer and cook for a further 5 minutes. Transfer the salsa to a bowl and set aside to cool.

Once cooled, place half the salsa in a blender and blend until smooth. Return it to the bowl and stir it through the remaining salsa.

The salsa will keep in an airtight container in the fridge for up to 1 week.

Taco salsa

Salsa Taquera

Makes about 500 ml (2 cups)

Enough for 20 tacos

Ingredients

- 300 g (10½ oz) fresh or tinned tomatillos
- 2 garlic cloves, peeled
- 1 tomato
- 3 tablespoons vegetable oil
- ½ white onion, halved
- 2 dried guajillo chillies
- 10 dried arbol chillies (or fresh cayenne or Thai red chillies)
- 1 teaspoon table salt

Method

If you are lucky enough to find fresh tomatillos, remove the husks and thoroughly wash the fruit.

Place the tomatillos in a saucepan with the garlic, tomato, 1 tablespoon of the oil, an onion quarter and 250 ml (1 cup) water. Bring to the boil and cook for 3 minutes. Remove from the heat, cover the pan and set aside to cool to room temperature.

Heat the remaining oil in a frying pan over low heat. Add the guajillo chillies and cook, stirring, for 3 minutes on each side, making sure the chillies don't burn. Using a slotted spoon, remove the chillies and add them to the tomatillo mixture. Repeat with the arbol chillies.

Using a blender or molcajete, blend or pound the tomatillo mixture until you have a chunky salsa.

Place the salsa in a serving bowl, finely chop the remaining onion quarter and stir it through, along with the salt, just before serving.

The salsa will keep in an airtight container in the fridge for up to 1 week.

Brave salsa

Salsa Macha

Makes about 300 ml (10½ fl oz)

Enough for 15 tacos

Ingredients

- 10 garlic cloves, finely sliced
- 1 teaspoon table salt
- 100 ml (3½ fl oz) vegetable oil
- 200 ml (7 fl oz) extra virgin olive oil, plus extra if needed
- 25 g (1 oz) dried arbol chillies
- 25 g (1 oz) dried pequin chillies
- 10 g (¼ oz) dried morita chillies

Method

Combine the garlic and salt in a small bowl.

Heat the vegetable oil in a frying pan over medium heat. Add the salty garlic and cook, stirring, for 4–5 minutes, until lightly golden. Do not let the garlic burn, or your salsa will be bitter. Transfer the garlicky oil to a heatproof bowl.

Heat the olive oil in a frying pan over low heat. Add all the dried chillies and cook, stirring, for 3 minutes, or until the arbol chillies darken in colour. Remove from the heat, set aside to cool slightly, then add the chillies and oil to the garlic oil. Set the mixture aside to cool to room temperature.

Transfer the chilli mixture to a blender and blend until smooth. Add a little more olive oil if you prefer a runnier consistency.

The salsa will keep in an airtight container in the pantry for up to 6 months.

Salsa Chamoy

Makes about 350 g (12½ oz)

Ingredients

- 150 g (5½ oz) dried apricots, roughly chopped
- 20 g (¾ oz) dried plums (see Note), chopped
- 20 g (¾ oz) dried hibiscus flowers (see Note)
- 2 tablespoons tamarind puree
- 1 dried guajillo chilli, stem and seeds removed
- 110 g (½ cup) brown sugar
- 2 teaspoons Tajin seasoning
- 1 tablespoon Mexican chilli powder
- juice of 2 limes
- juice of 1 orange

Method

Place the dried apricots and plums in a saucepan with the hibiscus flowers, tamarind puree, chilli and 250 ml (1 cup) water. Bring to the boil, then reduce the heat to medium and simmer, stirring occasionally, for 30 minutes, or until the mixture is dark red in colour. Add the sugar, Tajin seasoning and chilli powder and continue to cook, stirring, until the sugar has dissolved. Remove from the heat and set aside to cool for 30 minutes.

Add the lime juice and orange juice and stir until incorporated. Depending on how you're going to enjoy the sauce, you can blend it to a smooth consistency, strain it into a jar or leave it chunky – it's your choice!

The salsa will keep in an airtight container in the fridge for up to 6 months.

Variations

Chamoy is so much fun to eat, it'll make all your tastebuds have a party! Want to go a bit crazy? Try adding chopped fresh mango, pineapple, green apple, blueberries or even strawberries!

- Blend to a thick consistency that's perfect for a sticky michelada rim (see page 76).
- For a pourable chamoy that's perfect for drizzling over fruits and vegetables, stir through 125 ml (½ cup) water before serving.
- Stir in an extra 125 ml (½ cup) lime juice and you have a wonderful dipping sauce for freshly cooked seafood.

Note

You'll find dried plums in Asian supermarkets, and dried hibiscus flowers in spice shops and Latin American or African grocers.

Top: Salsa Verde de Chile Asado - Roasted green chilli salsa | Bottom: Salsa Negra - Black salsa

Roasted green chilli salsa

Salsa Verde de Chile Asado

Makes about 500 g (1 lb 2 oz)

Serves 4

Ingredients

- 10 fresh green serrano chillies, stems removed
- 5 fresh jalapeno chillies, stems removed
- ½ white onion, roughly chopped
- 1 garlic clove, peeled
- 1 teaspoon table salt
- cooking oil spray

Method

Place the chillies, onion, garlic and salt in a heavy-based saucepan over medium heat and spray the ingredients with cooking oil. Cover and cook for about 7 minutes, or until charred, stirring occasionally.

Using a blender or molcajete, blend or pound the charred chilli mixture with 250 ml (1 cup) water until smooth – the mixture should be quite thick.

The salsa will keep in an airtight container in the fridge for up to 1 week.

Black salsa

Salsa Negra

Makes about 420 ml (14 fl oz)

Ingredients

- 100 ml (3½ fl oz) lime juice
- 100 ml (3½ fl oz) Clamato
- 100 ml (3½ fl oz) Maggi seasoning
- 100 ml (3½ fl oz) worcestershire sauce
- 20 ml (¾ fl oz) Valentina hot sauce, Tapatio or sriracha chilli sauce
- 1 fresh habanero chilli, seeds removed, finely chopped
- pinch of freshly ground black pepper

Method

Simply mix all the ingredients together in a bowl.

The salsa will keep in an airtight container in the fridge for up to 2 weeks.

Guacamole

Serves 6

Ingredients

- 1 small garlic clove, peeled
- 5 small avocados, halved, stones removed
- 1 tomato, seeds removed, diced
- 2 fresh green jalapeno, serrano or Thai chillies, finely chopped
- large handful of coriander (cilantro), chopped
- juice of 3 limes
- 1 tablespoon olive oil
- 1 tablespoon table salt

Method

Gently pound the garlic clove using a mortar and pestle or molcajete, then add the avocado and mash to a chunky paste. Add the remaining ingredients and stir until you have a thick and luscious guacamole.

Guacamole is best eaten on the day it is made, as the avocado will start to discolour. If you have leftovers, combine it with the fake guacamole opposite and use as a salsa to top your tacos.

Fake guacamole

Guacamole Falso

Serves 6

Ingredients

- 5 fresh or tinned tomatillos (see Note)
- 2 Lebanese or green zucchini (courgettes), chopped
- 5 fresh green jalapeno or serrano chillies, roughly chopped
- ½ white onion, chopped
- small handful of coriander (cilantro) leaves, including a few stems
- juice of 1 lime
- 1 tablespoon vegetable oil
- 2 teaspoons table salt
- 1 teaspoon white vinegar

Method

If you are lucky enough to find fresh tomatillos, remove the husks and thoroughly wash the fruit. If using tinned tomatillos, drain and rinse them. Roughly chop the tomatillos.

Place the tomatillos in a blender with the remaining ingredients. Blitz to a creamy consistency.

The guacamole will keep in an airtight container in the fridge for up to 5 days.

Note

Instead of tomatillos, you can use finely diced green bell peppers (capsicums).

Top: Guacamole | Bottom: Guacamole Falso - Fake guacamole

Top: Salsa Macha Verde - Brave green salsa | Bottom: Salsa con Rajas de Poblano - Roasted poblano strips in red salsa

Salsa Macha Verde

Makes about 300 ml (10 fl oz)

Enough for 15 tacos

Ingredients

- 200 ml (7 fl oz) olive oil
- 1 white onion, cut into 4 cm (1½ in) chunks
- 10 garlic cloves, roughly chopped
- 10 fresh jalapeno chillies, roughly chopped
- 50 g (⅓ cup) pepitas (pumpkin seeds)
- 50 g (⅓ cup) shelled pistachios
- 30 g (¼ cup) raw skinless peanuts
- 1 teaspoon table salt
- 1 small bunch of coriander (cilantro), chopped

Method

Heat the oil in a comal or heavy-based frying pan over medium heat and fry the onion and garlic for about 4 minutes, until golden, stirring often. Add the chilli and cook, stirring, for about 10 minutes, until nicely browned. Using a slotted spoon, transfer the onion, garlic and chilli to a small bowl and leave to cool.

Add the pepitas, pistachios and peanuts to the pan and cook for 5 minutes or until lightly coloured. Set aside to cool.

Transfer the cooled chilli mixture to a food processor. Add the pepitas, pistachios and peanuts, along with the olive oil from the pan, and the salt. Blend to form a chunky salsa.

Transfer to a serving bowl and stir through the coriander.

The salsa will keep in an airtight container in the fridge for up to 10 days.

Salsa con Rajas de Poblano

Makes about 500 g (1 lb 2 oz)

Ingredients

- 3 fresh poblano chillies
- 3 roma (plum) tomatoes, roughly chopped
- 1 teaspoon vegetable oil
- ½ onion, diced
- 1 teaspoon table salt
- 1 tablespoon sour cream

Method

Preheat a barbecue grill or use a stovetop gas flame to char the chillies, turning occasionally, until the skins are blackened and blistered. Using tongs, immediately transfer the chillies to a large zip-lock bag and let them sweat for 5–10 minutes – this will make peeling them much easier. Once the chillies are cool enough to handle, cut off the stems. Peel away the skins and carefully remove and discard the seeds. Slice the chillies into strips.

Put the tomato in a blender, along with 250 ml (1 cup) water, and blend to a puree.

Heat the vegetable oil in a frying pan over medium heat and saute the onion for about 4 minutes, until translucent. Add the pureed tomato, reduce the heat to low and cook for 7–10 minutes, until slightly thickened. Gently stir in the poblano strips and season with the salt.

Remove from the heat and stir in the sour cream.

The salsa will keep in an airtight container in the fridge for up to 3 days.

Salsa de Cacahuate y Chile de Arbol

Makes about 300 ml (10½ fl oz)

Enough for 15 tacos

Ingredients

- 125 ml (½ cup) olive oil
- 4 garlic cloves, peeled
- 20 dried arbol chillies
- 50 g (1¾ oz) raw skinless peanuts
- 1 teaspoon table salt
- pinch of freshly ground black pepper

Method

Heat half the oil in a heavy-based saucepan over medium heat. Fry the garlic, stirring often, until browned on both sides, taking care it doesn't burn. Using a slotted spoon, scoop the garlic into a blender or molcajete.

Add the chillies to the hot oil and reduce the heat to low. Cook, stirring, for 3 minutes, until the chillies are dark red in colour – don't cook them any longer than that, or they'll taste bitter. Transfer the chillies to the blender or molcajete.

Pour the remaining oil into the pan and add the peanuts. Fry, stirring constantly, for about 6 minutes, until the peanuts are lightly browned. Add the peanuts to the garlic and chillies and set the oil aside to cool to room temperature.

Add the oil to the blender or molcajete, along with the salt and pepper, and blend or pound until smooth.

The salsa will keep in an airtight container in the pantry for up to 6 months.

Salsa de Siete Chiles

Makes about 500 g (1 lb 2 oz)

Ingredients

- 125 ml (½ cup) vegetable oil
- 1 dried pasilla chilli
- 3 dried morita chillies
- 2 dried chipotle chillies
- 3 dried cascabel chillies
- 2 dried guajillo chillies
- 3 dried arbol chillies
- 1 dried ancho chilli
- 2 roma (plum) tomatoes, quartered
- 6 garlic cloves, peeled
- 125 ml (½ cup) white vinegar
- 1 tablespoon dried epazote
- 2½ teaspoons table salt

Method

Heat half the oil in a saucepan over medium heat. Add all the chillies and cook, stirring constantly, for about 3 minutes, or until they have an oily sheen. Remove the chillies using a slotted spoon and drain on paper towel, then set aside to cool.

Add the tomato quarters and garlic to the hot oil and cook, stirring frequently, for 5 minutes, or until the garlic is lightly browned. Transfer the mixture to a blender and allow to cool. Let the oil in the pan cool to room temperature.

Remove and discard the stems from the chillies. Add the chillies to the blender, along with the vinegar, epazote and salt. Pour in the cooled oil from the pan, along with the remaining vegetable oil, then blend to a shiny, smooth salsa.

The salsa will keep in an airtight container in the fridge for up to 1 week.

Salsa de Zanahoria con Habanero

Makes about 500 g (1 lb 2 oz)

Ingredients

- 2 fresh habanero chillies (preferably orange, yellow or red)
- 2 carrots, roughly chopped
- ½ white onion
- 1 garlic clove, peeled
- 1 teaspoon table salt

Method

Char the chillies in a dry comal or heavy-based frying pan over medium heat for about 5 minutes, stirring constantly, until they begin to soften and blacken. Remove the chillies from the pan and leave until cool enough to handle, then remove and discard the stems.

Place the chillies in a blender with the remaining ingredients. Add 50 ml (1¾ fl oz) water and blend to create a chunky salsa.

The salsa will keep in an airtight container in the fridge for up to 1 week.

Habanero salsa with mango

Salsa de Habanero con Mango

Makes about 250 ml (1 cup)

Serves 4–6

Ingredients

- 1 ripe mango, flesh chopped
- 2 fresh habanero chillies, seeds removed, roughly chopped
- 100 ml (3½ fl oz) orange juice
- 200 g (7 oz) unsalted butter
- 100 g (3½ oz) white sugar

Method

In a food processor, blend the mango, habanero chilli and orange juice until smooth.

Melt the butter with the sugar in a saucepan over medium heat, stirring constantly for 5 minutes, until it forms a golden caramel. Stir the mango mixture through the caramel until completely incorporated, then simmer, stirring constantly, for a further 2–3 minutes. Season to taste with salt and freshly ground black pepper, then remove from the heat and allow to cool.

The salsa will keep in an airtight container in the fridge for up to 4 days.

Habanero & pineapple salsa

Salsa Habanero y Piña

Makes about 250 g (9 oz)

Enough for 15 tacos

Ingredients

- 150 g (5½ oz) peeled and cored pineapple, diced
- juice of 3 limes
- 1 red onion, finely sliced
- large pinch of table salt
- 5 fresh habanero chillies, finely sliced
- pinch of dried Mexican oregano (optional)

Method

Heat a comal or heavy-based frying pan over medium–high heat. Cook the pineapple, stirring occasionally, for 3 minutes on each side, or until slightly charred. Remove from the heat and set aside to cool.

Place the lime juice, onion and salt in a large bowl. Add the chilli and charred pineapple and stir to combine. Stir in the oregano, if using.

The salsa will keep in an airtight container in the fridge for up to 1 week.

BASICS

Tortillas de Maiz

Makes 20

Ingredients

500 g (1 lb 2 oz) masa flour (yellow, white or blue)

pinch of table salt

50 ml (1¾ fl oz) vegetable oil

600 ml (20½ fl oz) warm water

cooking oil spray

Method

Place the masa flour, salt and oil in a bowl. Pour in the water and mix together using your hands until you have a soft and non-sticky tortilla dough (see Note).

To cook the tortillas, lightly spray a comal or heavy-based frying pan with cooking oil and place over medium–high heat. Place a plastic food bag over the bottom half of a tortilla press. Roll 50 g (1¾ oz) of the dough into a ball (about the size of an apricot) and place it in the middle of the press. Cover with another plastic food bag, then close the tortilla press and gently press to flatten the dough into a 14–16 cm (5½–6¼ in) tortilla, about 3 mm (⅛ mm) thick.

Open the tortilla press, remove the top plastic food bag and flip the tortilla onto your hand and then into the pan. Cook for about 2 minutes each side, or until the tortilla puffs up and is just starting to change colour around the edge. Transfer the cooked tortilla to a tortilla warmer or wrap in a folded clean tea towel, then repeat with the remaining dough.

Leftover tortillas will keep in an airtight container in the fridge for up to 4 days. Gently reheat on a comal or in a heavy-based frying pan, or wrap up to eight tortillas in a tea towel and microwave on high for about 1 minute. Alternatively, use the tortillas to make tostadas or totopos (see page 318).

Note

The texture of the tortilla dough should feel like soft playdough, so you may need to add more water depending on the brand and coarseness of masa flour you use. To test if you have enough water, follow the quantities as stated in this recipe to start, then roll a small ball of dough and gently press to flatten it – if the edges crack, it means you need a little more water. Add only 4 teaspoons and mix it through the dough and try again. Keep going until you reach the right consistency.

Tortillas de Harina

Makes 20

Ingredients

- 500 g (1 lb 2 oz) plain (all-purpose) flour, plus extra for dusting
- 80 g (⅓ cup) vegetable shortening or pork lard, softened and chopped
- 2 pinches of table salt
- 1 teaspoon baking powder
- 220 ml (8 fl oz) hot water (as hot as your hands can handle)

Method

Place the flour in a bowl with the shortening or lard, salt and baking powder and mix well to combine. Pour in half the water and mix together using your hands to form a rough dough. Add more water as needed and knead until you have a soft and elastic dough – this will take about 15 minutes.

Completely cover the dough with a wet clean tea towel and set aside to rest for 20 minutes.

On a work surface lightly dusted with flour, roll the dough into 40 g (1½ oz) balls about the size of an apricot, then use a rolling pin to roll them out to 14 cm (5½ in) tortillas.

Heat a comal or heavy-based frying pan over medium heat. Add 1–2 tortillas and cook for about 20 seconds, then flip and cook the other side until the tortillas have a few light brown spots. Flip again and let the tortillas inflate like a balloon, then remove and place in a tortilla warmer or wrap in a folded clean tea towel. Repeat with the remaining dough.

Leftover tortillas will keep in an airtight container in the fridge for up to 5 days. To reheat, warm a comal or heavy-based frying pan over medium heat and cook the tortillas for about 2 minutes, flipping until warmed through. Alternatively, wrap up to eight tortillas in a tea towel and microwave on high for about 1 minute.

Tortilla chips

Totopos

Serves 4

Ingredients

500 ml (2 cups) vegetable oil

15 Tortillas de maiz page 314 →

table salt, to taste

Method

Heat the oil in a large heavy-based saucepan over medium–high heat to 180°C (350°F) on a kitchen thermometer.

Cut the tortillas into triangles. Working in batches so as not to overcrowd the pan, add the tortilla triangles to the hot oil and fry, flipping frequently, for 3 minutes, or until crisp and lightly golden.

Remove the totopos using a slotted spoon and transfer to a large plate lined with paper towel to drain. Season with salt and serve with your favourite salsas.

Fried corn tortillas

Tostadas

Makes 10

Ingredients

vegetable oil, for shallow-frying

10 Tortillas de maiz page 314 →

Method

Heat 100 ml (3½ fl oz) vegetable oil in a large heavy-based frying pan over medium heat to 180°C (350°F) on a kitchen thermometer.

Fry the tortillas, one by one, for about 2 minutes, until crisp and lightly golden – flipping frequently, and adding 50 ml (1¾ fl oz) extra oil to the pan after every three tostadas. If bubbles start to rise in the tortillas when they are cooking, use tongs to pinch them back together. Transfer the tostadas to a plate lined with paper towel to drain.

If you prefer, you can dry-toast the tortillas in a comal over low heat, flipping frequently, until crisp.

Black beans

Frijoles Negros

Serves 4

Ingredients

- 250 g (9 oz) dried black beans
- ½ white onion
- 1 bay leaf
- pinch of dried epazote (optional)
- 1 tablespoon table salt

Method

Rinse the beans and remove any grit or small pebbles, then place in a large bowl and cover with water. Set aside to soak overnight.

The next day, drain and rinse the beans, then place in a large saucepan with the onion, bay leaf and epazote, if using. Pour in 1.5 litres (6 cups) water and bring to the boil over high heat.

Boil the beans for 30 minutes, then reduce the heat to medium, add the salt and simmer for a further 40 minutes, or until the beans are soft and cooked through. If the pan starts to dry out during cooking, add up to 250 ml (1 cup) more water.

Drain the beans and reserve the cooking water if you need it for other recipes. Discard the bay leaf and onion.

Transfer the frijoles to a bowl and serve, or add to your dish of choice. Any leftovers will keep in an airtight container in the fridge for up to 5 days.

Refried black beans

Frijoles Negros Refritos

Serves 4

Ingredients

- 2 tablespoons vegetable oil
- ½ white or brown onion, finely chopped
- 3 tomatoes, finely diced
- 1 × quantity Frijoles negros (see opposite), plus 125 ml (½ cup) reserved bean cooking water
- pinch of dried epazote (optional)

Method

Heat the oil in a large frying pan over medium heat. Add the onion and tomato and cook, stirring occasionally, for about 8 minutes, until the tomato starts to collapse and the onion is soft.

Add the frijoles and reserved cooking water and, using a potato masher, crush the beans until they are half mashed, adding a little extra water if the mixture is very thick.

Add the epazote, if using, and stir the beans for 3 minutes, or until heated through.

Transfer the refried beans to a bowl and serve, or add to your dish of choice. Any leftovers will keep in an airtight container in the fridge for up to 5 days.

Frijoles Charros

Serves 4

Ingredients

- 500 g (1 lb 2 oz) dried pinto beans
- 1 bay leaf
- pinch of dried epazote (optional)
- 1 white onion
- 2 tomatoes, diced
- 1 teaspoon minced garlic
- 1 chipotle chilli in adobo sauce, chopped
- 1 tablespoon table salt
- 3 tablespoons vegetable oil or pork lard
- pinch of freshly ground black pepper
- pinch of chilli powder
- pinch of dried oregano
- 50 g (1¾ oz) diced bacon
- 3 skinless hotdog (frankfurter) sausages, cut into 5 mm (¼ in) dice
- 30 g (1 oz) cooked Mexican-style chorizo, crumbled
- 20 g (¾ oz) pork crackling, crumbled
- 375 ml (1½ cups) Mexican lager, plus extra if needed
- 4 fresh jalapeno chillies or long green chillies, finely diced
- coriander (cilantro) leaves, to serve (optional)

Method

Rinse the beans and remove any grit or small pebbles, then place in a large bowl and cover with water. Set aside to soak overnight.

The next day, drain and rinse the beans, then place in a large saucepan with the bay leaf and epazote, if using. Chop the onion in half and add a whole half to the pan.

Pour in 2 litres (2 qts) water and bring to the boil over high heat. Boil the beans for 30 minutes, then reduce the heat to medium and simmer for a further 40 minutes, or until the beans are just soft and cooked through. If the pan starts to dry out during cooking, add up to 250 ml (1 cup) more water (the beans are meant to be a bit runny). Remove from the heat and set aside.

Meanwhile, roughly chop the remaining onion half, then place in a bowl with the tomato, garlic, chipotle chilli and salt and mix to combine.

Heat the oil or lard in a frying pan over medium–high heat. Add the tomato mixture and cook, stirring frequently, for 5 minutes. Add the black pepper, chilli powder and oregano and cook for a further 3 minutes. Add the bacon, sausage, chorizo and crackling to the pan, along with the lager, and stir to combine. Cook, stirring, for 20 minutes, or until the beer has evaporated.

Transfer the sausage mixture to the pan of beans and cook over medium heat for 20 minutes. If the mixture starts to dry out, stir in a little water or more beer. When the beans are ready, remove and discard the whole onion half.

Transfer to serving bowls and top with the diced fresh chilli and coriander, if using. Any leftover beans will keep in an airtight container in the fridge for up to 5 days.

Tamales Verdes

Makes 10

Ingredients

20 sweetcorn husks (see Note)
200 g (7 oz) pork lard
1 teaspoon baking powder
500 g (1 lb 2 oz) masa flour, sifted (yellow masa is most commonly used here, but you can also use white or blue masa)
2 teaspoons table salt
650 ml (22 fl oz) chicken stock, warmed
500 g (1 lb 2 oz) cooked shredded chicken breast or thighs
2 × quantities Salsa verde page 286 →

Method

Soften the sweetcorn husks in a large bowl of warm water for about 5 minutes, then drain to remove any excess water.

Place the lard and baking powder in a bowl and use a wooden spoon to whip the mixture as fast as possible – the lard needs to soften and look spongy. Don't stress if this takes a long time; it can take up to 15 minutes to achieve the right consistency.

Once the lard is ready, add the masa flour, salt and warm chicken stock and mix well until completely combined. (Depending on the brand of masa flour you've used, you may need to add a little more water to achieve the right consistency.) To test if the dough is ready, drop a small ball of dough into a cup of cold water; if it floats to the top you're good to go! (If the dough doesn't float, mix the dough a little longer until it does float.)

Spread 80 g (2¾ oz) of the dough in the middle of a damp sweetcorn husk, leaving a 4 cm (1½ in) border around the edge. Add 50 g (1¾ oz) of the shredded chicken and 50 ml (1¾ fl oz) of the salsa verde, then cover with another 20 g (¾ oz) of dough. Place another sweetcorn husk over the filling, then wrap up the tamale by overlapping the sides and folding over the top and bottom ends towards the centre to enclose the filling. Secure the ends with kitchen string and set aside. Repeat with the remaining husks and ingredients to make 10 tamales.

Stand the tamales upright in a large steamer (do not stack them on top of each other). Fit as many tamales as you can into the steamer, but be careful not to pack them in too tightly as they can burst, leaving you with empty tamales. Place the steamer over a saucepan of simmering water and steam for 45 minutes.

The best way to check if your tamales are cooked is to remove one from the steamer, let it cool for 5 minutes, and then unwrap the husk. If the dough doesn't stick to the husk and it looks shiny and fluffy, your tamales are ready.

Let the tamales cool for 15–20 minutes inside the steamer, then serve.

Leftover tamales will keep in an airtight container in the fridge for 4 days.

Note

You can buy dried sweetcorn husks from Latin American supermarkets or online. It's better to buy more than you need, as they are unpredictable and can sometimes be small or break. They can be frozen, or kept in an airtight container in the pantry.

Mexican rice

Arroz Mexicano

Serves 4

Ingredients

- 250 g (9 oz) long-grain white rice
- 2 large roma (plum) tomatoes, roughly chopped
- ½ small white onion, roughly chopped
- 90 g (⅓ cup) tomato paste (concentrated puree)
- 1 teaspoon table salt
- 400 ml (14 fl oz) chicken stock or water
- 1 tablespoon vegetable oil
- 2 garlic cloves, peeled
- 2 fresh Thai green chillies

Method

Soak the rice in a bowl of cold water for 10 minutes, then drain and rinse.

Place the tomato, onion, tomato paste, salt and chicken stock or water in a blender and blend until smooth – you'll need 500 ml (2 cups) of liquid for this recipe.

Heat the oil in a large saucepan over medium–low heat. Add the garlic and cook, stirring, for 1–2 minutes, until lightly browned. Using a slotted spoon, remove the garlic cloves and discard them. Add the drained rice to the pan and stir for 8 minutes, or until lightly toasted. Stir in the blended tomato mixture until combined, then cover and bring to the boil. Reduce the heat to low and cook for 15 minutes.

Score 5 mm (¼ in) long slits all over the chillies, then add them to the pan. Gently stir the rice, then cover and continue to cook, adding more water if the mixture starts to look dry, for a further 3 minutes, or until the liquid has been completely absorbed and the rice is cooked through.

Any leftover rice will keep in an airtight container in the fridge for 3 days.

Blistered jalapenos

Jalapenos Toreados

Makes 10

Ingredients

- 10 fresh jalapeno chillies
- 1 teaspoon garlic salt
- 1 tablespoon Valentina hot sauce
- 1 teaspoon Maggi seasoning
- 1 teaspoon worcestershire sauce
- juice of 1 lime

Method

Char the chillies in a dry comal or heavy-based frying pan over medium heat for 15 minutes, stirring frequently, until they blacken.

Place the chillies in a clean 1 litre (34 fl oz) jar and add the remaining ingredients. Screw the lid on securely and shake the jar to combine everything.

Enjoy straight away, or store in the fridge for up to 1 week.

Chiles en Vinagre

Makes 2 × 500 g (1 lb 2 oz) jars

Ingredients

- 1 small bunch of dried marjoram
- 4 bay leaves
- 1 teaspoon dried thyme
- table salt
- 100 ml (3½ fl oz) vegetable oil
- 100 ml (3½ fl oz) olive oil
- 1 garlic bulb, cut in half crossways
- 3 carrots, sliced into 5 mm (¼ in) rounds
- 10 fresh jalapeno chillies
- 1 white onion, cut into big chunks
- 200 ml (7 fl oz) white vinegar
- 2 teaspoons dried oregano
- 10 whole allspice berries

Method

Soak the marjoram, bay leaves and thyme in 250 ml (1 cup) water with a pinch of salt for 20 minutes.

Meanwhile, heat the vegetable and olive oils in a large heavy-based saucepan over medium heat. Fry the garlic bulb halves for about 4 minutes, turning several times, until they release their aroma and turn golden. Transfer the garlic to a small bowl.

Fry the carrot slices for 2–3 minutes, stirring to coat them in the garlicky oil. Make a few small cuts in the whole chillies so they absorb the flavours and don't burst while cooking, then add them to the pan and cook for 3 minutes, stirring to ensure everything is evenly fried. Add the onion chunks and cook, stirring now and then, for about 7 minutes, until the onion turns translucent.

Return the fried garlic to the pan and pour in the vinegar and 1 litre (4 cups) water. Stir in 2 teaspoons salt, the oregano and allspice berries, along with the soaked herbs and their soaking water. Cover the pan, reduce the heat and leave to simmer gently for 10–15 minutes, until the vegetables are tender but still have a slight crunch.

Remove from the heat and leave to cool, then transfer the mixture to clean glass jars and store in the fridge. The pickled chillies are ready to eat straight away, but will taste even better the next day and over the following weeks, as the flavours deepen.

Store in the fridge for up to 6 months – the pickled chillies also make excellent homemade gifts.

Chiles Rellenos

Makes 8

Ingredients

- 8 large fresh or tinned poblano chillies
- 320 g (11½ oz) queso fresco or feta, cut into 8 sticks
- 150 g (1 cup) plain (all-purpose) flour
- 6 eggs, separated
- pinch of salt
- pinch of ground white pepper
- vegetable oil, for shallow-frying

Tomato salsa

- 6 roma (plum) tomatoes, roughly chopped
- ½ white onion, roughly chopped
- 1 small garlic clove, peeled
- 2 teaspoons table salt
- 2 tablespoons vegetable oil

Method

If you are using tinned chillies, select the biggest ones and very gently prise them open lengthways, keeping them intact for stuffing, and scrape away the seeds. Set aside.

If using fresh poblano chillies, preheat a barbecue grill or use a stovetop gas flame to char the chillies, turning occasionally, until the skins are blackened and blistered. Using tongs, immediately transfer the chillies to a large zip-lock bag and let them sweat for 5–10 minutes – this will make peeling them much easier. Once the chillies are cool enough to handle, peel away and discard the skins. Carefully slice open each chilli lengthways and remove the seeds, keeping the chilli intact for stuffing. Set aside.

To make the salsa, blitz the tomato, onion, garlic, salt and 400 ml (14 fl oz) water in a blender until smooth. Heat the oil in a saucepan over medium–high heat, add the salsa and bring to the boil. Reduce the heat and simmer for 5 minutes, until the salsa changes colour. Keep warm.

Place a cheese stick in the middle of each opened chilli, then close up and secure with toothpicks.

Tip the flour into a shallow bowl and set aside.

Using a stand mixer with the whisk attached, beat the egg whites on high speed for 7–10 minutes, until shiny and foamy. Add the egg yolks, one at a time, beating well between each addition, then add the salt and white pepper and mix until you have a foamy batter.

Meanwhile, heat enough oil to come halfway up the stuffed chillies in a deep heavy-based frying pan. Heat the oil over medium heat to 180°C (350°F) on a kitchen thermometer.

Working in batches, gently roll the stuffed chillies in the flour, then dip them in the batter. Lower the chillies into the oil and shallow-fry, turning occasionally, for 3–4 minutes, until golden. Drain on paper towel and serve with the salsa.

Carnitas

Makes about 1 kg (2 lb 3 oz)

Ingredients

- 3 tablespoons table salt
- 250 g (9 oz) pork ribs
- 1 kg (2 lb 3 oz) boneless pork shoulder, cut into 5 cm (2 in) chunks
- 250 g (9 oz) pork belly, cut into 5 cm (2 in) chunks
- 100 g (3½ oz) pork skin, cut into 4 cm × 1 cm (1½ in × ½ in) strips
- 3 kg (6 lb 10 oz) pork lard
- 375 ml (1½ cups) evaporated milk
- 1 orange, cut into 8 slices
- 500 ml (2 cups) cola
- 1 white onion
- 6 bay leaves
- 250 ml (1 cup) fizzy orange soft drink
- 1 teaspoon dried thyme
- 1 teaspoon dried marjoram
- 1 tablespoon cloves
- 1 tablespoon whole black peppercorns
- 3 garlic cloves

Method

Rub the salt into all the pork pieces and set aside.

Heat the lard in a large heavy-based saucepan over high heat to 120°C (250°F) on a kitchen thermometer. Once the lard is hot, slowly add the evaporated milk, orange slices and cola, stirring to combine. Reduce the heat to medium, add the onion, five of the bay leaves, the soft drink and 1 litre (4 cups) water and stir again. Place the remaining bay leaf with the thyme and marjoram in a small muslin (cheesecloth) spice bag and tie with kitchen string. Add the bag to the pan, along with the cloves, peppercorns and garlic. Continue to cook, stirring, for 5 minutes.

Add the ribs and pork shoulder to the pan and cook for 15 minutes. Add the pork belly and cook, stirring frequently so the pork doesn't stick to the base of the pan, for 20–30 minutes, until the meat has a lightly golden crust. Add the pork skin and continue to simmer for 30 minutes, or until all the pork is tender.

Remove the pork from the pan and set aside to cool slightly, then cut the meat into small pieces. The pork should be tender and juicy.

The carnitas will keep in an airtight container in the fridge for up to 3 days. Use in tacos and burritos, or serve with Arroz Mexicano (see page 327) and your favourite salsa.

Gracias

I can't thank enough the amazing team at Smith Street Books, they are like my Melbourne family. THANK YOU Paul, Lucy, Caro, Alicia, Deb, Jane, Katri and Evi for helping, inspiring and pushing me to do my best! I'm sure this cookbook has so much love from all of us on every page.

I had such an amazing time at the photo shoot at the Smith Street Books studio, from the delicious coffee and lots of people coming to try my food, to the laughs, the car shares and sourcing of ingredients from places I didn't know. I felt very lucky and definitely blessed to be in such good company – thank you!

To all my followers and the Mexican-food enthusiasts from all over the world who bought my first two cookbooks, *Comida Mexicana* and *CDMX,* and sent me photos of their amazing dishes. You have no idea how loved I feel every time I hear from you. I hope you enjoy this new collection of recipes.

To all my friends who took the time to talk to me about their family's cooking traditions, recipes and stories – I learned a lot and it was so important to have you there cheering me on, taste-testing my food or simply giving me a hug and encouraging me to keep going. Thank you to Graciela, Carla, Luis, Juan Manuel, Juan Pablo, Claudio, Mitzel, Alex and so many more!

To my family, thank you for always pushing me to grow professionally and give the best of me in everything I do.

To my son, Julio, this cookbook is deeply dedicated to you. Chiquis, you are my mini-me, my little treasured heart and my motor to do everything I do. I feel proud of the man you have become and I love having you around supporting my crazy ideas. You are my greatest creation and the best adventure of my entire life; watching you grow is a privilege – you have taught me so much about love, life, loyalty, trust, friendship and everything in between. My precious boy, I hope this book reminds you that you are capable of anything you set your mind to, and that my love and support will always be with you, no matter what. You bring so much light into my world. I hope you remember those days when we delivered food around Sydney and the long nights we spent making tamales, our Mexican heritage passing from one generation to the next, yet this time in a different country and in a different environment, but definitely with the same love.

And, finally, to everyone who buys this book, I hope you all love it as much as I have loved writing it, GRACIAS!

About the author

Rosa Cienfuegos is the passionate face behind Sydney's beloved Tamaleria and Mexican Deli. Opened by Rosa in 2017, with the enthusiastic encouragement from family, clients and friends who deeply connected with her authentic Mexican cuisine, it was the first of its kind in Australia.

Recognised as the 'Tamal Queen of Sydney' and a cherished food ambassador by the Mexican Embassy in Australia, Rosa is celebrated for her dedication to opening the path for a new wave of Mexican restaurants, inspired by her approach to recreating her country's traditional flavours here in Australia.

In her first cookbook, *Comida Mexicana*, Rosa introduced home-style Mexican dishes to a wide audience, with easy-to-follow recipes that not only celebrated the joy of cooking Mexican food at home, but also showcased the remarkable diversity of Mexico's rich gastronomy.

Following the succes of *Comida Mexicana*, Rosa started running cooking classes in her local community, teaching everything from the fundamentals of making tortillas to creating more complex dishes such as tamales. But she soon realised that having one cookbook was not enough to share the rich and diverse food of her homeland. She embarked on her second book: *CDMX*, a cookbook dedicated to her childhood in Mexico City and the local dishes she grew up eating. *CDMX* led Rosa to host master-chef talks across Australia where she shares a bit of her heart at every event. Being from Mexico City, there is so much to share and explain!

For Rosa, working in hospitality is a rewarding way to connect with individuals who share an interest in her culture, traditions and cooking methods. So, if you see her around, don't hesitate to say hello – she is always delighted to offer advice on preparing your favourite Mexican dishes! You can also follow Rosa on her YouTube channel: @RosaCienfuegos100

La Mesa Mexicana is filled with the same deep love and passion Rosa feels for her beloved Mexico. Its creation involved months of dedicated study, research and meaningful connections with people from different regions, allowing her to understand the local ingredients, cooking techniques and ancestral indigenous traditions that have contributed to and continue to shape modern Mexican cuisine. This latest culinary offering is undoubtedly not the last chapter in Rosa's flavourful journey.

Index

Note: English recipe titles are in *italics*

Smith Street Books

Published in 2025 by Smith Street Books
Naarm (Melbourne) | Australia
smithstreetbooks.com

Distributed outside of ANZ, North & Latin America
by Thames & Hudson Ltd., 6–24 Britannia Street,
London, WC1X 9JD
thamesandhudson.com

EU Authorised Representative: Interart S.A.R.L.
19 rue Charles Auray, 93500 Pantin, Paris, France
productsafety@thameshudson.co.uk; www.interart.fr

ISBN: 978-1-9232-3942-5

Smith Street Books respectfully acknowledges the Wurundjeri People of the Kulin Nation, who are the Traditional Owners of the land on which we work, and we pay our respects to their Elders past and present.

Publisher: Lucy Heaver
Recipe editor: Katri Hilden
Content editor: Jane Price
Design, layout and illustrations: Evi.O Studio
Photographer: Alicia Taylor
Food stylist: Deborah Kaloper
Photography chefs: Rosa Cienfuegos, Caroline Griffiths,
Melanie Ryan and Amanda Menegazzo
Proofreader: Elena Callcott
Indexer: Max McMaster
Prepress: Megan Ellis
Production manager: Aisling Coughlan

Printed & bound in China by C&C Offset Printing Co., Ltd.

Book 411
10 9 8 7 6 5 4 3 2 1